Recruiting, Educating, and Training Librarians for Collection Development

Library of Congress Cataloging-in-Publication Data

Recruiting, educating, and training librarians for collection
    development / edited by Peggy Johnson and Sheila S. Intner.
        p. cm. — (New directions in information management, ISSN
    0887–3844 ; no. 33)
        Includes bibliographical references and index.
        ISBN 0–313–28561–6
        1. Collection development (United States)—United States.
    2. Librarians—Recruiting—United States. 3. Library education—
    United States. 4. Librarians—Training of—United States.
    I. Johnson, Peggy. II. Intner, Sheila S. III. Series.
    Z687.2.U6R43 1994
    023.9—dc20   93–35839

British Library Cataloguing in Publication Data is available.

Library of Congress Catalog Card Number: 93–35839
ISBN: 0–313–28561–6
ISSN: 0887–3844

First published in 1994

Greenwood Press, 88 Post Road West, Westport, CT 06881
An imprint of Greenwood Publishing Group, Inc.

Printed in the United States of America

The paper used in this book complies with the
Permanent Paper Standard issued by the National
Information Standards Organization (Z39.48–1984).

10 9 8 7 6 5 4 3 2

Recruiting, Educating, and Training Librarians for Collection Development

Edited by Peggy Johnson
and Sheila S. Intner

New Directions in Information Management, Number 33

Greenwood Press
Westport, Connecticut • London

Recent Titles in
New Directions in Information Management

To Lee, Carson, and Amelia, who firmly believe one can never have too many books, videotapes, and recordings.

—Peggy Johnson

To Jordan, Rachel, Leif, Tyler, and Caitlin, for whom I hope collections are being developed.

—Sheila S. Intner

Contents

Acknowledgments

Many people helped bring this book to completion and publication, and they have our deepest appreciation. While it would take too much space to name them all, it is impossible to finish this text without mentioning the following:

Robert D. Stueart, Dean of the Graduate School of Library and Information Science, whose wise counsel helped develop the foundation for this book;

Shmuel Sever, Director of the University of Haifa Library, whose enthusiasm for collection development was an inspiration, and whose resources were generously tapped by the editors;

Richard Rohrer, Director of the St. Paul Campus Libraries, University of Minnesota, whose support for research provided continuing encouragement;

Lynn Sipe, whose collection development Listserv was (and is) a continuing source of valuable information and insights;

and the fifteen authors whose chapters appear in this book, without whom there would be no book at all.

Introduction

Agreement is by no means universal on what collection development librarians should know, where they might be sought, how they might best be prepared for this specialty, or how they ought to function once they have been hired to work in a library. Some believe that the most important credential a collection development librarian can bring to the job is a Ph.D. in one of the traditional disciplines. We could not agree more with these colleagues that a doctorate, representing the successful completion of a major scholarly study involving years of disciplined intellectual activity, is a splendid background for many endeavors in librarianship, including this one. But when we enquired among groups of collection development officers gathered at professional conferences whether they thought the problems of recruiting, educating, and training librarians for our specialty would be solved by concentrating on hiring Ph.D.'s, they were appalled. The problems they were experiencing were serious and diverse enough to warrant a multifaced response in which hiring people with additional degrees was helpful but in no way sufficient by itself to solve them. When we suggested that we ask leading collection development librarians to contribute solutions to these problems and put them into a book, the reaction was enthusiastic and we were urged to move full speed ahead with the project. This volume is the result.

For many patrons, collections *are* the library. Several authors writing for this book echo the notion. Some patrons may be too timid to approach librarians for service or too uncomfortable with catalogs and indexes to search those venerable tools. But they can approach the materials without fear. That is why they come to the library. Even when patrons feel free to ask for help and confidently consult bibliographic tools, their ultimate objective nearly always is to obtain some piece of library material, some part of the collections that librarians have brought together for their use.

In the last several decades, collection development has grown more complex and more challenging. The definition of collection development now includes much more than the selection of books to purchase (if ever it was just that), although this delightful task remains central to building library collections. It includes making decisions of a different nature and requires that collection officers play a leadership role in developing their libraries as well as their collections.

The introduction of computers into collection development processes has altered the way they operate by expanding the information base with which collection officers work and enabling them to solve problems that were not even identifiable before automation. Yet despite the new sophistication of the specialty, certain fundamental issues remain, and since the introduction of automation, they have become clearer, sharper, and more insistent in demanding our attention and our best thinking. Thus, in preparing this book, we asked the authors, all familiar with the basic problems, to give us not only their careful, disciplined analyses of the problems, but also their most creative solutions. They present issues for the future that must be considered today. Collection development as it is practiced now, and as it will continue to be practiced, is presented in its varying aspects.

If the title and format of this book sound vaguely reminiscent of an earlier work focusing on cataloging—*Recruiting, Educating, and Training Cataloging Librarians: Solving the Problems* (Greenwood, 1989)—the resemblance is intentional. We also would have liked to hold an event similar to the 1989 Simmons College Symposium on Recruiting, Educating, and Training Cataloging Librarians on which that book was based, but we knew such a project would take a great deal of time, energy, and significant monetary support to reach, perhaps, a maximum of 150 people. So we opted to prepare this book, which we hope will reach many more interested library administrators, collection development librarians, library educators, and students learning about the field of library and information science and the specialty of collection development. One can understand much about the special nature of the area by examining the issues its practitioners face in preparing a new cadre of colleagues.

Bill Katz begins by asking the Big Questions: For whom are we building our collections, and why? Are library collections ends in themselves or are they means to ends determined by persons other than the librarian? The answers provide a foundation for recruitment and educational efforts, shaping a framework of attributes and attitudes the ideal collection development officer might possess. Terry Allison and Marion T. Reid bring together in one paper the scattered literature on organization of collection development and explore the genesis of the related areas of acquisitions librarianship and collection development. They demonstrate how these two areas merge and diverge in practice, what professional advantages and disadvantages each role offers, and what practitioners face in undertaking to perform one or both of them. Eugene L. Wiemers, Jr., offers a persuasive argument for collection development as a career choice. Michael A. Keller develops this perspective while considering a career in collection development for those who prepared for work in a subject specialty before coming to librarianship. He concludes with suggestions for the recruitment process.

Library materials to be collected may be interpreted to mean books and journals—scholarly and otherwise—and videos, computer software, sound recordings, interactive multimedia, and other diverse kinds of items. Sheila S. Intner alleges that libraries' built-in bibliocentricity precludes the adequate collection of non-book materials and challenges recruiters to seek non-bibliocentric people for the specialty to counter these tendencies. Michael T. Ryan scrutinizes the "I" world—the world of interdisciplinary studies—and suggests how to prepare collection developers who can operate successfully in it.

Analyzing education issues in depth, Paul Metz examines the place of collection development in library school curricula, how it has developed over more than half a century since the establishment of graduate education for librarianship, and where it might go in the future. In this same section, Thomas E. Nisonger considers the educational alternatives for combining or distinguishing education for the two specialties of acquisitions and collection development. Peggy Johnson details the competencies contemporary collection development officers should possess, acknowledging a need for financial, statistical, and communication skills, plus an understanding of organizational behavior and the ethical considerations underlying decision making. Elizabeth Futas presents the debate over the practicum in education for collection development. She points out that the difficulty in utilizing practicums effectively goes beyond their intrinsic educational value and offers an assessment of the ultimate cost-benefit tradeoffs.

Regardless of formal educational preparation, newly hired collection development librarians require introduction to and training for responsibilities when beginning in a position. George J. Soete proposes a training program for new bibliographers and identifies the competencies that should be covered in the program. Anthony W. Ferguson turns to the Conspectus, a familiar tool for collection assessment, and identifies its uses and benefits as a training tool. An astute plan of action for training existing staff in collection development responsibilities is suggested by D. Whitney Coe and Joseph Consoli. These authors provide a thorough look at current trends and summarize two classic monographs on collection development. Gay N. Dannelly concludes the section on training with practical advice in the important area of continuing education, stressing its importance as well as detailing options.

In the final chapter, Wilf Lancaster stargazes a little, forecasting what might be a likely collection development scenario in the year 2025. Who better than the author, who correctly predicted the advent of electronic information transfer more than fifteen years before it occurred (he called it "the paperless society" then), can suggest now which strands are significant in the warp and woof of contemporary librarianship?

The chapter authors draw from the literature of collection development in crafting their contributions, citing some of the best from an extensive body of work. Taken in total, the chapter endnotes and suggested readings, which accompany some chapters, provide a comprehensive approach to the literature. To aid the reader, we also provide a concluding bibliography of selected works compiled from the chapters.

We hope the ideas presented here will prompt action in three areas: (1) consideration of the specialty by students and entering librarians; (2) curriculum development by library school faculty and administrators; and (3) organizational development and innovation in libraries by senior decision makers. The positive effects of successful changes in recruiting, educating, and training a new cadre of collection development librarians will help shape a new future for libraries.

Part I

OVERVIEW

1

Book Selection and Collection Building: Evolution of the Art

Bill Katz

The heart of collection building is a matter of people making choices—and, at the end of the day, they cannot help but be subjective choices laden with all the attitudinal baggage carried by the persons who make them. Librarians, being ordinary humans, take a great deal for granted about their choices. In this overview chapter, Bill Katz asks that we examine more than the processes by the which the choices are made. He suggests we go beyond decision-making processes to investigate the kinds of persons making the decisions and the assumptions under which they operate. Librarians' views of their collections are colored by their visions of the library as well as by their professional assumptions and their professional outlook.

Bill Katz asks that librarians examine the fundamental assumptions they hold about libraries when they approach the decision-making processes central to all collection building. What are these collections? Why do they exist? Who are they designed to serve? Most of us take the answers to these simple questions for granted. We think everyone knows why libraries exist, why collections are in them, why librarians add and subtract materials as they do, and why the materials on library shelves are read, viewed, and heard. But if one does not question basic assumptions, one may miss the whole point of collection *development*. If what librarians have been doing all along is so correct and so good, why should libraries need *development* at all?

Katz makes very clear his belief that librarians should concentrate on the educational role of libraries, not to the exclusion of popular materials, but as their primary mission. Exercising judgment and discretion is central to the art of collection building. Katz concludes that the spread of computers and electronic information means that the role of librarian as mediator between "garbage" and information is needed more, not less.

In the construction, or more likely the evaluation, of existing selection policies, one quickly realizes these are the best and the worst of times: best in that more people are using libraries, worst in that budgets are being guillotined.

Pressures and delights vary from library to library, and while generalizations are in oversupply, there are a few traditional truths about selection. Some of these determinants of success or failure include the following:

- Selection must be recognized as an art form that, as such, rejects universal laws and formulas.

- The successful selector of materials is an expert who may solve many problems now delegated to spinners of formulas and theories. A case in point is the current plethora of recommendations on how to deal with a shortage of funds and a flood of periodicals.

- There is a problem with deciding who among the public is served and is not served, and this often reflects badly considered selection policies.

- There should be a return, particularly by public libraries, to selecting materials primarily for educational purposes rather than for recreation. Too many libraries are trying to be too many things without thought for their main mission.

- More attention should be paid to book reviews and what they can and cannot do in the selection process.

- Technology will neither replace libraries or librarians. In fact, it is likely to create the need for more librarians, but at a higher intellectual level than in the past.

The intricacies of acquisitions, which may be compared to dining with the Jabberwocky, are skipped in this overview because (1) acquisitions is covered in great depth in the literature and in any meeting of more than two librarians; and (2) the technological aspects of jobbers, spreadsheets, and budgets deserve more attention than can be suggested in a short chapter. With that premise, though, to divorce acquisitions from selection is to lay the foundation for a librarian mausoleum. Worse, the librarian becomes the appetizer, not the host, for the Jabberwocky.

THE ART OF SELECTION

Material selection is an art form, corrected and controlled by many variables, from the imagined audience to realistic budget limitations. The possibilities are without number. Conventional formulas fail, as do comparative guidelines. One may probe the literature, spend a life attending meetings, and know no more about the art form than the illusory dimensions of a unicorn.

While this is hardly news to even the most myopic librarian, for distressed students and bellicose critics of libraries it is difficult to understand. Infatuated with "science," "information," "technology," "policy," and computers, the self-righteous, if not always self-confident, partisans attempt to budget selection into fixed formulas. The solicitous attention to universal laws is touching, although faithless to daily library activity.

Support for selection as art rather than science may be found in a deceptively simple question: "What constitutes a good collection?" The grouchy individual who considers this a trivial query is locked into a specialized, limited collection of monographs on gnats with a limited budget. For all others, the question is the very stuff of selection. And it can never be completely answered.

Much to the dismay of those from poets evaluating the Alexandria Library to computer conquistadors striving to understand the local university library, "good" presents too many variables for a definitive or even an approximate answer. In an amazing list of questions designed to define "good," Elizabeth Futas and David Vidor conclude, "Many unanswerable questions were raised for us by our research, and those that were answerable often left us uninformed." This confirms that notion that selection defies analysis, or as Futas and Vidor put it, "We hope this exercise encourages others to . . . question how far empirical research can take us along the path to understanding."[1] The cheerful implication is that research will get you nowhere. Common sense and intuition are better guides when supported by education and intellect.

THE SELECTOR

The next proposition is that the person who succeeds in selection moves from the uncertainties of the art to the firm ground of continuing self education, experience, knowledge and confidence. One may become an expert. What are some characteristics of the expert librarian concerned with purchasing libraries materials? First, to paraphrase Dr. Spock, "You know more than you think you do."[2]

Trusted with selection of novels or government documents, the individual, if only through osmosis, can soon find the fiction section or appreciate the characteristics of a document's classification. Beyond that, constant reading, constant attention to people who wander in and out of the library, and constant awareness of developments in fiction and government soon turn the selector into a formidable expert.

Second, every librarian understands the assumption that books may change a life—or, at least, help in repairing a toilet. Whether it be books, films, or other deserving media, the librarian knows the forms and which is best to serve a given audience, a given purpose.

Third, the concept of being sure that anyone using the library will find what is needed requires selection skills based on understanding format and sources.

Fourth, the concept of helping someone find the right book may be an old-fashioned notion. No matter, it is much required. An appreciation of readers is a felicitous major step in the education of any librarian and is an absolute must for the person charged with selection. Other qualifications for such a professional include patience, regular habits, and a licensed sense of humor.

Moving away from the ideal, consider the profile of selection people in some libraries. This is a short, cautionary description that one trusts will serve as a warning, not as a model.

- Some librarians themselves don't read. If so, how can they select for others?
- Others have only one notion of selection—give the public want it wants. Yet they have no real idea of those wants.
- A few rely on mechanics—from jobber lists to approval plans—to do their work.
- And there are those who are so occupied with keeping the library from crashing down around them that they give no real thought to long-range planning.

Fortunately, the types just listed are more rare than normal, yet there are enough around to detract from the claim of us all to be professionals.

The professional who selects material regularly is a decided asset in times of tight budgets. One example will illustrate the value of such people. Consider the fact that journals, particularly in academic libraries, are devouring the budget. Something has to give. The problem is what—personnel, building improvements, periodicals, or . . . ?

The question of balancing fewer dollars with more titles has taken as much space in library journals as the articles on compact discs or censorship. Obviously, there is no general, easy answer. At the same time many otherwise astute authors who are bent on formula construction miss an important point.

Rather than rely on formulas, dust on bound volumes, what is or is not left behind at closing hours, or the element of chance associated with the sound of a title in a language other than English, it might be better to determine what is to be chopped or added by giving the librarian the helm. Divided into specific subject areas, turned over to library experts, the listing of deletions and additions may be examined and cut back as needed in less than an hour or two. The designated drops should be passed on to teachers, students, guests, and involved stray dogs. They may or may not have ideas, but chances are most will be more than content to leave it to the librarian. One may call this the benevolent dictatorship of the subject expert, but it will save hours, days, weeks of time. The result, too, will be considerably more satisfactory than what is churned out of countless meetings.

Actually, this approach is now used in many libraries, although it may be hidden behind circulation figures, curriculum, professor's cough, and mysterious visits to the bindery. Someone committed to serious selection can be equally trusted to weed, deselect, chop, and cut, however one wishes to describe the process.

Accurate, intellectual, often intuitive decision making is a major benefit of having a first-class collection person on the staff. Not incidentally, the same librarian will apply similar skills to related matters from identifying the best online/CD-ROM texts to suggesting what printouts are of greatest value to the philosopher seeking the meaning of green tomatoes.

One should not be so presumptuous as to answer all problems about what to collect, what to drop, or what to consider. Nor should one try to circumvent the participation of groups in the process. But in this confederacy of opinion, leadership is required. A congenial, assured, and intellectually confident librarian who will ratify personal views is the validation of the meaning of professionalism.

THOSE WHO ARE SERVED . . . AND NOT SERVED

Most people charged with selection have problems with determining audience needs. The difficulty of defining "user" diminishes as the library becomes more specialized, but anyone who has participated in drawing up an approval program profile realizes even a self-selected group of students and teachers suggests unresolved questions. As one moves into the public library sector, the generations of users (and non-users) are presumably without number.

Generally, about one-third of the public wanders into a library, and these tend to be middle class, college exposed or educated, and more often than not in some type of professional work. There are surprising exceptions. Only one-quarter to one-third of a faculty will go to the library, and sometimes the student body uses it only for a social center.

According to people who should know, the Democratic National Committee, a voter who falls into the much-wooed middle class is described as a suburbanite, in a household with about a $35,000 income, younger than forty-five, with a child or two, and in a marriage in which both partners work. The Congressional Budget Office considers about 60 percent of the population middle class, with incomes from $19,000 to $78,000. Beyond that, study after study shows what every librarian knows: People who read tend to go to more movies, attend more political rallies, and are generally more involved with this side of the television than are others. They are stout defenders of libraries. One heartening aspect of budget slashes is that when really pushed to close down the library, most librarians can rally the necessary support to reverse city hall or the school administrators.

The middle-class stereotype may not fit all readers, although even those with higher or lower incomes and higher or lower education usually classify themselves as middle class. As a matter of fact, when was the last time you heard anyone call himself or herself upper class or lower class?

One common historical mistake is to equate middle class only with WASPs (white Anglo-Saxon Protestants). Today, multiculture, in all its definitions and facets, strongly determines the definition of middle class. By now librarians know, too, that middle-class minorities need not be illiterate, poor, or out of touch with society. Feminists fought long and hard, and the battle continues, to show that women are part of the reading middle classes without the support of men. Ironically, of course, women make up the majority of public library readers, and until only a few decades or so ago this was thought to be primarily a matter of supplying them with romances and cookbooks.

This is not the place to argue the necessity or the moral duty of the librarian to reach out for community members who are desperately in need of help. It is the place, however, to ask the reader to recognize that there is more to America than the middle. Various cultures whose members suffer economic, social, and educational deprivation require a library. Equally important, they require a librarian who is constantly pointing out to them that the library is a first defense against their isolation. Assistance for minorities and multicultural groups, as yet locked out of the middle class, starts with selection of materials to meet their often unexpressed, yet desperate, needs.

MORE EMPHASIS ON EDUCATION

Americans are getting dumber, and they know it. They don't like not being able to read well or being baffled when asked to find Mexico. Even the children of the middle class may feel left out, and certainly this is the case with many minorities. There are many roads back to self-esteem for Americans. The schools, the family, and the library are important in the quest for pride.

A real loss, particularly in public libraries, is the traditional focus on helping to educate the community. This comes, in part, from a lack of interest in seeing people as individuals rather than circulation statistics.

Another loss to public libraries, although equally applicable to schools and academic situations, is the lack of affirmative publicity in the local papers, the lack of an occasional article such as "Former Idaho Resident Recalls Boyhood Days in Weyerhauser Public Library." From time to time there is an equivalent piece, such as New York Times columnist Anna Quindlen's tribute to books: "I would be most content if my children grew up to be the kind of people who think decorating consists mostly of building bookshelves. That would give them an infinite number of worlds in which to wander."[3]

Little is to be found these days about the sometimes pressing needs of people inside and outside the library for guidance in choosing books. It has not always been that way. Turning to back issues of Library Literature one discovers that a few generations ago, such interests as "Books and reading" fascinated librarians. There are whole columns devoted to this and related matters from "ways into books" to "accent on the individual readers." In 1991 there is no subject heading "Books and reading," and "Reader guidance" has been supplanted by other interests.

There is a need to find *more*, not fewer, entries under "Reader guidance" or "Readers' advisory services." This will come about when three things happen:

- Librarians, particularly those working closely with the public, take a second, hard look at their library goals, particularly the collection and its part in those goals. No one, it seems, will argue with the triad information, education, and recreation. It should be a matter of emphasis, and that emphasis must be on education.

- Education, rather than entertainment, becomes a focus of the community.

- Concentration is centered on educational matter rather than on the popular, regardless of format. If some sacrifice of videos, films, and other audiovisual affectations is necessary, so be it. Knowledgeable selection will identify the appropriate non-print, as well as printed, acquisitions.

This is not, repeat *not*, to eliminate recreational reading from libraries. Even Wittgenstein, after all, enjoyed westerns. It is to suggest a better balance between budgetary problems, a cry for help from many Americans, and a return to cultural leadership. More attention must be spent on reader relations and on discovering books and other materials that will make us wiser, not dumber.

It need not be an either/or situation—either all of the materials are guides to a better personal world *or* they are similar to television's game shows. It can be a blend, although, again, the light novel or biography should take second place. Buy all best sellers, for example, but put the most effort into quality.

Education is not antithetical to relaxation. Education does not mean the end of fiction. On the contrary, it simply means more and better novels that enlighten and entertain as they go along. Education does not imply the loss of humanity and delight. It does show a deep interest by the librarian in the unfulfilled needs of culturally starved Americans.

E. J. Josey explains, "Librarians . . . need to integrate their goals with the goals of greatest importance to the American people."[4] There are many views of those goals, but in collection development they should first, foremost, and always support education. Here one should factor in information. Recreation, all too often the focal point of selection, has a place, albeit a narrow one.

Lest anyone believe the mission of the library as a schoolroom is past, consider an otherwise discouraging National Opinion Poll on Library Issues (1992): Some 93 percent of those polled believe public libraries should provide adult literacy programs. Simultaneously, 87 percent approve of a library collecting educational videos, but 75 percent oppose spending money on recent entertainment flicks. And while close to 70 percent disapprove of girlie magazines and related materials in libraries, a majority (85 percent) strongly urge the library to have educational data on Acquired Immunodeficiency Syndrome (AIDS).[5]

Actually, the public library as a bastion of education rather than an entertainment palace is the view held by most people. As Russell Baker puts it:

The dumbness is spreading, so naturally they are closing the libraries. "A few muddled thinkers," they said, wanted to close the schools. They said that since the schools were the source of the dumbness while the libraries were keeping learning from going out of style, it was the schools that ought to close.[6]

The phrase "keeping learning from going out of style" should be, and usually is, the battle cry of dedicated librarians. So to ask for reaffirmation of the obvious in constructing collections is hardly unusual.

It is more a failure of nerve on almost everyone's part. Homogenized culture has limited appeal, and then primarily to the people selling goods and trying to shape the U.S. consumer. More success has been evident in convincing Americans that the only game in town is television, a bad film, or a tattered copy of *Reader's Digest*. Librarians, locked in as much by lack of funds and personnel as by the lack of will, have done little to fight back to rescue Americans from themselves.

People may or may not use the library, but a growing number do turn to it for help. According to one 1991 study of 846 public libraries, it was no surprise to find that circulation was up close to 10 percent and budgets were level or down. Typical: "The California State Library's budget was cut $7,990,789 from last year" and "Worst year in a decade" was the cry from Arizona.[7]

The point is clear. If use rises and budgets fall, one must be more persuasive than most to get additional funding or reassign priorities. Here the easy yet difficult way is the Sunday closing, shutting down at nights, and halting other services. That is a favored approach, but a more difficult, realistic one is cutback on the purchase of books and audiovisuals considered useful solely because they are entertaining. Concentrate limited funds on the expressed needs of Americans by offering one-to-one educational materials.

Glutted with pablum television, films, and books, most Americans are desperately seeking help, even guidance, toward more challenging ways to spend leisure time. Publishing conglomerates and television producers argue this is not true, that the public is truly happy with the sad programming it receives. Unfortunately, some librarians buy the same sick, elitist argument. "Give 'em what they want" is the battle cry. Just how elitist can you get? All these experts on needs of people think they know, yes *know*, what the public wants. Actually, they are saying that as elite evaluators of public bad taste, they can dictate what the public wants. The old argument is that bad programming, bad books, bad anything, draws. Quality only draws yawns.

The purveyors of pulp, both inside and outside the library, not too cleverly turn the argument on its head by proclaiming that anyone who believes in American good taste is an "elitist." In a democracy, the term is poison to most, as well it should be when it has such a pejorative connotation. But the next time this descriptor is used in an argument, ask who is using it, and for what reason. Ask, "Just who around here has faith in the American people?"

More damage is done because the attitude creates a less-than-pleasing image of the professional qualities of the librarian, of the person making choices of materials. A critic's observation in England seems equally applicable in too many places in the United States:

My own town's public library, which is in this no worse than many another, has a shelf of CDs labelled "Easy listening." That sits well with the shelves of popular novels and the failure to buy almost anything worthy of serious consideration. A display of "hard listening—but worth it" would be more tonic and more true to the libraries' origins and purposes. Woolworth's, H. W. Smith (booksellers) and the rest can handle the easy listening side far more effectively. Point this out and the staff probably will ignore you politely, if hardly comprehendingly. Or they may suggest, with a mild air of reproof coupled with the assurance that they, not you, are going the way the world is going, that—misusing the language yet again—their principles for purchase are "democratic."[8]

Selection can have another dark side. Out there are people trying to put unacceptable books into the library or, more often, to take books off the shelves. The censor may be the otherwise rational, kind, and well-educated father or hordes of upset followers of the Ayatallah Khomeini ready to kill Salman Rushdie for his *Satanic Verses*. The outrage of parent and nation needs attention, although one can't help but agree with the expert who concludes: "I can see no way to bring this censorship battle to an end. No argument, however cogent, will ever be universally persuasive."[9] Still one must continue to fight.

REVIEW OF THE REVIEWERS

Few librarians, possibly too few, take the time or have the energy to read even a few of the books considered for purchase. There are several proven ways to go around this problem, at least in part. The most obvious is the use of reviews.

Librarians selecting books for people, not for statistical holes in Dewey or Library of Congress classification schemes, should consider it a professional duty to read certain reviews. There are basic sources of information about books for all types of libraries. Every person trusted with selection must read these regularly.

Following, in order of importance, are recommended review sources:

1. *Library Journal*, because the evaluators are librarians who know the needs of a public, and equally important, are able to evaluate the intrinsic quality of the book in terms of that need. The judges usually pull no punches, and one has respect for non-professional writers who write that well. Added features, particularly "Word of mouth," a reader's advisory service for patrons, and Michael Rogers's "Classic returns" remind the librarian about books this side of best sellers. One minor drawback—not enough reviews of magazines. (*LJ*: no comment.)

2. *Booklist*, as much for the section on reference books as anything else, but also because of the witty, well-written descriptive reviews. Also, there are more of them—up to 9,200 a year as contrasted with about half that number in *Library Journal*.[10] The one catch is that only approved books are reviewed. It would be helpful to include the "Others," which many read and are found in bookstores. The one-sided "cop out" policy is much dated and in need of change.

3. *Kirkus* is required for anyone concerned with middlebrows who may be less than involved with social issues, yet are avid readers looking for a book to entertain and inform. The satirical, hard hitting reviewers at *Kirkus* are given the space to express strong opinions. Agree or not, at least the librarian knows precisely what is thought of the book. Fault: too many words about really bad titles. Brand them and quit.

4. *New York Times, New Yorker, Time, Newsweek*, in no particular order. All these appeal to middle-class readers, often with similar tastes, although just as often different political and social viewpoints. A book reviewed favorably (and almost all titles are so evaluated) should be automatically purchased. The reviewers pretty well know Mr. and Mrs. Middle Class America, and while they may not offer more than a hint of the 55,000 plus titles out there, the ones they do review are usually those of interest to average readers. The catch for long time readers: too much blah and not enough bite.

5. *New York Review of Books (NYRB), Times Literary Supplement, London Review of Books*. These are leaders in dictating or reflecting (take your pick) the tastes of better educated, often highly selective readers. Not to know them is not to know the best essay-length book reviews available anywhere. One does not have to agree with the politics of the reviewer to appreciate the skills of the analysis. Question: Are those personals really necessary in the *NYRB*? Excellent spinoffs of these sources, but at a more local level, include the *Boston Review, Hungry Mind Review,* and *San Francisco Review of Books*—to name only three out of a dozen or more available.

6. *Choice* is the last best hope of the academic and large research library librarian who wants more current reviews than found in specialized,

subject journals whose reviews are always late. They are as necessary to selection as fiber is to diet, but this does not mean one has to enjoy either. The problems: no appreciation for fiction; primarily reviewers who are professors often do not understand library needs; and focus on many books that would be better off forgotten. The positive: fine comparisons with other titles and useful features and bibliographies.

7. *Small Press*, *Small Press Book Review*, and *Small Press Review* remind librarians that while the conglomerates control most of American publishing, there are over 5,000 small presses out there turning out marvelous titles from first novels to travel to methods of fixing skates. These titles review the more likely books for an average library, thanks, by the way, to national jobbers for the small press. There no longer is the excuse that these are unavailable. To miss any of these works is to miss an important section of American life.

8. *Publishers Weekly* is in some ways as important as any review source in this short list. As a trade journal of publishing, it is of major interest for the advertisements (particularly in the announcement issues), as are the concise forecasts and descriptive reviews of books likely to do well in a bookstore.

9. And while hardly a frontline review source, *AB Bookman's Weekly* is absolutely a marvelous habit for the librarian who wanders in and out of used book stores and has an appreciation of why the poet Callimachus settled down in the library at Alexandria. There may not be that many book reviews, but the articles are by readers all.

THE COMPUTER IN THE LIBRARY

Now for something not so completely different—the computer in the library.

The computer plays two major roles in selection. First, foremost, and always, it saves time, energy, and frustration. Where would anyone be these days without OCLC and friends? Second, electronic full text for magazines and newspapers opens up all sorts of possibilities either for balancing budgets through cooperative access or going bankrupt with each and every library buying the same CD-ROM. At any rate, within the next few years most libraries will have access to full text journals in some electronic form.

The future? If one gazes only into the reference crystal ball, one sees indexes, abstracts, data, statistics, archives, and so on, available online (or in some similar form). The average reference librarian will be concerned primarily with selecting electronic books rather than those in print. Browsing types of texts that are in constant use—from general encyclopedias to biographical sources—may or may not be best on a computer; but that's another debate.

So much for reference. Selecting for the general reader is quite another thing. Almost any work that one enjoys reading in bed will continue to be in print. Of course, there are those who envision the whole library as one massive screen. These computer cadets are primarily

- nonreaders confused by traditional bookworms
- computer salespersons, engineers, or stockholders who see billions arising from the destruction of print
- people desperately in need to find a new topic for conversation, particularly if most of their time is spent talking silently with a dead screen

The all-or-nothing computer fan is someone you are not likely to invite to an intimate dinner party. On the whole, he or she is about as fascinating as a VCR manual. Indeed, the person who invented the dishwasher deserves more honor. As imaginative forecasters, such fans are as reliable as your stockbroker or the weather reporter.[11]

With that, consider another point. Until someone convinces authors, researchers, and, more important, big publishers that there is more money in a computer chip than in a bound volume, you can rest comfortably in a room surrounded by books. To be sure, the day will come when virtual reality and a keyboard will help the million-year-old person pass the time, but only if there is a buck on longevity and tigers burning bright.[12]

In this world of software, hardware, and masses of undifferentiated information, what's going to happen to the library? More important, what happens to the librarians who have been selecting materials? Some see disaster, others see paradise—that is, the closing of the library. Some imagine librarians as trained engineers, cousins to Hal and the 2001 generation. More shiver in the shadow of George Orwell and Jonathan Swift. Speculation runs from suggestions of quick suicide by librarians to sailing off to the Outer Hebrides to go fishing.[13] The automation Cassandras may be right, particularly if librarians continue with strategies "based on a diminution of mission," as Arthur Curley puts it.[14]

There is a quick, realistic response to the pessimistic argument that turns on the mistaken notion that a computer chip will, in a few years, destroy a heritage of libraries that goes back to the Sumerians collecting versions of *Gilgamesh* some 5,000 years ago. Even with newly developed cuneiform, someone had to explain to non-experts and non-bibliographers the meaning and the importance of the different versions of the epic. In a period when all knowledge was readily captured on clay, judicious interpretation, selection, and evaluation were needed. That is little changed. Most of the world's information is not being mass produced for people with less than delicate discretionary abilities. The librarian as mediator between garbage and information is needed more, not less.

There is so little time and so much to read. The familiar refrain now becomes a scream for expert and layperson alike. The rapid multiplication of information, whether on a computer screen or book page, requires precise choices. Again, the librarian is needed to make those vital choices. Simple or complex technology is useful, but it is illusory as an evaluation aid. The theory problems of what to collect, what to read, what to remember, and what to discard are as fundamental as ever.

Service, economists proclaim, is a growth industry. And no wonder. Never, but never, have people needed the services of skilled librarians more as selectors and interpreters of data. There will be more, not fewer, librarians, and they will be better trained, intellectually alert, and certainly considerably more needed than they are now.

In conclusion, "to meet the challenges ahead, greater attention must be paid to expanding the skills of our current staff. We need to redouble our efforts to attract outstanding individuals to the profession."[15] That, or so it seems to me, is what library education is all about. One should salute the bright future. There is no better place to start than in collection development.

NOTES

1. Elizabeth Futas and David L. Vidor, "What Constitutes a Good Collection?" *Library Journal* 112 (April 15, 1987): 47. This title fits among the classical queries, many of which are right up there with the first (and last) question, "What is truth?" "Something that is good is valuable, but to whom? "How many times does an item have to be used in order to make it useful?"

2. "At 88, an Undiminished Spock," *New York Times*, March 5, 1992, C1. This is the Spock of baby book fame, not the space cadet.

3. Anna Quindlen, "Enough Bookshelves," *New York Times*, August 7, 1991, A21. A short, splendid essay on the joys of reading and encouraging children to read.

4. E. J. Josey, *Librarians, Coalitions, & the Public Good* (New York: Neal Schuman, 1987), 2.

5. National Poll, *Library Journal* 117 (February 15, 1992): 108–109.

6. Russell Baker, "A Blow for Ignorance," *New York Times*, April 23, 1991, A21.

7. "Library Budgets Survey '91: Hard Times Continue," *Library Journal* 117 (January 1, 1992): 14.

8. Richard Hoggart, "The Abuses of Literacy," *Manchester Guardian Weekly* 145: 1 (July 7, 1991): 22.

9. Richard A. Gray, "Case Studies in Censorship: Censoring *The Merchant of Venice*," *Reference Services Review* 19 (Fall 1991): 68.

10. "Book Review Media Statistics," *Library and Book Trade Almanac, 1991* (New York: R. R. Bowker, 1991). Figures for 1989–1990: *Booklist*, 9,217; *Library Journal*, 4,470; *New York Times Sunday Book Review*, 2,300; *Kirkus*, 4,000; *Choice*, 6,737.

11. These comments are not a lapse in manners but, rather, a response to the pretentious, inflated prose of numerous technocrats who cannot tell the difference

between Goethe and the telephone book. Fortunately, there are others (such as the pioneers of OCLC, CD-ROMs, online, etc.) who appreciate diversity as well as fidelity to economic reality. See just about anything written by Wilf Lancaster, with whom one does not necessarily have to agree, but whom everyone respects; and the series of wrong-headed yet fascinating articles by Raymond Kurzweil on "The Future of Libraries," beginning with the February 1, 1992, issue of *Library Journal* 117: 80ff. An all-time favorite, though, is the intellectual research and inspiration of the Chudnovsky brothers; see, for example, "Profiles: The Mountains of Pi," *New Yorker* 68 (March 2, 1992): 36–67.

12. The so-called realists who write about the future of the automated library inevitably miss a major opportunity to explain the economics of it all. See, for example, Erik Davis, "Cyberlibraries," *Lingua Franca* 2:3 (February/March 1992): 46–52. For an example of someone making too much, much too much, out of the automated library, see Roma M. Harris, "Information Technology and the Deskilling of Librarians or, The Erosion of Woman's Profession," *Computers in Libraries* 12 (January 1992): 8–15. (*Computers in Libraries* is an excellent magazine for keeping up with such matters.)

13. The fear that technology will create unemployment for librarians is a common one, and badly grounded in lack of understanding about what librarians do, particularly in direct one-to-one meetings with individuals. The misunderstanding, one suspects, comes from too many years of teaching people that they can use the library as well as the librarian and suggesting that librarianship is primarily a profession devoted to cataloging and dusting.

14. Arthur Curley, "Funding for Public Libraries in the 1990s," *Library Journal* 115 (January 1, 1990): 67.

15. Richard M. Dougherty, "Exploding Myths," in *Acquisitions, Budgets, and Collections*, ed. by David Genaway (Canfield, Ohio: Genaway & Associates, 1991), 19. This is a perceptive, intellectual approach to the basic issues in collection development.

Part II

RECRUITING FOR COLLECTION DEVELOPMENT

2

The Professionalization of Acquisitions and Collection Development

Terry L. Allison and Marion T. Reid

One of the Great Debates in our field is over the question of whether librarians practice a profession or simply perform tasks comprising an occupation. The issue lurks just below the surfaces of the fusses made about the librarian's image, the way librarians are portrayed in the media, and the frequently heard complaints that "we don't get no respect." Library work has evolved steadily throughout the years since Melvil Dewey, Charles A. Cutter, Charles Coffin Jewett, John Cotton Dana, and other early library leaders began formalizing their ideas about the library field and what constitutes appropriate management, services, and collections, and, by example, demonstrated what librarians do.

In recent years, the pace of change continues to move faster. New specializations have emerged; familiar ones have changed. Terry L. Allison and Marion T. Reid probe the history and character of the twin specializations of acquisitions and collection development, enquiring about the professionalism of the work they involve, the bodies of learning they require, and the ways in which they have been intertwined or separated in the library world. One point of agreement is that both contribute to building library collections.

To some degree, individual library organization patterns determine the closeness of the bond between acquisitions and collection development work. In very small libraries, the issue may be moot, since one librarian may wear both hats and perform all the tasks involved in building the collections—as well as organizing them for use, assisting in that use, and managing and controlling the use process. But in larger libraries—even those of modestly larger size—the issue is an important one, certainly for the librarians involved and also for the organization itself and the efficacy of its collection-building operations.

Marion Reid and Terry Allison examine more than just the two options of *together* versus *separate* for acquisitions and collection development work. They analyze each specialization into its component functions and responsibilities, then match selected combinations against models they observed in place, currently, in libraries. Exploring the advantages and disadvantages of each model, the authors offer several possible answers to questions about the professional relationships between acquisitions and collection development. It remains for the reader to decide which answers apply to his or her individual situation as well as exploring interesting alternatives.

Librarians continue to wrestle with image. The "AL Aside—Image; How They're Seeing Us" column in *American Libraries* reports on how often the stereotypical old-maidish librarian reappears to demand quiet and on how sometimes "The Librarian" is viewed in a positive light. Within librarianship, some individuals shape their professional self-esteem according to the level of status they perceive their specialty to have among librarians. It is doubtful that discussion about image does much to improve that image; however, examining individual specialties may help to emphasize the professional aspects that provide their practitioners with sustained interest, excitement, and challenge throughout their careers.

After offering some basic definitions, this chapter describes image perceptions of acquisitions and collection development functions, outlines components of both acquisitions and collection development, reviews the literature on acquisitions and collection development organizational models, and outlines the benefits and drawbacks to professionalization of basic organizational models of acquisitions and collection development.

DEFINITIONS

As soon as a library is created, someone must think both about what its collection will contain and how to obtain that material. These selection and procurement tasks may initially be handled by the same individual, but if the library grows to any size, they will be handled by different people. Over time, the selection process and related activities have become known as *collection development*; the ordering and receiving functions are referred to as *acquisitions*.

Of the two, collection development is the more difficult to define. No one term is consistently used from library to library to describe the process. Terms used as synonyms for collection development include "collection management," "resources management," and "collection building"; people who practice this specialty may be called "collection developers," "bibliographers," "subject bibliographers," or "subject specialists," and the individual primarily responsible for the activity may be called "collection manager" or "chief bibliographer." It is not surprising that each of these terms has a slightly different definition. What is surprising is that the same term can have different meanings in different libraries. Inconsistency in terminology may be explained by the fact that collection development, a specialty that has blossomed in the last twenty-five years primarily in academic libraries, has changed focus. People in collection development in the 1960s and 1970s concentrated on building their collections and wresting from the academic faculty the authority over spending the library materials budget. Money for collection building was abundant; spending it wisely before losing it was a challenge. When budgets began to decline in the mid-1970s, collection developers expanded their activities. Louis Pitschmann points out that "the past decade has witnessed a major shift in emphasis from selection-driven collection development activities to a more inclusive management approach to collection issues."[1] Charles Osburn describes collection development as "a public service system, characterized by a process of decision making to determine the desirability of acquiring or retaining library materials."[2] Working in collection development now means caring for the existing collection in addition to making decisions about what new materials to buy.

IMAGE PERCEPTIONS

The literature suggests that those practicing acquisitions and collection development may not be perceived to hold valued positions. Karen Schmidt refers to acquisitions as the "neglected stepchild of librarianship";[3] Jean Sohn states that "collection development has a history of being something of an organizational stepchild."[4] Joe Hewitt explains the acquisitions image problem in detail, saying that

acquisitions work, for a variety of reasons, tends to be undervalued and misunderstood; it may occupy a vulnerable position organizationally; it has minimal self-determination of its objectives and control of its work flow; and, regrettably, it receives less respect and exerts less influence than it deserves. Taken together, these conditions may lead to excessive stress on acquisitions staff, oversensitivity on the part of staff to certain management measures, defensiveness, and a general insecurity or vulnerability that may require special support and accommodation from upper-level administrators.[5]

Comments on the status of collection development do not reflect so severe a problem. They imply that negative aspects of collection development image perceptions relate more to the visibility of the function within the library than to the tasks its incumbents perform. Bonita Bryant says that collection development retains its invisibility if the director hears few complaints, funds are spent promptly, and few personnel problems are presented for resolution. She continues, "Perhaps invisibility is a comfort to all, but it hardly enhances their perceptions of the importance of their daily contributions to the library."[6] Osburn concurs: "A constant nagging problem of collection development has been its projected image as a 'soft' area. . . . [This has meant] that it is the activity that can be foregone or delayed when one of the more normalized or visible activities requires additional attention."[7] Results of Sohn's study of collection development organizational patterns suggest that the "image of collection development as the stepchild within the organization is disappearing among ARL [Association of Research Libraries] libraries, and the unit has established a definite and legitimate place for itself."[8]

It appears that the acquisitions librarian's self-esteem problem may be more severe than the collection developer's. Indeed, acquisitions seems to rank below collection development. Hewitt points out that the separation between collection development activity and acquisitions activity "is sometimes expressed as a division of the intellectual [versus] the clerical aspects of building library collections."[9] The perception, then, is that collection development work is more substantive—or more professional—than acquisitions work.

COMPONENTS OF ACQUISITIONS AND COLLECTION DEVELOPMENT

Rose Mary Magrill and John Corbin list acquisitions functions as obtaining information about materials; initiating the purchasing process by selecting the appropriate vendor, encumbering the funds, and preparing and despatching the order; maintaining records for materials ordered; receiving and checking materials; authorizing payment for materials; clearing order records; claiming and canceling orders; handling materials that need special treatment; dealing with special situations; and developing and analyzing performance statistics.[10] In their description of the role of the professional in technical services, Marion Reid and Walter High identify professional acquisitions activities as designing and evaluating workflow; determining format of order information files (including serials control); establishing and evaluating exchanges; monitoring expenditures; evaluating vendor performance; setting guidelines for searching and verifying, selecting vendors, authorizing payment, and disposing of unwanted materials; and resolving issues not covered by guidelines.[11] In other words, the acquisitions librarian's duties may be viewed primarily as managerial.

Carolyn Bucknall outlines collection development functions as selection, faculty liaison, collection management including preservation, collection evaluation, fund management and library use instruction.[12] Sheila Creth's list specifies weeding, which Bucknall included within collection management, and adds reference and access, "an important adjunct to ownership."[13]

One responsibility that can be found in either acquisitions or collection development is the pre-order search function, which could be included either in Magrill and Corbin's first function (obtaining information about materials) or as part of Bucknall's first function (selection). Within a library, it is important that tasks involving verification of material to be ordered be clearly assigned to either one area or the other to ensure it is done, but not done twice.

Note that fiscal management is included as a responsibility of both acquisitions librarians and collection developers. Usually, both contribute to fiscal management, but from different perspectives. Typically, collection development librarians allocate library materials budget funds and acquisitions librarians make certain that they are expended within the proper period and according to the regulations that apply to their institution.

In addition, when more than one individual is handling acquisitions and collection development, the person responsible for the unit assumes administrative tasks. Reid and High identify these as strategic and short-term planning; coordinating and establishing policy; hiring, dismissing, and evaluating personnel; and preparing management reports.[14]

Acquisitions and collection development each incorporate distinct professional responsibilities that provide variety and intellectual challenges.

ORGANIZATIONAL MODELS

Most of the literature describing organizational models pertains to collection development within academic libraries, for academic libraries are those most likely to have a critical mass of staff with collection development responsibilities. As Bucknall states, "The type of organization likely to have a collection development function is determined by several factors, most of which relate to size: size of the collection, size of the book budget, and size of professional and support staff. Generally, the smaller the library, the smaller the collection development program."[15]

The first description of types of collection development organizations was done in 1973 by Elaine Sloan, who studied the placement of the collection development function in twenty-three libraries in the northeastern United States. She identified three types of collection development models: a selection unit within public services with responsibilities for allocation and fund monitoring being placed in acquisitions or technical services, a separate collection development unit whose head participates in top management, and a collection development head participating in top management who works with specialists drawn from various departments to work part time on collecting responsibilities.[16] Articles by James Cogswell and Bryant reiterate these organizational types and offer more variations of these models.[17]

Bucknall divides the models into two categories: *centralized* (with the responsibility carried by an individual or unit, usually reporting to the library director) and *coordinated* (responsibility attached to an individual working with others throughout the library who assume work on collection development activities part time).[18] Articles by Carol Cubberley and Midori Kanazawa advocate the centralized approach; Karin Ford and Jasper

Schad espouse the coordinated approach.[19] Variations on categories within
the two types abound. Results of Sohn's study of collection development
organizations in libraries belonging to ARL conclude "that ARL members
seem to have almost as many organizational patterns as there are ARL
libraries."[20] Pitschmann, who offers a comprehensive overview of collection development organization patterns, concludes that it is not the organizational "method per se but rather how the method works, how its
function and components are carried out, and how they are coordinated
that determine a method's success."[21]

The place of acquisitions within the library is more consistent. Although
the ordering and receipt functions may be divided by format (e.g., monographs, serials, nonbook formats), they are generally found reporting to the
assistant/associate director in charge of technical services. With the arrival
of local automated systems, some acquisitions departments are beginning
to assume copy-cataloging duties; however, this additional responsibility
does not affect their place within the organizational hierarchy.

BENEFITS AND DRAWBACKS OF ORGANIZATIONAL
MODELS

As described above, various authors have explored the pros and cons of
organizational models for both acquisitions and collection development.[22]
The purpose here is not merely to reiterate the organizational models but
to reevaluate them in terms of the range of professional activities and
responsibilities each type of collections or acquisitions position within the
library either demands or promises. The following section will examine
various models of collections and acquisitions librarianship, not to judge
their efficiencies within different library settings or organizational models,
but to illuminate the various benefits, drawbacks, and possible professional
future for each range of responsibilities.

Bibliographer Only

The professional activity of the bibliographer only model is most commonly practiced in large research libraries, specialized libraries, or the
largest of public libraries. With collection budgets consistently waning, at
least compared to the rate of inflation for library materials, this library
specialty of bibliographer with no other duties becomes increasingly rare.
Yet as Haskell describes it, the specialty of bibliography can provide some
of the most fulfilling professional library work.[23]

In the bibliographer only model, the librarian's tasks likely include
reviewing approval plans, initiating new orders based either on requests
(from faculty, students, the public, or private user of the library) or on the
bibliographer's reading of reviews, publishers' announcements, or search

of bibliographies. Depending on the subjects covered or the depth of the collection, the bibliographer may select from more esoteric or specialized literature, including auction catalogs, specialized journals, and out-of-print catalogs.

The bibliographer only model has at least two substantial professional benefits. First, in devoting full energy to collecting in a subject or range of subjects, the bibliographer often develops or extends his or her own knowledge of the field(s) of collection. Second, this bibliographer model describes work that is typically performed independently. Although surely one measure of the librarian's professionalization has been the increased commitment to participation in joint activities, such as local, state, or national planning committees, the bibliographer's sometimes wide freedoms to conduct the business of developing and managing the library collection are also a mark of professionalization.[24]

On the other hand, the independent bibliographer is likely to work on a collegial or professional level with the faculty, students, and public or private clientele whom he or she serves. In some areas of librarianship, such as public services, there is a constant debate about how to structure the job such that librarians perform consistently high-level professional activities, such as providing in-depth reference rather than routine directional services. Although this same demanding public may sometimes treat the bibliographer as an ordering clerk, the typical bibliographer, with the power of the purse, is more likely to experience collegial, professional interactions in which not only the buying power but also the intellectual power of the bibliographer is acknowledged. In a specialized library (e.g., hospital, architectural or design, military intelligence) there could be a great and vital dependence on the bibliographer's professional knowledge. In such situations the bibliographer's professional knowledge of a field becomes a significant factor in the success or failure of the enterprise.

The bibliographer only model, though working independently in selection and some collection management functions, may also work quite closely with other bibliographers in building and managing a library collection. When looking for a professional model of librarianship, bibliographers who work independently, performing similar functions at similarly high levels of responsibility, can be compared to other professionals, such as lawyers or accountants who also function this way within an institution or corporation.

The bibliographer may come to have the degree of specialization in library collections through his or her own interest in one or more professional areas or fields of scholarship. Thus, the bibliographer only model actively participates in two professions, librarianship and another field. As part of pursuing professional activities in other arenas, the librarian may belong to or participate in non-library associations, give papers at conferences, publish, teach, lecture, and consult. In other words, the bibliographer has a dual career as librarian and as scholar or professional in another field. This extended connection to the other field not only boosts the librarian's professional esteem (or image among other professionals or academics) but also is likely to improve his or her ability to manage a collection.

Returning to the independent vein of bibliographers, the bibliographer only model may have total management responsibility for a collection, including selection, acquisitions, budgeting, and storage and preservation of materials. This range of activities still concentrates on collections, but it also provides the bibliographer with professional challenges beyond selection. Independence within an organizational model, in other words, does not necessarily imply a narrow specialization or job focus.

The bibliographer only model may have organizational drawbacks (one already mentioned is that fewer libraries can afford this degree of specialization, as all staff are requested to work at many functions), but it may also have some drawbacks in providing professional-level work. The bibliographer only model may in some libraries translate to "only bibliographer." The librarian working as the only bibliographer can have so many subjects to collect and manage that in-depth, specialized, or professional attention to every subject is impossible. If the bibliographer has a wide range of subjects to collect but a narrower range of professional or specialized interest, she or he might naturally spend more time, energy, or money on the familiar. Conversely, the relatively unknown subjects, since unknown, might be collected more indiscriminately or inappropriately. In other words, the wider scope of knowledge the bibliographer covers, the more likely that professional-level collection development and management cannot be sustained.

The prized independent role of the bibliographer may isolate the bibliographer not only organizationally but professionally. If there is no mix of public services in the bibliographer's responsibilities, the bibliographer can lose contact with the new interests of the library's clientele. If there is no extended contact with technical services, the bibliographer may acquire collections without considering when or how the collections will be made available to the library user. Bibliographers who become too specialized or isolated from other library activities may lose the mark of professionalism, to "create an active, visible, and critical role for themselves in the education and scholarly process."[25]

Bibliographer with Additional Responsibilities

The bibliographer with additional duties can experience all of the benefits and drawbacks of the bibliographer only model, but now mixed with the responsibility to perform other library functions. Perhaps the bibliographer/reference librarian or the bibliographer/cataloger or even the holistic bibliographer/cataloger/reference librarian model would provide a more satisfying or complete range of professional activities than the bibliographer only model. Seeing the benefits of the collection by connecting the library user to the material sought, either through reference interviews or by providing appropriate cataloging or other description, may be seen as providing equal, if not more, professional satisfaction than merely collecting materials.[26] Like the bibliographer only model, however, the bibliographer-with-other-responsibilities position has its own professional benefits and drawbacks.

As noted above, one hallmark of librarianship as a profession, which has been described as what separates the M.L.S. holder from even the most-skilled non-M.L.S. library worker, is the theoretical knowledge and practical responsibility (usually shared) for the whole of library operations.[27] The bibliographer who also has one other or a range of other responsibilities may be in a much better position than the bibliographer only model to gain the integrated, theoretical approach that is the mark of a professional.

One drawback of this mixed set of responsibilities is the potential for diffusiveness. Is it professional to handle a variety of duties without being able to devote extended time or energy to any one of the tasks? Or is this variety itself and the expertise required to handle the mix of duties the very mark of the professional? If there are two major sets of responsibilities, does the librarian need to become a "double professional" and master all of the skills in depth, forming professional networks and so on for both areas of specialization?

Our belief is that the librarian can perform professionally in these multifunction or dual professional models. However, the potential for burnout is great. Expectations of the bibliographer who has additional responsibilities may not consider the additional professional-level work required by each librarian specialization. Too often, the bibliographer's work is characterized as "selection only," while what is demanded of the bibliographer is the full range of professional responsibility for and knowledge of the collection.[28] To make the dual or multiprofessional model work, the bibliographer must be able to devote dedicated time in the library workday to bibliographer responsibilities, rather than spending lunch, commuting, or using free time going through approval forms, publishers' catalogs, or reviews. In the mixed model, collection development or management may not receive the professional level of attention it deserves, although the librarian is perfectly capable of this professional level of collection management.

Collection Development Officer

One collections activity clearly recognized as professional, probably because of its management component, is the overall responsibility for library collections. In a public, college, or special library, this responsibility may rest with the head of the library. Primarily within university or research libraries, but possibly in other types of libraries, this position might be part of top administration or rest with a single librarian at the department head level. In either case, the administrator responsible for collection development and management might also have administrative responsibility for other library activities, such as acquisitions or preservation; he or she might manage other departments, such as special collections, or any number of library departments either in public or technical services.[29]

The primary professional benefit of the collections officer model is that authority and responsibility clearly rest with this collections librarian. Collections officers typically develop and defend the total "book" budget, which, in reality, is a book, serials, audiovisual, and, sometimes, computer or optical disk and CD-ROM budget. They allocate resources based on the perceived need of the entire library-user community and frequently have the authority to initiate new sources of funding for the collection. They initiate and coordinate weeding and storage projects, as well as the always difficult serials cancellations projects (though they likely work intimately with acquisitions and/or serials departments in this task). In short, the look of a collection, how much of what types of material are displayed or stored in which places, is the professional responsibility of the collections officer.

The professional skills of management, hiring, training, supervision, and evaluation all involve extensive coordination both within the library and with its client base. Budgeting and allocation of resources is a particularly sensitive area of professional work. Budgeting requires not only the allocation of available dollars (which, again, may have to be justified each year or supplemented through grants) but also professional-level knowledge of publishing trends (output, pricing) and the ability to weigh compelling but competing needs. Fund raising or gift solicitation requires negotiating skills and even the diplomatic skills of refusing certain gifts. Another typical administrative function, to evaluate the effectiveness of library functions, is now made easier with automated tracking of budgets, circulations, and even in-house use of periodicals collections. The collections officer must then decide when to initiate such reports, how to evaluate them, and how to adjust collections policies or procedures to the newly gathered information.

The professional drawbacks of the collections officer position are likely to be similar to that of other managerial positions. The collections officer may feel like a professional manager more than a professional librarian. The collections officer, who may have entered the library profession because it allowed the hands-on contact with library materials, may now lose most of that contact. Just as a head of public services *may* no longer work at a public desk serving the public, the collections officer *may* no longer collect library materials. The collections officer, therefore, has to depend more on managerial skills than bibliographic ones to evaluate the success of collection-building efforts. Like any other move into management, the bibliographer considering collection development responsibility has to evaluate the change in the nature of duties. What is clear, however, is that the management responsibilities are likely to bring more recognition as a professional.[30]

Acquisitions Only

Hewitt outlines well the "mutually reinforcing perceptual and role conditions" that, in effect, are the primary drawbacks for the acquisitions librarian. They are the following:

1. A characterization of acquisitions as predominantly routine and clerical in nature, resulting in a serious underestimation of the professional and managerial aspects of acquisitions work
2. Relative isolation of acquisitions librarians both in terms of a strong immediate support group and a knowledgeable and understanding community of users
3. Lack of academic recognition as a specialization in the profession and the absence of an acknowledged, coherent body of theoretical or codified expert knowledge
4. An intermediate service role that calls for the execution of decisions made by others and an ongoing accommodation to goals determined by others
5. The need to accommodate to fiscal and workflow cycles, which leads to an emphasis on short-term objectives and expedients, an orientation differing fundamentally from that of acquisitions' most closely associated functions
6. A dependence on external entities to meet objectives and the need to meet externally imposed regulations while also serving as the channel through which these constraints are imposed on others in the library[31]

After seeing this list, one might wonder what is beneficial about being a librarian who handles acquisitions responsibilities only. Basically, the acquisitions librarian must turn the drawbacks into advantages. The acquisitions librarian can explain to upper management some complexities of the business of acquisitions. However, doing this in excruciating detail will have negative impact. Describing processes from the perspective of the library as a whole or providing explanatory articles might be the best approaches. Having no internal colleagues who understand the full gamut of acquisitions responsibilities, the librarian in charge of acquisitions can enjoy being the library expert on publishing and acquisitions issues. The acquisitions librarian with good interpersonal skills can maintain good relations with staff in both collection development and cataloging; and he or she can explain to acquisitions staff how important it is to maintain flexibility. The acquisitions librarian who plans well can save special projects that accrue during peak workloads to be done when the workload is at low ebb. The acquisitions librarian who deals well with the institution's accounting department can serve as one of the library's primary contacts with the institution's business services staff. The acquisitions librarian who explains external problems (e.g., mail strikes, vendor error) as they arise can avoid having the acquisitions operation blamed for circumstances beyond its control.

The acquisitions librarian, then, is often responsible for the professional operation of the business side of collecting library materials. The acquisitions librarian is the library's most likely contact with book vendors, serials agents, and out-of-print book dealers and may handle gift acceptance and acknowledgment. The acquisitions librarian can be charged with the task of pursuing ephemeral material and difficult formats or acquiring collections from parts of the world where the book trade is not organized along U.S. and European models. A professional task of the acquisitions librarian may be, then, the mastery of the world book trade.

Acquisitions librarians have also been in the forefront of the serials pricing issue. In fact, acquisitions librarians also often act as the library's serials librarians. The definition of acquisitions librarianship can include serials acquisitions, so that some or all of the professional attributes of the serials librarian can be seen even in the acquisitions only model.

Acquisitions and Collection Management Together

As suggested above, there are many possibilities for combining different library functions with either acquisitions or collection development. In describing the professional functions and responsibilities of either the bibliographer only, mixed bibliographer, collections officer, or acquisitions only librarian, one should not forget that responsibility for collections and acquisitions together may provide a satisfying professional position.

The obvious professional benefit of integrating these two functions is the integration itself. Since the functions of selecting, acquiring, and managing materials are so interdependent, the librarian who supervises or performs all these functions (within a manageable job) would gain in knowledge and expertise. For the acquisitions librarian who may be "desperately seeking status,"[32] the connection to higher-esteemed collections work may provide a professional boost, though Christian Boissonnas, among many others, defines acquisitions work as professional. Conversely, the collections librarian may find that more extensive knowledge and practice of acquiring material and the understanding of the crucial impact that acquisitions has on collection building leads to that wonderful holistic experience of librarianship described above in other integrated models.

The sole drawback of the acquisitions/collections librarian appears to be the feasibility of mastering these dual functions. An attempt to integrate completely acquisitions and collections development at Yale University continues to be controversial. Some literature is in preparation that will examine the source of the debate about the effectiveness of this integrated model.[33] What is now clear about the debate is that a lack of organizational success for a particular model of librarianship is likely to signal a lack of professional success for an individual librarian, so that the proposed merits of an integrated job need to be weighed against the practice of trying to perform professionally within the model.

IMPLICATIONS FOR RECRUITMENT

When an acquisitions and/or collection development position opens within a library, those managing the search should be aware of the acquisitions/collection development model being used. They should review all the models and decide if they wish to develop a different model instead of continuing the one that is in place. They should consider carefully whether they want to recruit an individual interested in and capable of performing a variety of tasks or whether they want someone who will work in a job that is more single-task oriented. James Neal indicates applicant pools were more significant for positions that offered both reference and cataloging duties when recruiting new M.L.S.'s for cataloging positions.[34] Certainly many factors (e.g., size and type of library, geographic location) influence why individuals apply for a certain position, but this interest in variety by new librarians suggests that a post with both acquisitions and collection development responsibilities will attract more interest than one that concentrates solely on either acquisitions or collection development.

CONCLUSION

Obviously, neither acquisitions nor collection development librarianship is on a smooth course. If librarians are to continue in their traditional roles of selecting, acquiring, and organizing information for the benefit of the public or private clientele whom they serve, they must shift their professional practice to match changed realities in the publication and distribution of information. Several writers predicting future trends in academic libraries strongly advocate leadership roles for acquisitions and collection development librarians.

Ross Atkinson writes that "acquisitions administrators—who, along with circulation, interlibrary loan, and preservation officers, have primary responsibility for delivery in the paper-based academic library of today— need to begin planning now to expand their knowledge and responsibilities to respond to the new requirements for information delivery in the rapidly approaching age of networked information."[35] He further explains that acquisitions leaders, so as to assume a major role, must broaden their knowledge in the economics of publishing and scholarly communication; in electronic publishing; in information technology and telecommunications.[36]

Osburn, who describes collection development as "central to library operations and pivotal in library community relations," states that

> success in the future will depend upon librarians' assumption of the role of information and service brokers rather than continuation in the role of maintainers of an intellectual utility. It is up to C[ollection] D[evelopment] librarians, foremost, to lead in this movement toward the adoption of a new role and the establishment of a new image, since their processes are central internally and pivotal externally.[37]

Creth suggests a new paradigm for academic library organizations. Instead of continuing with the traditional segmented approach of splitting into two primary areas of public services and technical services, she recommends that the organization use collection management as a bridge to establish an integrative approach. In this model, those with appropriate subject knowledge would be appointed to teams by discipline. They would use their knowledge of the collections and information sources as the basis from which to accomplish both public and technical services responsibilities.[38]

The two 1991 articles in *Library Resources & Technical Services* that review the literature of acquisitions and the literature of collection development, respectively,[39] as well as the articles cited above, represent current thinking about the challenges to acquisitions and collections librarianship. Models of acquisitions and collection development organization that reflect the shift to non-traditional formats will undoubtedly arise. Most libraries, despite the worst budgetary picture in years, continue to acquire traditional materials and thus will require both acquisitions and collections librarians in professional positions. Monitoring and managing change in the publishing and information worlds will be added to the professional responsibilities described in this chapter. To respond professionally to change, acquisitions and collection development librarians will have to show more initiative and take more risks when executing their responsibilities. Despite reservations about how sweeping or immediate the changes in publishing and information accessibility will be,[40] there is no doubt that electronic publishing, document delivery, and other access strategies will become an increasingly important part of the professional repertoire of the acquisitions and/or collection development librarian.

NOTES

1. Louis A. Pitschmann, "Organization and Staffing," in *Collection Management: A New Treatise*, ed. by Charles B. Osburn and Ross Atkinson. Foundations in Library and Information Science, vol. 26 (Greenwich, Conn.: JAI Press, 1991), 138.

2. Charles B. Osburn, "Toward a Reconceptualization of Collection Development," *Advances in Library Administration and Organization* 2 (1983): 175.

3. Karen Schmidt, "Buying a Good Pennysworth? A Review of the Literature of Acquisitions in the Eighties," *Library Resources & Technical Services* 30 (1986): 333–340.

4. Jean Sohn, "Collection Development Organizational Patterns in ARL Libraries," *Library Resources & Technical Services* 31 (1987): 123.

5. Joe A. Hewitt, "On the Nature of Acquisitions," *Library Resources & Technical Services* 33 (1989): 105–106.

6. Bonita Bryant, "The Organizational Structure of Collection Development," *Library Resources & Technical Services* 31 (1987): 118.

7. Osburn, "Toward a Reconceptualization," 180–181.

8. Sohn, "Collection Development Organizational Patterns," 131.

9. Hewitt, "On the Nature of Acquisitions," 106–107.

10. Rose Mary Magrill and John Corbin, *Acquisitions Management and Collection Development in Libraries*, 2nd ed. (Chicago: American Library Association, 1989), 78–80.

11. Marion T. Reid and Walter M. High, "The Role of the Professional in Technical Services," *RTSD Newsletter* 11 (1986): 59.

12. Carolyn Bucknall, "Organization of Collection Development and Management in Academic Libraries," *Collection Building* 9 (1988): 13.

13. Sheila D. Creth, "The Organization of Collection Development: A Shift in the Organization Paradigm," *Journal of Library Administration* 14 (1991): 74–75.

14. Reid and High, "The Role of the Professional in Technical Services," 59.

15. Bucknall, "Organization of Collection Development and Management," 13.

16. Elaine F. Sloan, "The Organization of Collection Development in Large University Research Libraries," Ph.D. dissertation, University of Maryland, 1973, 130.

17. Bryant, "The Organizational Structure," 111–122, and James A. Cogswell, "The Organization of Collection Management Functions in Academic Research Libraries," *Journal of Academic Librarianship* 13 (1987): 268–276.

18. Bucknall, "Organization of Collection Development and Management," 13.

19. Carol W. Cubberley, "Organization for Collection Development in Medium-sized Academic Libraries," *Library Acquisitions: Practice & Theory* 11 (1987): 297–323; Midori Kanazawa, "Organization Theory and Collection Management in Libraries," *Collection Management* 14 (1991): 43–57; Karin F. Ford, "Interaction of Public and Technical Services: Collection Development as Common Ground," in *Library Management and Technical Services: The Changing Role of Technical Services in Library Organization*, ed. by Jennifer Cargill (New York: Haworth Press, 1988), 45–53; Jasper G. Schad, "Managing Collection Development in University Libraries That Utilize Librarians with Dual-Responsibility Assignments," *Library Acquisitions: Practice & Theory* 14 (1990): 165–171.

20. Sohn, "Collection Development Organizational Patterns," 131.

21. Pitschmann, "Organization and Staffing," 142.

22. See, for example, Bucknall, "Organization of Collection Development and Management," 13–14.

23. John D. Haskell, Jr., "Subject Bibliographers in Academic Libraries: An Historical and Descriptive Review," *Advances in Library Administration and Organization: A Research Annual* 3 (1984): 73–84.

24. Ibid., 81.

25. Sheila D. Creth, "Personnel Issues for Academic Librarians: A Review and Perspectives for the Future," *College & Research Libraries* 50 (1989): 151.

26. Creth implies this in "The Organization of Collection Development," 78.

27. Creth, "Personnel Issues for Academic Librarians," 145–146.

28. Creth, "The Organization of Collection Development," 74.

29. Sohn, "Collection Development Organizational Patterns," 125.

30. Although Creth describes the evolution of management from an authoritative center in the library to a more collegial, dispersed model, that is, the "professional" model, in "Personnel Issues for Academic Librarians," 147.

31. Hewitt, "On the Nature of Acquisitions," 114.

32. Christian Boissonnas, "Desperately Seeking Status: Acquisitions Librarians in Academic Libraries," *Library Acquisitions: Practice & Theory* 15 (1991): 349–354.

33. Joyce L. Ogburn, "Organizing Acquisitions: The Yale University Experience," *Library Acquisitions: Practice & Theory* 16 (1992): 367–372.

34. James G. Neal, "The Evolving Public/Technical Services Relationship: New Opportunities for Staffing the Cataloging Function," in *Recruiting, Educating, and Training Cataloging Librarians: Solving the Problems*, ed. by Sheila S. Intner and Janet Swan Hill (Westport, Conn.: Greenwood Press, 1989), 111–119.

35. Ross Atkinson, "The Acquisitions Librarian as Change Agent in the Transition to the Electronic Library," *Library Resources & Technical Services* 36 (1992): 7.

36. Ibid., 17.

37. Osburn, "Toward a Reconceptualization," 182–183.

38. Creth, "The Organization of Collection Development," 78.

39. Richard P. Jasper, "Challenge, Change, and Confidence: The Literature of Acquisitions, 1991," *Library Resources & Technical Services* 36 (1992): 263–275; William S. Monroe, "Redefining the Library: The Year's Work in Collection Development, 1991," *Library Resources & Technical Services* 36 (1992): 277–289.

40. Timothy B. King expresses reservations in his "Impact of Electronic and Networking Technologies on the Delivery of Scholarly Information," *Serials Librarian* 21:2/3 (1991): 5–13.

3

Recruiting as Competition: Why Choose Collection Development?

Eugene L. Wiemers, Jr.

Many people begin library school with some idea of a specialty. Potential librarians tend to think of specialization in terms of the types of libraries in which they'd like to work—school media centers, medical libraries, special libraries, academic libraries, or perhaps public libraries. They are more likely to define their future occupation by distinguishing between client or user groups instead of between functional specialties. Once students begin a library and information science program, they will find courses that have these same user group orientations. Students soon realize that they have more choices to make about specialization as they discover courses that concentrate on functions, such as library automation or reference work. By taking courses in many areas, students have the chance to learn about each and to gather impressions about which type of library and which type of work appeals to them and to which they are best suited. If a student is fortunate, he or she has the opportunity for internships or insider's visits to libraries. Even when students decide to pursue a particular specialty, their choice is often influenced by the job market upon graduation. Someone who had not thought of collection development as a specialty in library school might adopt it if his or her first job happens to include some collection development responsibilities.

One of the most effective ways of learning about a specialty as a career choice is talking to someone in that area—and the most persuasive is someone who thoroughly enjoys his or her work. Eugene L. Wiemers's chapter presents such an opportunity. He offers a complete picture of the many sides of collection development work, drawing in detail the tasks, responsibilities, demands, and joys of being a selector. Here is someone who understands the complicated nature of collection development work and describes it as both entrepreneurial and connective. Wiemers does not ignore the drawbacks— the pressures to satisfy library users, to evaluate and select materials from constantly changing possibilities, to balance time and priorities. Yet he finds that the intellectual and personal rewards far outweigh the stresses and frustrations. Wiemers's chapter is an essay recruiting individuals to the field of collection development. As he concludes, "Why not you?"

A librarian can choose multiple career paths within the profession, paths that lead to computer programming and cataloging that share common traits with puzzle solving; paths that lead to reference work and direct public service that share common traits with social work; and paths that lead to administration and management that share common traits with any executive position. This chapter is a personal statement of what collection development is about, what it offers, and what it is like to be a collections librarian. It explores the nature of the work, the features that make it attractive, and the frustrations that make it both difficult and worthwhile. Above all, it is an explication of why the bibliographer's job is simultaneously one of the least understood and one of the most interesting jobs in the library.

THE ACADEMIC OFFICERS OF THE LIBRARY

One can fuss about nomenclature and titles—collection development, collection management, chief collection development officer, director of collections, bibliographer, curator, selector—but the essence of the collection development role in the academic library is captured by the introduction one collections officer got at a faculty meeting. This individual was introduced as "the chief academic officer of the Library." To the speaker and the listener, this was both accurate and descriptive.[1] The collections librarian is the librarian who is most likely to be in continuing contact with the faculty, and the one who manages the resources the faculty most closely associates with the library—the books, journals, and other resources that form the body of scholarship essential to the scholar and researcher. The bibliographer or subject librarian is the one who tries to know what the members of the faculty need, who tries to shape the information resources to meet that need, and who most directly provides support for their academic work. The bibliographer is also the one most likely to be in contact with their graduate and advanced undergraduate students—showing them how the literature of the field is organized and helping them find specialized materials that are needed for their theses and research projects. The bibliographer also directly shapes the collection that is immediately available for undergraduates. The collection development officer is the one who pays attention to the substance of the academic programs of the institution, leaving the business end, the processing end, and the on-demand desk service to others, thus putting the paying of bills, the managing of "bureaucratic procedures," and most of the handling of complaints to other harried administrators. So who wouldn't want collection development jobs?

In most library settings, it is the collections librarian who selects the materials that define the substance of the information resources of the library.[2] For that reason, although few users know that someone actually chooses the things that end on shelves or are available to users, the selector has the most visible job in the library. At least the results are visible. They are also permanent. Through their choices, collections librarians construct from what is presently available the future resource base of the library. If selectors do not unnecessarily constrict their horizons and do manage to keep up with changes in formats, tastes, possibilities, and combinations of resources, they will continue to be central to the information structure of the library and continue to build the unique features that people come to libraries to use.

Why? Because collections librarians, bibliographers, selectors, curators, no matter what they are called, are in the *choice* business and, by their own choices, guide and direct the library and to a great extent determine the potential the library has to solve information problems and inform users' sensibilities.[3] The work may be prosaic and hidden from view, but its results are valued and visible—something that people see and something that if done well, people will use today in ways we know and in the future in ways not yet imagined. Though not a career choice that is obvious to the uninitiated, most who think about it can imagine what the job of selecting a library's collection must be. What is amazing is that it is a job they pay you to do!

YOU GET PAID TO DO THIS JOB?

Many collection development librarians will tell you this story. Asked what they do by a child, a colleague, or a stranger, they say that they review the available material in, say, modern literature, physics, or African studies and choose what the library will acquire or make available. The enquirer thinks about it for a minute, then asks, "They pay you to do that?"

For some, it is an ideal job, one that asks you to take all you know about a subject area, an institution, and a clientele and put it together to make a library. It is a job that will take what you know and put it to work, and one that demands imagination and continued growth.[4] What you get in return is the joy and excitement of creating bodies of primary materials that make scholarship possible, of amassing the secondary literature that helps define a field, or of bringing the best of art, literature, or popular material to the public.

Perhaps unique among library specializations, collection development offers the possibility of unlimited professional growth without changing positions. It is a field that lets the practitioner use subject knowledge in an immediately useful way, and to continue to do so as that knowledge expands. It is a field that allows practitioners to improve as they get older, and the more they know, the better they can get. It is one in which opportunities for professional advancement derive from knowing something and putting it to work, not just from rising higher in an organization and supervising larger numbers of staff.

Moreover, collection development librarians have latitude for self-direction as professionals that often makes their positions the envy of colleagues in other fields. At least in the subject-matter aspects of their work, collections librarians' positions are usually defined as the library's expert on an assigned field. They are expected to know how to choose what is needed for the collection in the subject area or know how to find out and to act on that information. As a practical matter, the choices they make are rarely scrutinized in detail. Selectors are expected to make informed choices and take responsibility for them. They are expected to articulate the plans for the future of the collection and to work with considerable autonomy to set goals and timetables to realize those plans.[5] No matter how a particular position is defined in a library, whether as a so-called "full-time bibliographer" or as a collections librarian who mixes this role with others, he or she functions as the library's expert on an assigned field and is allowed, in fact required, to know more about what needs to be done in that field than anyone else. By definition, selectors set priorities both for building the collection and for finding out what users need.

This autonomy often translates into control over the work schedule, and this control is a very important aspect of the position. One source of jealousy within libraries and among librarians is resentment of the autonomy that collections librarians have and the control they have over their own time. Unlike catalogers, who are often tied to workstations and output quotas, or reference librarians, who face the stress of dealing with an unpredictable public that has the right to ask any question any time, the collections librarian often decides the mix of activities that go on during each day—selection routines, working with users with complex inquiries, finding out what the public needs—and chooses the order in which they will be handled. This is real freedom. It is not freedom from routine work, nor freedom from hierarchy and supervision. It is, however, the freedom to schedule activities in the way that makes sense, such as writing at the times when the body is alert, and doing the rough screening to select new items late at night if that fits the body's need. It may also mean spending an afternoon at a seminar or meeting with a faculty group, which looks like pleasure to many colleagues, but which is real work, important work, and work that makes a late night selection session a virtual certainty.

They pay you for this work. They pay you to deal with the challenge of an unpredictable clientele and to try to mold the library's collection to an unpredictable future. This puts you face to face with the unpredictable nature of the library enterprise, and it generates a lot of fun. These are some typical examples:

- Good ideas make successful grant proposals, proposals that usually require some informational support and that may themselves strengthen the library's resources. Nearly every library grant requires some statement of collection strength, which involves the collection development librarian in its writing (and in doing the work to make sure that what the text says is true *is* true).

- Involvement with the faculty can result in joint projects or joint publishing ventures. This work may not be directly in the job description, but it cements the library's relationship with the faculty as an information provider and a supporter of their work.

- In most academic settings, the collection development role can result in teaching opportunities and the chance to put students and young scholars together with research materials. Teaching can take many forms, from the singular encounter with an individual student to an organized program of regular bibliographic instruction for students within fields of the collections librarian's specialty. There is probably no more rewarding way to assure the utility of a research collection than the opportunity to design an instructional program that touches every student in a teaching department. What you learn from the students helps make the collection better and helps you appreciate and improve access tools. This kind of teaching is a comfortable supporting role. The instructor or graduate adviser provides the direction and critical judgments about the students' work. The bibliographer gets the fun of helping a student explore the literature and find new approaches. The faculty person gets to be the harsh critic; the collections librarian can be the supportive coach.

All these examples are opportunities for collaborative work. In essence, the bibliographer's role is entrepreneurial and connective. The work "brings things together" and enables others to do things that they cannot do by themselves. Collections work brings living scholars and students in contact with dead ones, it brings current researchers in contact with earlier ones, and it brings people together with others working on or interested in the same subject areas. In a unique way among librarians, the collections librarian's role brings him or her into contact with all aspects of the library and its public. He or she is expected to know about and cultivate good relationships with scholars, students, booksellers, publishers, authors, grants administrators, donors, lawyers, book lovers, academic administrators, program planners, program evaluators, catalogers, acquisitions librarians, computer center staff, library assistants in all areas, accounts specialists, budget officers, and librarians from other libraries. Doing the work requires joining the present state of a subject with its past and requires close collaboration with preservationists to make sure that those connections remain intact. It is connective work that aggregates, consolidates, and grounds a field in its past, that joins people who share common interests, and that brings people into contact with materials that change the shape of what they produce.

The collections librarian is not pigeonholed. He or she is expected to know a lot about a lot of things. The work provides the chance to do something with that knowledge. Unlike most non-administrative library positions, collections librarians have considerable budget management and decision-making authority. There are plenty of uses for creativity and opportunities for statistical and other types of analysis, if you are so inclined. The work requires broad and deep institutional knowledge, the essential background against which all choices for the collection are made. The successful practitioner combines knowledge of bibliography and subject matter in ways that are neither constrained by current fashion nor limited by conventional scholarship. And if possessed with a practical sense, a flair for logistics, an entrepreneurial approach, and, above all else, the capacity to integrate new kinds of information sources and new ideas with old, the bibliographer faces a future with limitless possibilities for creative librarianship—and gets paid for it!

THERE'S SOMETHING OUT THERE

One principal attraction of collection development work is the boundary-spanning nature of the work itself. Collection development has the ability to draw librarians' attention away from the frequently mundane and routine side of the job and to focus on activity outside the sphere of libraries altogether. So often in librarianship, the object of attention is the librarian and his or her colleagues and supervisors—discussing and planning new ways to deal with the public or new procedures to handle problems. When there is a reference to a body of knowledge, it is on the knowledge of practice of the librarians' specialty. What collection development work offers, however, is an added dimension—the scholarship and substance of the collections librarian's assigned field, a field that has its own discourse, its own growth characteristics, and its own human embodiment in the form of users.

Thus there is more to the librarian's work than "me and thee." There is an "it"—an assigned field and an assigned clientele.[6] There is an object of attention outside the library, outside the control of the library administration, and outside the control of the bibliographer. The subject librarian's work is to make connections with an ongoing, ever-expanding, and changing academic enterprise and a volatile user community. This can be frustrating because scholars are usually steps ahead of their current publications and interested in new areas. An added complication is the way in which clientele needs are defined in terms of the future, yet the bureaucratic structures that support their work are usually defined in terms of the past. The essence of a collections librarian's work is putting scholars and research materials together, which means continuous involvement with a discipline or public and personal involvement with engaged individuals—people who think ideas matter.[7]

In an academic library, the subject librarian is expected to know the academic gossip and to spend an appropriate amount of time to get it. To someone who is not a bibliographer, watching this kind of discourse take place "on company time" may be troublesome. Much of what transpires in these conversations is transitory and of dubious value. Buried in the sometimes petty talk, however, is insight on where a department, academic program, or research project is heading; what new programs or research centers are planned; where the opportunities for involvement of the library and the information infrastructure will be; and what new demands are likely to be placed on the library in the process. Moreover, intrinsic to the exchange of information is the development of relationships between the library and its clientele that will help each build for the future. Moving from the informal arena to the formal, this kind of information exchange may eventually get the bibliographer directly involved in program planning for the discipline.

The bibliographer has a unique niche in the academic enterprise. Faculty users have gradually relinquished to librarians the role of discovering and selecting new information sources. Filling this niche requires curiosity about what is needed and assertiveness to attack the problems. Until now, this has meant knowing the world of print publishing and subject bibliography. As electronic resources expand, the role will encompass knowledge of an increasing array of information products available for purchase, as well as everything that is available on the national networks for "free." When electronic collections were novelties, or when they primarily substituted for printed reference works, a bibliographer could leave their selection and evaluation to others. Increasingly, however, basic scholarly resources—books, journals, research reports and reviews, and primary source data—are available in electronic formats in a variety of ways. This has reached the point that a detailed knowledge of what they are and how to get to them is necessary to choose new materials for the library.

Like the knowledge of the institution and its background, familiarity with the electronic information landscape has become a basic requirement for a collections librarian. Particularly when the user community is marginally familiar with the newly available electronics, the bibliographer must be knowledgeable if the same level of expertise can be employed in making selections decisions as has been employed in the past. What the collections librarian brings to this new set of choices is both the background and skills to balance the new with the old and the responsibility to hold flashy new products to the same standards of value that are used to assess print sources.

There is something compelling and exciting out there for a collections librarian—the constantly changing information environment, knowledge of which is crucial to the successful performance of an essential role. It is an environment that cannot be mastered but can be grasped, one that must be constantly examined and reevaluated. The difficulties in assessing electronic collections are only the most recent example of the challenge, even frustration, of choosing materials and access to materials in a changing universe of possibilities. The source of frustration, however, is also the source of reward as it provides the opportunity to keep stepping across conventional boundaries and into new professional territory.

THE DRAWBACKS

So why doesn't every librarian want this dream job? While it shares some characteristics with the role of scholar or teacher and draws on similar subject expertise, collection development librarianship is still essentially a service role and not for everyone. Not everyone who has the requisite subject knowledge is willing to work in the sometime subordinate position to scholars. The work requires people with the interpersonal skills to build good working relationships with all kinds of people and to deal occasionally with demanding and unreasonable clients, who have an entitlement view of their relationship to the library. These clients may treat the collections librarian as their own "personal librarian," leading to inappropriate requests for personal research services. Nevertheless, at its best, the bibliographer is a peer and an integral part of the academic enterprise, a service professional who helps make the enterprise work.

The nature of selection is also not for everyone. The work involves constantly making judgments about the appropriateness of resources, and most of them are negative. A typical bibliographer in a research library, for example, can easily make 200,000 selection decisions in a year, mostly decisions not to acquire an item. The weight of the routine can be exhausting and, at times, demoralizing. The work is by its very nature solitary and sometimes isolating. Each selector must devise an efficient strategy to keep up with the relevant literature in the field and to identify new publications. He or she will not be able to delegate this reviewing and sifting to others. Sources need to be read, in a concentrated way. This work is singular and disciplined, and only the collections librarian will be aware of the dimensions of the workload. Selection can be scheduled, but it cannot be planned, and since much of the rest of the work also cannot be planned, much of the actual selection takes place in odd hours and odd places and often when there are much more enjoyable things to do. The very aspects that make a subject librarian's role exciting—the clientele, the subject knowledge, and the diversity—also often mean a work life with too many demands and too many difficult choices.

The design of collection development positions creates its own drawbacks. Nearly any subject area, however small or large, can be constructed into a full-time position. It is a matter of how much interaction with faculty, students, and other users the library can afford; how much time is available to spend on working with colleagues at other libraries on cooperative projects; and how much time can be set aside for ferreting out obscure materials. If the subject assignment carries the usual responsibilities—user liaison, instruction of students, selection, and coordination with other librarians and other libraries—the work will expand to fill any amount of available time. The question is how much time is intended. Typical practice in many libraries is to create a position with impossible dimensions and demands and then ask the collections librarian to use all the skill and knowledge he or she has to do the most important things first. The subject knowledge and the knowledge of the clientele become the determinant not only of what to do but also of the priorities that govern the work. This allows the library to set general collecting priorities by assigning subject areas narrowly or broadly, and to assign the responsibility for setting priorities within a subject area to an "expert" librarian. This practice should mean that priority setting is well informed at an operational level. It also means that some tasks will not get done, some tasks will get done only superficially, and the most important tasks will be accomplished. Ultimately the bibliographer is responsible for making these choices. Since the bibliographer is never an expert in all the subjects assigned (no library can afford a specialist in every field it serves), informed choice of priorities can be especially difficult to achieve in a field that is not one's own.

This method of assigning professional responsibilities gives the bibliographer the autonomy and professional latitude that make the job so interesting. It also makes the job stressful and frustrating.[8] Not only is the selector the only person in the organization who takes the responsibility to build a specific collection, the selector is also the only one who knows what is not being done and what could be done if there were only more time. It is an individual and often troubling responsibility to decide what will not be achieved.[9] It sometimes seems that nothing is ever finished.

THE REWARDS

At the end of the day, the rewards in the bibliographer's job are both intellectual and personal. The intellectual challenge of working in a subject specialty, of rebuilding the library's collection daily, of balancing new sources with old, and of applying durable standards of judgment to constantly changing resources is continuous and deep. The personal rewards of working with people to whom ideas matter and whose ideas are part of the subject matter of the relationship are impossible to estimate. Someone needs to talk with users and try to understand their needs. Someone needs to make the decisions about what information products to make available. Someone needs to learn how to assess these products against the standards of what has been available in the past, decide which new products are needed, and put those decisions in priority order. Someone needs to manage the budgets that pay for them and manage the time it takes to achieve all this. Why not you?

NOTES

1. Accurate and descriptive titles for collection development librarians are not so simple. This chapter cuts through this complexity, using the titles bibliographer, selector, collections librarian, collection development librarian, and subject librarian interchangeably. This convention is intended to convey the idea that the role transcends the title and not that titles do not matter. The lofty title "curator" could also be used, though that imprecision would violate the conventions of most library settings.

2. The examples used in this chapter draw from the author's own experience working with more than 100 subject librarians over the past dozen years. The roles that collections librarians play in academic libraries are often mixed with other roles in reference and technical services. The fact that such combinations exist does not diminish the essence of the role itself. The role also generalizes to library settings in public and special libraries, but the author cannot authentically conjure examples from these domains.

3. Carrigan argues that choice is the "essence of collection development." Dennis P. Carrigan, "Librarians and the 'Dismal Science,'" *Library Journal* 113:1 (June 15, 1988): 22.

4. Ross Atkinson reminds the reader that underneath any framework used to understand the selection process, "creativity and interpretation" are essential to selections. See his "Citation as Intertext: Toward a Theory of the Selection Process," *Library Resources & Technical Services* 28, 2 (April/June 1984):109–119.

5. Schad argues that planning is now the primary function of the collections librarian, not selection. Jasper G. Schad, "The Future of Collection Development in an Era of Fiscal Stringency: A Symposium," *Journal of Academic Librarianship* 18:1 (March 1992): 4–7.

6. The metaphor is taken from David Hawkins, "I, Thou, and It," in *The Informed Vision: Essays on Learning and Human Nature* (New York: Agathon Press, 1974): 48–62. Hawkins develops this idea in the context of teacher and child. Obviously there is substance within the discipline of librarianship that comprises an "it" in ordinary supervisory relationships. The collections librarian's focus outside librarianship provides a more remote object of attention that can be an effective, long-term diversion from what Hawkins calls "an affair of mirrors confronting each other" in relationships without content (p. 52).

7. Hazen argues that understanding users is the greatest challenge for collection development. Dan C. Hazen, "Is Money the Issue? Research Resources and Our Collections Crisis," *Journal of Academic Librarianship* 18:1 (March 1992): 13–15.

8. This was described in detail by David G. Null, "Robbing Peter . . .: Balancing Collection Development and Reference Responsibilities," *College & Research Libraries* 49:5 (September 1988): 448–452.

9. Null says, "Often the problem is to convince people who have never done collection development that such activities are worthwhile and essential for the library as a whole." Ibid., 451.

4

Late Awakenings: Recruiting Subject Specialists to Librarianship and Collection Development

Michael A. Keller

People choose to become librarians for many reasons: Some prepare initially for a career in librarianship, and others come from other positions and fields of study. In-depth knowledge of a subject, language, or geographic area is a wonderful plus in any area of librarianship—from cataloging to reference work. It is particularly beneficial for those building and managing collections. How can we encourage individuals who have advanced knowledge in particular disciplines, either through formal education or practical experience, to consider pursuing a career in collection development?

Michael A. Keller looks at this question and suggests practical steps for recruitment. He begins by exploring the responsibilities of subject specialists who hold collection development positions in academic libraries. Keller presents their tasks and areas of activity, drawing both from library literature and an unpublished position description questionnaire completed by bibliographers at Yale's Sterling Memorial Library.

Keller considers qualifications for subject specialist bibliographers, looking at the distinctive skills that subject specialists bring to the position and the qualifications a library will likely want when hiring a new bibliographer. He looks at the benefits, perquisites, career paths, and satisfactions for those who choose positions in collection development. Finally, he discusses the recruitment and interview process as it works in the larger academic libraries. His suggestions for the conduct of both libraries and candidates and their responsibilities during the search for new bibliographers are adaptable for all libraries.

An abstraction that informs the activities of all collection development officers to one degree or another is that of the "library of the mind," the idealized bibliography on any given topic. It is the "library of the mind" against which scholars measure their satisfaction with any collection. The "library of the mind" is not everything ever written or published on a topic but, instead, the works, sources, and commentaries necessary to complete research. This concept relinquishes notions of comprehensiveness in favor of other notions of quality and relevance. The idea of the "library of the mind" played out over many topics and disciplines by generations of scholars, students, and bibliographers building library collections influences selection or, better, selectivity.

Since we acquire library materials in our research libraries to meet current needs for subject coverage, to respond to expressed needs for individual titles, and to anticipate future needs, any mechanisms—especially those of access to remote collections through interlibrary cooperation and the expanding universe of digitized sources available through networks, which allow us to move titles or sources in any scholar's "library of the mind" to the collection, logical, virtual, or actual—extend our grasp. Because as bibliographers we select to build collections and because topics are expanding and hybridizing at a greater rate as there are more scholars and scientists, we cannot rely solely upon selections made in the past.[1] This chapter considers the work of subject specialists in collection development, the need for people with expert knowledge in research libraries, and the means to attract them to librarianship.

INTRODUCTION

One has only to read the biographies of the contributors to the excellent series of volumes on the selection of library materials published by the American Library Association (ALA) to realize the proportion of bibliographers, curators, and other selectors who have come to collection development from a discipline other than librarianship.[2] Presumably this is true because knowledge of the discipline or subject or region of the world for which or from which a collection is being developed is an important qualification for success in that work.[3] A corollary is that at least among the small group of bibliographers whose advice on selection for research libraries appeared in the ALA *Selection* series, most turned to librarianship after serious involvement in the discipline for which they became selectors. There is remarkably little written about this phenomenon per se in the literature of librarianship and little available about it in the literature of other disciplines and trades. This contribution is intended to discuss the practical aspects of recruiting subject specialists to collection development in research libraries, but little of the historical and sociological factors of the phenomenon itself.

"RE-TREADS"

The population of professionals who work in research libraries can be characterized in many ways. More study on this population is warranted, especially as this generation will have been responsible for stewardship of a great transformation of human civilization, involving the addition of digital resources and methods to the traditions of collecting, providing access to, and interpreting printed materials and their analogs.[4] Those of us who have worked in research libraries even for a short time recognize that professionals engaged in librarianship can be divided into two groups with ease: those who "heard the call" early and prepared from the beginning for a career in libraries and those whose postgraduate interests were elsewhere and came to librarianship after preparing for work in another field, often earning the M.L.S. as a requirement of continuing employment. The latter group might be called "re-treads."

A survey published in 1983, but completed in 1978, of degrees earned by members of the Association of College and Research Libraries (ACRL) showed that 93.5 percent of the members surveyed were earning or already had master's degrees (presumably the M.L.S. or its equivalent), 37.6 percent were earning or already had a second master's degree (second only in the sense of another degree besides the M.L.S., which might well have been earned before the library degree), and 16.2 percent were earning or already had a doctoral degree.[5] Another survey of advertisements for professional positions in academic libraries over a twenty-year period showed that in 1979, 27.6 percent of advertised positions required a subject master's degree.[6] These are tantalizing evidence of our subjective appreciation of the phenomenon of persons coming to research librarianship after education and perhaps experience in another discipline, "re-treads" awakening late to career possibilities as subject specialists in libraries.

Such specialists are desired because they have the experience necessary to make qualified decisions to build research collections. To make more explicit Ross Atkinson's model of selection:

The reader [with an advanced degree in a subject or specialized language qualification working as a selector] is very much the product of the texts he or she has come upon before; an individual's ability not only to understand but also to evaluate and make other decisions about newly encountered documents (or other utterances) [including the decision to acquire the text in question] depends upon his or her reference to such personal textual experience.[7]

Some of us are self-taught specialists, but most of us came by our specialty through the mills of academe.

ROLES AND RESPONSIBILITIES OF SUBJECT SPECIALISTS IN COLLECTION DEVELOPMENT

Recruiting subject specialists is most successfully accomplished with an understanding of the roles and responsibilities for such people in general and the detailed duties of any given position. The following descriptions of roles and responsibilities present generic aspects of the work of subject specialists. Further reading of the cited sources and the related literature of collection development might strengthen one's understanding, but recourse is advised to specific position descriptions from institutions employing subject specialists devoted to the desired coverage. Recruiters are wise also to consult with senior practitioners of the specialty at other institutions for advice on qualifications and nominations.

Subject specialists build research library collections using a three-dimensional matrix of knowledge:

1. knowledge of local curricular and research programs in the assigned fields, subjects, regions of the world, and/or languages;
2. knowledge of the literature of the fields covered, including methods and techniques of scholarship or science of the predominant and developing sub-specialties;
3. knowledge of the publications trade *and* the "invisible college" of the disciplines assigned.

With this matrix of knowledge secure (and noting that different, though related, communication and learning skills are essential to achieve useful knowledge in each dimension cited above), the subject specialist must then make judgments to develop policy and/or selection criteria to select titles for local readers in the assigned disciplines. Such selection activities occur within the institutional constraints of budgets and, ideally, the abilities and capacities of local technical processing colleagues to provide intellectual access via cataloging and classification. Thus, the subject specialist must satisfy the assigned responsibilities in a web of local and remote, real and virtual, and budgeted and unlimited opportunities and limitations.

There are several descriptions of the role of subject specialists that provide helpful background information in recruiting new bibliographers or curators. One must keep in mind, however, that most literature on this topic was written before the great debate on "access instead of ownership" as the new paradigm for research libraries and the related visionary presumptions on the role of electronic publishing and digitized resources for scholarship. The debate and the vision of an electronic future for libraries have strong implications, at least superficially, for the role of subject specialists in research libraries. At least one recent article by two influential leaders in librarianship draws what I believe to be a false dichotomy between "knowledge professionals" and "collection professionals."[8] My conception of the role of subject specialists in research libraries depends upon content rather than medium and includes notions of virtual and logical collections, electronic and optical resources owned locally or accessed remotely, and a most extensive exploitation of whatever resources there are for supporting and even stimulating growth of scholarship in any discipline, however broadly or narrowly defined.

John Haskell's review of the roles of subject specialists in libraries identifies five main areas of activity:

1. selecting materials;
2. establishing contacts with the book trade in foreign countries;
3. specifying and performing various processing and cataloging functions;
4. providing reference support and bibliographic instruction;
5. liaising with faculty.[9]

Bonita Bryant identifies nineteen tasks assigned to collection development officers, meaning selectors of all sorts, but these apply also to subject specialists who are presumably engaged in collection development for a greater portion of their time.[10] Paramount among these is selection, of course, and Dan Hazan's recent article on that function provides the most extensive description and theoretical foundation for it.[11] Bryant's list neglects one task that is increasingly important as the national efforts continue to preserve the huge portion of our collections printed on self-destructing acidic paper—selection for preservation; Paul Mosher provides a pragmatic introduction to that task.[12]

The literature on collection development rarely provides a generic description of the work of subject specialists written *by* subject specialists. A "Position Description Questionnaire [for] Managerial and Professional Staff" at Yale University distributed in June 1989 prompted the following extensive description by the bibliographers responsible for development of the main stack collections in Yale's largest library, the Sterling Memorial Library:

1. Primary Purposes [of bibliographers] are to develop, manage, supervise and preserve collections with enormous capital value in addition to unmeasurable value for scholarship. Using advanced knowledge of academic subjects, we select materials to support library collections of national and international standing in the fields of the humanities and social sciences. Through work with faculty and students, we develop and make accessible materials to support the research and teaching that is the primary mission of the university. Through cooperation with colleagues outside Yale, we work to develop and maintain "national research collections" to support scholarship.
2. Duties and Responsibilities—
   a. Develop, manage, supervise and preserve collections with enormous capital value in addition to unmeasurable value for scholarship;
   b. Select materials in traditional as well as new formats, i.e., books, serials, microforms, newspapers, maps, as well as machine readable data files, software, and CD-ROM products, that support and enhance scholarship;
   c. Evaluate existing collections to identify strengths and areas of weakness and needed growth; evaluate materials in need of preservation and conservation

and decide on appropriate format (Xerox copy, microform, or extent of repair);

d. Manage collections, decide on cataloging priorities and location in cases of special need;

e. Participate in interviews and evaluation of candidates drawn from national pools for positions within department and across library;

f. Serve on committees and task forces addressing issues and formulating policies in areas of current and future interest to the library system, e.g., automation and public relations, management of software collections, retrospective conversion of collections, etc.;

g. Maintain relations with publishers and representatives of the book trade, e.g., suggesting ideas for microform projects and evaluating theirs;

h. Select and evaluate performance of vendors; maintain communication and working relations with vendors;

i. Establish and monitor approval plans and blanket orders; this includes articulating needs of collections; determining subject and format profiles to guide vendors' selection of materials for the library, evaluating offers from vendors, and negotiating terms and practices of fulfillment and reporting of these complex arrangements;

j. Initiate and monitor exchange agreements and evaluate appropriateness;

k. Manage funds in the range of $250,000 to—, including both general appropriation and endowed funds with legal restrictions as to subjects; assign funds appropriate to materials ordered; control expenditure, pacing outflow across year; forecast financial needs over fiscal year;

l. Provide advanced specialized reference services to faculty, graduate students, undergraduates, visiting scholars and faculty;

m. Maintain public relations with faculty and students, donors, alumni, visiting scholars; represent the library to the university and in the world in national and international meetings, and forums of various sorts such as scholarly and professional meetings, edit library newsletter *Nota Bene*, prepare and mount exhibits of library materials;

n. Accomplish job without regard to scheduled work hours and with minimal supervision;

o. Supervise special collections and rooms, e.g., Judaica, Andrew Study;

p. Provide general service to Library through reference and consultation with other departments and libraries; provide direction to other professionals and units in processing and managing the collections;

q. Apply general concepts of collection building and interdisciplinary knowledge to other subject areas on a temporary emergency basis to assist colleagues and fill in for missing colleagues;

r. Maintain scholarly and professional activities that benefit the library directly (staying current in fields of responsibility, involvement in professional associations, consortial relations, etc.), that contribute to the larger intellectual and cultural life of the university (college fellowships, advising new freshmen, guiding senior essays, talks, courses), and that contribute to learning and library service outside Yale (professional associations both scholarly and library, reviewing books, delivering papers at conferences, broadcast and library presentations, consortial relations).[13]

LIBRARY ENVIRONMENTS

A crucial aspect of recruiting subject specialists to collection development is the library environment in which the new bibliographer is expected
to work. We are familiar with the position description prose that begins
"The Library at Everyone University is the center for scholarship." Yet
much more than advertising cant is required to describe any library's
working environment. Too often we make available the detailed description of the library environment only in response to questions during the
interview. Perhaps this is good, since any candidate failing to make such
an obvious query would most probably not fit well in any research library
environment. Nevertheless, consideration of the working environment for
the subject specialist may prove useful not only for recruitment now but
for sustained health of the entire library organization. Digital resources are
a new, permanent part of library environments and may require different
modes of access and service than more traditional library materials. Consequently, the recruitment of any new professional, particularly a new
subject specialist, is an opportunity to review and, if necessary, revise
organizational structure.

Louis Pitschmann provides the most up-to-date review of the organizational environment for collection development and much of his description
is valid for subject specialists.[14] Wilmer Baatz's report of a Council on
Library Resources fellowship concerning performance of the function of
collection development describes the organizational variants and actual
decision points for collection development in eighteen Association of Research Libraries (ARL) members. His presentation, though dated, nevertheless provides a nearly complete outline of questions on the institutional
environment in which subject specialists work.[15] Status of subject specialists and resentment or ill-feeling arising from perceived different status by
other library staff is addressed by Baatz in his section on "elitism vs 'no-one
cares' " and by Barbara Henn in her more recent article on acquisitions
management.[16] The consequences of the perceptions of stratified classes of
library professionals eventually confront all subject specialists.

Mutual respect among research librarians with different functional specialties can be enhanced by deliberate efforts to communicate, not only
through daily decisions and advice needed to move materials through the
selection and processing streams but also through discussion of policies
and philosophies across functional or organizational boundaries. Collections result not only from selection decisions but also from the work of
catalogers, who create access records, thereby making actual the relationships of any single title to other titles through subject analysis and classification decisions. Without catalogers, the work of collection development
officers would reside in more or less inaccessible mounds. Further, the
profession has developed such complex modes of bibliographic description, classification, and subject access that the work of collection develop-

ment officers *and* catalogers would be much diminished without reference librarians to interpret and conduct extensive searches. Frequent acknowledgment of one another's functional dependencies and reliance on one another to serve the specific and general needs of readers will help reduce the negative aspects of envy and enmity occasionally apparent among professionals in research libraries.

The research library environment is complex enough to allow varying expectations for staff with different roles and responsibilities. To minimize resentment and ill-will among those of different backgrounds and assignments, several means for communication and appreciation should constantly be employed. Moreover, the attitude of library administrators in showing equal understanding and respect for staff at different levels and with different kinds of work should be a significant example for the rest of a research library staff to follow in working effectively with one another. For subject specialists covering many disciplines, broad regions of the world, and sources in a variety of new and old formats in living and dead languages, as is the norm, what becomes necessary is latitude about daily schedules, clear understanding of the projects to be done or underway, and collegial communication among selectors—all important intangible qualities of the work environment. Subject specialists are expected to talk with faculty in their offices, at departmental meetings, before and after lectures, at symposia and seminars. They ought to attend annual meetings of the key scholarly societies in the several disciplines for which they are responsible. Subject specialists must read and digest key articles and, in the best of circumstances, review all incoming materials in their disciplines, often forwarding certain works of interdisciplinary nature to colleague bibliographers.

In these ways, they keep current their individual three-dimensional matrices described above. Evaluation of the performance of subject specialists can occur using the generic annual evaluation criteria most research libraries employ, but with expectations adjusted to fit the particular assignments. Recurring criteria of relative frequency are satisfaction of immediate requirements of the library (such as appropriate use of library processes), attention to budget and financial requirements, and availability to readers for advanced reference consultation. Satisfaction of scholars and students with collection building by an individual can be observed only after the subject specialist has had an obvious impact on the actual shape of collections owned or available; this usually takes years.

QUALIFICATIONS

In 1969 Robert Haro provided a succinct statement of qualifications for subject specialist bibliographers, lacking only the requirement that subject specialists in nearly all library settings need a library science degree, particularly because of technological advances in the profession.[17] He mentions subject competence, foreign language proficiency, and knowledge of the book business; he specifically disclaims the need for the M.L.S. degree. Haro could not have foreseen the impact of digital resources on research libraries, but if we admit the digital medium *and* notions of leased access to remote electronic files to the phrase "book trade," his qualifications are entirely valid, but for his disclaimer of the library science degree. Occasionally subject specialists are recruited without an M.L.S. either because of equivalent experience or with the requirement that such lacuna in their qualifications will be remedied within a specific period.

In the questionnaire stemming from the Yale classification and salary review, Yale's bibliographers described their specialized knowledge and skills required to perform their responsibilities:

- Educational background is highly relevant, indeed intrinsic to the job of selecting materials for a large academic and research library. We have years of experience in our fields as scholars, teachers, collection builders and researchers in academic libraries.

- Advanced degrees are required for the job of selector. All selectors have advanced graduate degrees (M.A.s or Ph.D.s in our subject areas and/or library science degrees).

- Language skills are especially relevant. Most of us are skilled in several European and/or Near Eastern languages and have a working knowledge of others. Knowledge of ancillary disciplines . . . is also useful.

- Computer skills are increasingly important and required in our daily work; we use computers for bibliographic searching, ordering, monitoring collections, word processing, electronic mail, etc. We also assist readers in the use of electronic data bases.

- Knowledge of the book trade is vital to the job. This is gained through years of experience, often requiring foreign travel, not from formal presentations. This is a complex knowledge as the book trade varies from country to country and changes over time.

- Also vital is knowledge of the scholarship, literature, methodologies and ongoing trends and developments of the disciplines and subject areas for which we select materials. These may differ from country to country, for each discipline has a national tradition of content and methodology.

- The skill of keeping up with fields and disciplines must be accompanied by the ability to learn new skills (such as the computer skills associated with increasing automation) and to adapt to a changing work environment.

- Beyond knowledge of the current state of a subject field or discipline, the ability to imagine and provide for newly developing areas and future interests is essential for building excellent collections.

- Important to the performance of the job are mastery of academic research library organization, operation and service; negotiating and diplomatic skills; knowledge of years of past practice at Yale (whom to ask and how to reconstruct . . .).[18]

A statement of required, desired, and preferred qualifications is an essential element of position descriptions. Such statements should be as objective and as impersonal as possible. Moreover, requirements for evidence of satisfaction of the stated qualifications should be explicit and equally objective.

REWARDS AND PERQUISITES

Subjects specialists and other specialists in research libraries are typically paid for the qualifications and experience that differentiate them from entry-level positions. Beginning with J. Perriam Danton, there has been acknowledgment that subject specialists are "expensive to secure and keep."[19] In many ARL institutions, subject specialists are hired at least one rank above entry-level librarians and are frequently brought in at ranks involving continuing appointments after a probationary period of rarely more than a year. Beyond rank, pay, and the ordinary benefits associated with any appointment as a professional librarian, other rewards and perquisites are available.

Attendance at scholarly meetings and the usual round of professional gatherings is important to assure that subject specialists stay current with research trends. Since most subject specialists have multiple assignments, annual attendance at any given society's meeting is usually not supported. However, as the papers given at such meetings are often early reports of new research, attention to this layer of any discipline is important for attentive bibliographers because it provides early warning of developing trends. Of course, some of these reports are published in scholarly journals; but with the lead time in many journals exceeding a year, dozens of relevant sources could be missed by reliance on published papers only.

Occasional domestic and foreign travel to visit institutes, publishers, collections, and book sellers and to develop contacts with colleagues beyond the frenzy of professional meetings also offers subject specialists the means to refresh their three-dimensional knowledge matrices and to find or evaluate collections for eventual acquisition. For sources "out of the trade"—like many government documents, particularly at the subnational levels—grey literature, ephemera, and nonprint media publications, trips by subject specialists contribute directly to the development of distinctive collections that attract and assist in the retention of faculty.

Bibliographers in some institutions work directly with donors of materials and, sometimes, endowments ear-marked for collection development. If subject specialists have adept social skills, employed daily in conversations with faculty, students, and library staff, these same skills can be turned to the intense and often pleasant tasks of engaging collection-oriented philanthropists in the enrichment of library holdings. At some institutions, Yale foremost among them, the tradition of alumni devoting themselves to the creation of collections that fill gaps in the college or university library collections is strong enough that lifelong relationships spring up between bibliographer and patron. This is highly valued and to be encouraged, but relationships and contacts involving the people responsible for doing the work to be encouraged by a magnanimous gesture could be nourished as well. For many subject specialists, this kind of responsibility is a prized asset in their list of duties.

The demographics of the baby-boomers passing to middle-age and the current economic situation present conflicting possibilities. The near-term seems to offer fewer employment opportunities, especially for highly trained professionals in research librarianship. Alternatively, the prospects are brighter further out in time due to the apparent renewal of increased government commitment to training and education. My experience in many searches for subject specialists in the past decade suggests that any search is a fortunate one if it produces *one* well-qualified candidate actually willing to move to a new location. Rhoda Garoogian's comments are well taken and are as relevant now as they were a decade ago: "If highly qualified people are to be tempted away from other fields, more money and prestige must be available to them."[20]

IMPACTS AND CONSEQUENCES

Subject specialists in collection development straddle chasms. On the one hand, the career is one in an applied art (or craft or trade), namely *building* collections. On the other hand, the intellectual and practical aspects, the ideas and notions, the facts and formulas, the techniques, philosophies, histories, and myths of the fields assigned to bibliographers, these are the stuff of their work. Ideally, subject specialists moving into collection development continue contributing to the development of their first discipline.

Scholarship of one's own and the promotion of scholarship are inextricably related. Librarians who see themselves as links in a long scholarly tradition will not stop at promoting and transmitting learning by assisting others in their efforts. They themselves will seek to contribute directly, and that direct contribution will better enable them to promote the scholarship of others.[21]

Collection development is under increasing pressure to adapt to more stringent fiscal resources, function under tighter accountability for collection building directly in support of current programs of research and teaching, and accommodate new varieties of resources (owned as well as leased), sometimes even providing workstations for digital resources from book budgets. A recent survey of the history of collection development by Robert N. Broadus and an article on "value and evaluation" of collections by David Henige are recommended as guides to current thinking about the function of collection development and its place in research libraries.[22] Among the pleasures of working in collection development are handling books and other library resources, seeing collections grow and observing their various uses, using money (and often sizable sums) as a tool to improve possibilities for scholarship, and, as with other librarians, coming to work assured that there is plenty to do. The task of winnowing possibilities to the small proportion of material to be made accessible to scholars is always daunting and (more often than not) satisfying, as well.

Bibliographers at Yale provided the following ideas on influences and consequences in the classification and salary review mentioned above:

The Library is the principal educational resource center of the University, research and teaching depend on the quality of the collections, their currentness, breadth and depth. Our collection building activities and our cooperative efforts with colleagues in other academic and research libraries contribute to the development of national collections and the availability of resources for scholarship and teaching.

We contribute directly to the research and teaching mission of the University through advanced references services to faculty, scholars and students, through advising and through teaching. Our intimate knowledge of the library's resources and means of access to them gives us a special role in this mission. The part we play in relations between the library and the wider Yale community is articulated through departmental and faculty/student contacts, college fellowships, publication of newsletters, . . .

Allocation of resources to large expensive collections requires research and judgment. One must evaluate the fit between newly available materials and existing resources and programs as well as judge the utility of these materials for future research.

The library acquires 5–7% of the world's publishing output; selectors must exercise judgment in choosing one item out of sixteen published. To this end daily decisions involve the selection of materials, the choice of vendors, the assignment of funds.

Without specific written policies guiding this work, the scope for independent judgment is great. The aim is to spend wisely the $250,000—to enable the library's collections to support current and future research and teaching. To this end one must devise, using creative strategies, ongoing acquisitions programs to support these programs and the strengths of the collections.

Regular decision-making sessions about the way most usefully to preserve deteriorating materials, especially books and newspapers, involve judgments about the relative value of these materials, the most appropriate format for preservation and the habits of readers.

We contribute in a collegial way to the elaboration of departmental organization and procedures surrounding the important selection and collection building process.

Our contribution to personnel evaluation and selection in our own department as well as others is vital to the health of the library.

The effects of errors in the selection process weaken the library and affect the ability of scholars to do research and to teach, the ability of the university to attract faculty, the prestige of the institution—both now and in the future.

In the short term, errors in judgment can mean a waste of money or conversely the loss of a unique opportunity to build a strong and perhaps special collection. In the long run, the national standing of the university, its departments, programs and collections depend on the strengths of library collections and the good judgment exercised now. The implication of error is not in the individual decisions so much as in the aggregate of decisions and opportunities seized or missed over time.[23]

One might wonder about the ethics of recruiting subject specialists to collection development in an era when many leaders of the profession are proclaiming an end to the era of "ownership" and the primacy of an era of "access." An excellent introduction to the question of the future of collection development is found in a symposium of the *Journal of Academic Librarianship*.[24] There is a logical inconsistency in the access paradigm that may be summarized by the question, "Access to what?"[25] Given the problem in logic, one can assume that the function of collection development will continue, with modifications, in North American research libraries. Given the expansion of publications of all sorts of interest to scholars in North America, one can even see a need for more specialist bibliographers, especially in area studies.

CAREER PATHS

Many research libraries' promotion policies for professional personnel are equivalent to those for faculty in an important respect: allowing for promotion in place. The subject specialist bibliographer enters a career in service of the subject originally chosen for his or her life-work. The range of responsibilities, as made apparent above, can be attractive to some and should not be daunting to those who are good candidates for a career shift. On the other hand, no one becomes well-to-do as a subject specialist, or for that matter, in any assignment in research librarianship. While we do not take a vow of poverty, our specialty, like most of the faculty ranks, is one in which a good many rewards are, if not spiritual, at least in the realm of "qualities of life." Librarians do socially useful, intellectually challenging, and rewarding work, and they live, especially but not uniquely among subject specialists, the life of the mind.

RECRUITMENT

In the halcyon days following Sputnik and into the early 1980s, internships and other "try-out" positions presented opportunities in which a subject specialist might discern by working in a research library whether a career as a bibliographer would be interesting. Plummeting budgets and decreasing numbers of professional positions in research libraries have made such positions rare. For the foreseeable future, recruitment of subject specialists to collection development is most likely to occur in an open position. Therefore, the following discussion of recruitment techniques is written without regard to previous possibilities for encouraging Ph.D.'s and Ph.D. candidates from other disciplines to librarianship by way of temporary positions. Some applicants to library schools do have advanced degrees in other subjects before they apply to library schools; such people are often good candidates for subject specialist positions in collection development, but are treated equally with all other applicants in a formal search to fill a vacant professional position.

Once the roles and responsibilities of subject specialists are understood for an institution, the library environment in which they are expected to work is established, qualifications defined, and rewards specified, recruitment for candidates for specific positions can get underway. The remainder of this chapter is concerned with practical steps in recruiting subject specialists to collection development in research libraries. The topics covered below are recruitment plans; position descriptions; search committees; passive and active recruitment; interviews; decision making; and, throughout, the care and treatment of potential recruits to collection development. An overarching concern is that all applicants and candidates are given equal courtesy and the appropriate information about the recruitment process and schedule; all applicants should be informed of their status in the search as the process reaches the later stages of winnowing applicants to a small pool of candidates and perhaps a final few to be interviewed. All candidates to be interviewed should be notified of the outcome of the search as quickly as appropriate.

Recruitment Plan

Once a decision has been made to recruit, the appointing official, usually a department head or more senior library administrator working with the library's personnel officer, should prepare a recruitment plan. Attention to this bureaucratic step in a process that can become creative (within bounds) is important because it makes clear to all concerned the parameters for the recruitment and appointment. Elements of the plan are

- position control information (new position or replacement for an incumbent), specifying permitted salary range and fund source for salary and benefits;
- permitted date of appointment;
- position description;
- home department and reference to any coordinating departments;
- names of appointing official, personnel officer responsible for mechanics of the search process, and search committee members (including faculty) if a committee will be employed;
- advertising scheme (including titles of journals and newspapers in which an advertisement will be placed and dates for submission of advertisements);

reference to distribution of positions descriptions to library school, professional *and* scholarly society placement services; expected dates of appearance and run-dates for advertisements; this element would identify, by the extent of the advertising scheme, the search as internal, local, regional, national, or international;

- reference to person-to-person recruitment (including appearances at professional and scholarly society meetings by key people in the recruitment) and to informal solicitation of nominations from library and faculty colleagues;
- budget for advertising;
- date of first formal review of applications;
- preliminary schedule and roster of participants (including faculty) in interviews;
- preliminary information on receiving and housing candidates during the interview;
- equal employment opportunity specifications;
- information packets for interviewers and candidates.

Many elements of the recruitment plan are likely to be modified as the recruitment proceeds. Salary ranges can and will be adjusted during negotiations, especially if the hiring institution is responsive to market conditions.

Search Committee

The composition of the search committee is a key factor in ensuring success in a recruitment. Paul Gherman provides a comprehensive overview of the various functions of the search committee in any library recruitment.[26] Some particular considerations to bear in mind in recruiting subject specialists are adequate representation of colleague bibliographers, the presence and active participation of faculty members in relevant disciplines, and inclusion of reference librarians and catalog librarians, whose responsibilities involve access to and interpretation of the subjects to which the new bibliographer will be assigned.

Search committee members should inform themselves of the key issues facing the successful candidate for the position in question; the preparation of a briefing paper by colleague bibliographers or the chief collection development officer may be in order. Reading and interpreting résumés and reading the candidates' publications are part of a search committee member's duties. Roles and responsibilities of persons on the search committee should be defined each time a search committee is formed; particular attention is needed to confidentiality, and the committee chairperson and personnel officer should conduct the official business of the search, including preparation of documents. I do not favor appointment of students or support staff in search committees, although they can be productively engaged in a search during the interview stage. The selection of a professional colleague should reside in the community of professionals; students' life in any institution is ordinarily short, whereas support staff are often, by definition, not committed to the profession as much as they are to particular functions. An appointment as a professional librarian in a research library is potentially one for life; thus, others with similar appointments ought to be engaged in recommending appointments. The search committee should be charged and discharged with thanks, as should those included in the interviews who are not members of the search committee.

Position Descriptions

A complex document containing institution-specific elements, the position description should always include title and rank of the position, titles and ranks of persons to whom the incumbent will report and/or those reporting to the incumbent, description of the institution, with more details provided on the portion of the institution for which the position has most relevance or responsibility, position duties and responsibilities (stating collegial, collaborative, and coordinating units or persons), position qualifications, salary and benefits, other perquisites, and starting date. Information on tuition-aid programs, resources of the university available (e.g., athletic facilities), insurance and medical programs, mortgage programs, sabbatic and other leaves, promotion policies, and coverage of relocation expenses should be included in the information packet sent to each candidate invited for an interview.

Passive and Active Recruitment: Advertising and Personal Contact

The advertising scheme is a critical yet curiously passive element in a recruitment campaign. The appointing official, working with the members of the search committee, needs to identify the journals and papers that are most likely to be read by a reasonably wide swath of potential applicants. The advertising campaign should be designed to create a wave of interest in the position itself so that the collegial network can take up and distribute further the availability of the position. Lately various library Listservs and similar electronic communication schemes have been employed directly and indirectly to advertise positions and to gather preliminary information for justifying positions and writing position descriptions.[27] The *Chronicle of Higher Education* is a particularly good journal for advertisements, as it appears weekly and has wide circulation. Depending upon the importance of the position and the budget available for advertisement, a display ad might be employed. Advertising copy should derive directly from the position description.

Recourse to placement services of scholarly societies can produce some candidates and assists in spreading the word of an available position to persons who may previously not have considered a career as a bibliographer in a research library. Another means of advertising is for the appointing official or search committee chair to send letters to faculty requesting nominations for the advertised post. In a recent Yale search, over 300 such letters resulted in a dozen nominations. The nominations were so useful both in advertising the position and in making credible the library's determination to be responsive to the university's curricular and research programs that the results were worth the effort. Whatever the use of informal networks to advertise the position and pursue leads, attention to the position description as the defining document is very important. Anything more than a gloss on the position description could lead applicants and candidates to expectations that cannot be fulfilled, and some of those unfulfilled expectations could be actionable. Due care to describe accurately the realities of any position is always repaid by the trust and cooperation of the candidates, even those not chosen.

Usually the advertising campaign is supplemented with appeals to colleagues and the community of bibliographers for nominations. One's network of colleagues is effective for recruitment because of the trust and frankness invested in it. Very often, recourse to the network produces the best-qualified candidates.

One can supplement the extent of one's own network of contacts by sending letters of enquiry and making telephone calls to the officers and representatives of the appropriate sections of ACRL (beginning with Afro-American Studies Librarian and ending with Women's Studies), ACRL discussion groups (beginning with Academic Librarians' Association and Australian Studies through Undergraduate Librarians), and the Affiliates of the American Library Association (from American Association of Law Librarians to the Urban Libraries Council), all of whom are listed in the *ALA Handbook of Organization*. More contacts can be made to officers of organizations not listed in the *ALA Handbook* through the information provided in the *Bowker Annual Library and Book Trade Almanac* directory of organizations.

The informal network can help identify informants in libraries who are most often pleased to make nominations of colleagues. The most effective way to get this assistance is to write or call before initiating a deep conversation, provide a copy of the position description, and begin the conversation by enquiring of the informant's own interest in applying for the available post. In order for this method to work, one must be ready for the tables to be turned, providing suitable nominations when asked. With nominations in hand, one can write or call the nominees, provide position descriptions, and encourage applications. Telephone calls and letters used together effectively encourage the nominated individuals to submit an

application. Nurturing relationships by telephone conversations and fol-
low-up letters takes time, money, and attention; missing a promised moment of contact or a long delay in getting a letter to a prospect can ruin the
possibility that the nominee will apply. Nevertheless, this mode of discovering suitable candidates and then getting some to apply has been remarkably successful. Occasionally, personal visits to prospective candidates can
be very powerful acts of flattery. In-person solicitation of applications
should be employed with great care, since the prospective candidate may
overinterpret this to mean the position is assured despite the operation of
an open search process through which appointment decisions are reached
by participation of many colleagues.

Practice concerning "due dates" for applications vary. However, "first
review dates" as distinct from due dates seem to offer the institution more
latitude in accepting applications during a search. First-review dates are
often stated this way: "Applications received on or before (date) will receive
first consideration." This specification allows rolling review in searches
involving several different pools of interviewed candidates. In effect, the
search is not closed until the position is filled. First review dates also allows
for an advertising campaign with phases depending on the match of
candidates' qualifications to those in the position description.

To the degree of its breadth, the public advertising campaign assures that
all who believe they are qualified have equal access to information about
the opening; the campaign is therefore essential. For some searches and
some individuals, a coy "dance" develops in which an intermediary dis-
closes the name of the candidate who desires a nomination, either for
personal satisfaction or to make his or her participation in the search at
another institution plausible to his or her home institution. Potential candidates are flattered to be nominated and even more flattered to receive a
letter inviting an application. To the extent that such flattery encourages
the discourse between qualified candidates and those conducting the recruitment, it is a good thing.

Interviews

The interview schedule and participants in the interview are key elements in learning whether a candidate matches the qualifications of the
position description and is suited to the working environment. Candidates
and institutions alike should understand that the interview process begins
whenever the candidate encounters for the first time a person involved in
the search, whether that is greeting someone at the airport or meeting with
the library personnel officer at a conference or arriving at the library
moments before the first appointment on the interview schedule itself.
While candidates do not need to be met at airports or train stations every
time, doing so is an obvious symbol of concern and hospitality. Especially

in remote places, such a gesture tells the candidate something about the institution's care for staff.

Since most interviews for subject specialists involve at least a full day of appointments, the practice of inviting a candidate for a meal the night before the interview allows the persons conducting the search the opportunity to discuss the search and the interview schedule and, in a social setting, to describe in glowing fashion the special attributes of the job and the institution. Given the requirements for communication inherent in subject specialist positions, assessing the candidate's ability to conduct himself or herself in a social setting is important. Simultaneously, the candidate gets an opportunity to explore themes and details he or she has found significant. As mentioned, however, all contact between candidate and institution is part of the search, so honesty and avoidance of aspects of a candidate's personal history are as important in the informal setting of a meal as in the formal interviews.[28] Often spending a little time or even another meal at the end of the interview day to recapitulate the day's findings on both sides and to offer each side another opportunity to develop better understanding can be useful, as well.

The formal interview should be conducted so that each candidate gets essentially the same treatment, even to the extent of preparing lists of questions to be asked. Candidates should be given a formal introduction to the interview procedure and encouraged to ask questions, as the interview is a process of mutual investigation. The intent of the institution to learn how well the candidate matches the specified qualifications and judge how well the candidate might perform the specified duties should be made explicit. Persons and groups representing the institution in the interviews should be aware of what topics need to be covered and of the requirement to write evaluations of each candidate. Such evaluations might or might not involve the ranking of candidates, but they should always stress the relevance of the candidate's own qualifications to those qualifications specified in the position description.

At the same time, the interview is intended to provide the candidate with a clear picture of the job and how success is measured in its performance. Candidates and interviewers share responsibility for seeing that both aspects of the interview are covered. Two practical matters need attention: Each interview segment, if a group interview is at hand, should involve a designated convener; and an individual should be assigned to accompany or pass the candidate on the next appointment in the schedule.

Time should be allotted to show candidates the office or other work space they would occupy. Unless the candidate already knows the collection or collections for which he or she would be responsible, time should be made to show the collection; any documents (annual reports of previous incumbents, published collection descriptions) relating to the collections can be presented as well. Care should be taken to provide candidates to be interviewed with extensive and relevant background information before the interview, including the names, titles, and, if needed, brief descriptions of the persons included on the interview roster. Truly interested candidates prepare for their interviews by reading everything they can about the institution, its collections, and especially the colleagues who will interview them. Likewise, members of the search committee and particularly the appointing official should read and reflect upon recent writings of each candidate. Copies of the candidate's publications should be made available to everyone on the interview schedule.

Careful questioning and skillful shaping of conversations with candidates can usually reveal the strengths that predict success and the weaknesses for which colleagues and the institution must either compensate or otherwise account. No candidate is perfect (and, indeed, perfection can be a most aggravating attribute), so there should be no expectation of perfection. On the other hand, candidates who require the most extensive and patient questioning to get information have rarely been appointed; candidates need to be forthcoming with information and with questions of their own. In one memorable interview when the candidate had exhausted a list of questions, the interviewers decided that they had no further questions and ultimately employed that candidate. The most effective interviews involve many people, especially those with whom the successful candidate will work or on whom the candidate will depend. The involvement of many people protects against the occasional blind spots any individual has and serves to begin the acculturation process for the successful candidate who accepts the position.

The best interviews allow for formal and informal evaluation of the interview by the candidate, the library personnel officer, and the appointing officer. This is best accomplished by a closing session with the candidate that is pre-arranged to allow for such an evaluation and the identification of open issues or unanswered questions. Each candidate should have some idea of the schedule for succeeding events: How many more candidates are to be seen in what period; how long the search committee will deliberate; when the choice of candidate to receive an offer will be made and by whom; with whom and when negotiations are likely to begin. Each candidate should also be informed how well he or she matches the diverse requirements for the position.

Since covering everything in an interview of a day or even two is very difficult, a quiet meal with the appointing official, the library personnel officer, and a key member or two of the search committee can give the candidate another opportunity to make a point, ask a question, and share concerns made palpable by the interview. As mentioned already, all such occasions are part of the interview, and correct behavior, especially concerning soliciting irrelevant personal information, is expected. For more senior appointments, time and resources need to be allotted to show candidates possibilities for housing and the institution's or region's amenities.

Role playing, trick questions, deliberately discourteous behavior, disapproval of a candidate's positions, and tactics intended to "wear down" candidates are to be avoided. Candidates, too, need to take care to present themselves accurately, even in the heat of the interview "performance." The best interviews proceed as extended conversations among friends.

Decision Making

The decision-making process is always two-sided. While the institutional process is the one with which this chapter is most concerned, the candidate, too, engages in decision making. Given the cosmopolitan nature of subject specialists and those who might become subject specialists, institutions are involved to one degree or another in marketing their openings. Thus, while candidates in one sense are supplicants, they are also agents with a free will. Keeping the candidates informed to a reasonable degree on the nature and timing of the decision-making process on the institutional side is another way of cultivating trust and proving institutional concern for the candidates' own situations. Offering this kind of information encourages candidates to be similarly open about their own thinking and critical issues in deciding whether to accept an offer.

Experience has shown that the search committee's role in advising the appointing official is fundamentally important. All those on the interview roster should submit written reports and advice, and the search committee itself should consider such reports, all of its observations, the candidates' résumés and publications, and the facts and opinions provided by the candidates' references. This welter of information should be examined in the light of the position's stated qualifications and its duties and responsibilities. The search committee's deliberations should be strictly confidential, and the written report to the appointing official should be secret as well.

The appointing official and the library personnel officer generally work together to review the advice of the search committee, sometimes expressed as a list of candidates suited for the position, and to arrive at the candidate to receive an offer. The offer is most often transmitted orally, and negotiations proceed with either the appointing official or the library personnel officer, but not both. Speaking with a single voice at this juncture is critical for the institution. Once verbal negotiations have reached a mutually acceptable conclusion, the offer can be put and accepted in writing and the professional life of the bibliographer will begin in the new venue.

CONCLUSION

A review of the literature of librarianship since 1960 reveals that research libraries have almost always faced declining budgets for collections and for staff, that there has been constant expansion, even explosions, of publications suitable for acquisition or access, and that there has never been a truly adequate supply of specialists and generalists to work in and lead these complex institutions.

We seem to be the profession of furrowed brows. Yet for many of us, research librarianship and collection development for such libraries require daily grappling with the great issues of all times. Despite the possible dominance of digital resources on our functions and services, we and our successors will be custodians of culture in all of its ramifications. This is good work of which we can be proud, and there is every reason to wish to recruit a few good persons to join us in it.

NOTES

1. This paragraph derives from one in Michael A. Keller, "Digital Preservation: Some Reflections upon Its Implications for Collection Development Officers," an unpublished paper delivered on November 18, 1991, to the Advisory Council of the Commission on Preservation and Access in Washington, D.C. The idea of the "library of the mind" is well described by Vincent H. Duckles in "The Library of the Mind: Observations on the Relationship between Musical Scholarship and Bibliography," in *Current Thought in Musicology*, ed. by John W. Grubbs (Austin: University of Texas Press, 1976).

2. Patricia A. McClung, ed., *Selection of Library Materials in the Humanities, Social Sciences, and Sciences* (Chicago: American Library Association, 1985); Beth J. Shapiro and John Whaley, eds., *Selection of Library Materials in Applied and Interdisciplinary Fields* (Chicago: American Library Association, 1987); and Cecily Johns, ed., *Selection of Library Materials for Area Studies, Part I. Asia, Iberia, the Caribbean, and Latin America, Eastern Europe and the Soviet Union, and the South Pacific* (Chicago: American Library Association, 1990). About sixty contributors are listed among the three volumes, the preponderance of whose careers in librarianship began with education in another field.

3. McClung writes in the introduction to *Selection of Library Materials*, "Basic knowledge of a discipline is important; command of the principles and techniques is essential," xiv.

4. Surprisingly, there has been little in library literature on the human dimensions of the coming of automation to research libraries. Articles abound on training and retraining, but descriptions of knowledge, education, and language qualifications for librarians in the new age are not easy to find. Even the sages of adapting libraries to technology and vice versa do not dwell regularly on the "people issues." See the article first presented in 1983 by Richard de Gennaro, "Shifting Gears: Information Technology and the Academic Library," in *Libraries and Information Science in the Electronic Age*, ed. by H. Edelman (Philadelphia: ISI Press, 1986), 23–35, and *New Information Technologies and Libraries*, ed. by H. Liebears, W. J. Haas, and W. E. Biervliet (Dordrecht: D. Reidel, 1985), as examples of otherwise excellent works that fail to consider librarians as individual professionals.

5. R. D. Swisher, P. C. Smith, and C. J. Boyers, "Educational Change among ACRL Academic Librarians," *Library Research* 5 (Summer 1983): 195–205.

6. Mary Baier Wells, "Requirements and Benefits for Academic Librarians, 1959–1979," *College & Research Libraries* 43 (November 1982): 450–458.

7. Ross Atkinson, "The Citation as Intertext: Toward a Theory of the Selection Process," *Library Resources & Technical Services* 28 (April/June 1984): 109–119. I've added the bracketed text to clarify my point.

8. Richard M. Dougherty and Carol Hughes, "Library Cooperation: A Historical Perspective and a Vision for the Future," *Advances in Library Resource Sharing* 1 (1990): 16.

9. John D. Haskell, Jr., "Subject Bibliographers in Academic Libraries: An Historical and Descriptive Review," *Advances in Library Administration and Organization* 3 (1984): 73–84.

10. Bonita Bryant, "Allocation of Human Resources for Collection Development," *Library Resources & Technical Services* 30 (1986): 149–162.

11. Dan C. Hazen, "Selection: Function, Models, Theory," in *Collection Management: A New Treatise*, ed. by Charles B. Osburn and Ross Atkinson, 273–300, Foundations in Library and Information Science, vol. 26 (Greenwich, Conn.: JAI Press, 1991).

12. Paul B. Mosher, "Reviewing for Preservation," in *Collection Management: A New Treatise*, 373–391.

13. "Collective Response of Bibliography Dept. Bibliographers to Position Description Questionnaire [for] Managerial and Professional Staff," unpublished document for the so-called Hewett Study, Yale University Library, June 1989. Responses offered here are to questions 1 and 3. Question 2 concerned place of respondents in the organizational structure. Bibliographers contributing to the collective response were Susanne F. Roberts, Humanities; Susan J. Steinberg, American and Commonwealth Studies; Linda P. Lerman, Judaic Studies; Jeffry K. Larson, Romance Languages and Literature; Åke I. Koel, Germanic Languages and Literature; Martha Brogan, Social Sciences.

14. Louis A. Pitschmann, "Organization and Staffing," in *Collection Management: A New Treatise*, 125–143.

15. Wilmer H. Baatz, "Collection Development in 19 Libraries of the Association of Research Libraries," *Library Acquisitions: Practice & Theory* 2 (1978): 85–121.

16. Barbara J. Henn, "Acquisitions Management: The Infringing Roles of Acquisitions Librarians and Subject Specialists—An Historical Perspective," *Advances in Library Administration and Organization* 8 (1989): 113–129. See p. 117 for a paragraph on "the conflict of the specialist's role as a scholar versus that of a manager."

17. Robert P. Haro, "The Bibliographer in the Academic Library," *Library Resources & Technical Services* 13 (Spring 1969): 163–169. See especially the last paragraph on p. 165 and the first full paragraph on p. 166. The article following Haro's, that of Helen Welch Tuttle, "An Acquisitionist Looks at Mr. Haro's Bibliographer," pp. 170–174, is an example of a misperception of the role of subject bibliographers so great that the author undertakes an etymological or semantic examination of the word *bibliographer*, returning to the question of function only for a few concluding sentences.

18. "Collective Response," response to question 3.

19. J. Periam Danton, "The Subject Specialist in National and University Libraries, with Special Reference to Book Selection," *Libri* 17 (1967): 44. Also Dennis

W. Dickinson, "Subject Specialists in Academic Libraries: The Once and Future Dinosaurs," in *New Horizons for Academic Libraries* (New York: G. K. Saur, 1979), 439. Dickinson's main thrust of the redundancy and unjustified cost of subject specialists has not been borne out as the constant reliance upon subject specialists by North American research libraries demonstrates.

20. Rhoda Garoogian, "The Changing Role of Library Schools in Recruitment and Selection: Implications for the Profession," *Drexel Library Quarterly* 17 (Summer 1981): 90–91.

21. Paul Raabe, "Library History and the History of Books: Two Fields of Research for Librarians," in *Books and Society in History*, ed. by Kenneth Carpenter (New York: R. R. Bowker, 1983), 252.

22. Robert N. Broadus, "The History of Collection Development," in *Collection Management: A New Treatise*, 3–28; and David Henige, "Value and Evaluation," in *Collection Management: A New Treatise*, 111–124.

23. "Collection Response," responses to questions 4 and 5.

24. Jasper G. Schad et al., "The Future of Collection Development in an Era of Fiscal Stringency," *Journal of Academic Librarianship* 18 (March 1992): 4–16.

25. For a rejoinder to the question and a response founded on cooperative collection development on a continental basis, see Michael A. Keller, "Foreign Acquisitions in North American Research Libraries," published as a supplement to *Focus on the Center for Research Libraries* 12 (September/October 1992).

26. Paul N. Gherman, "Selection Committees and The Recruitment Process," *Drexel Library Quarterly* 17 (Summer 1981): 14–25.

27. Of particular note in this regard is *Library Collection Development List* [electronic listserv], moderated by Lynn Sipe. Available from COLLDV-L@USCVM.BITNET and COLLDV-L@VM.USC.EDU.INTERNET. Lynn Sipe, Chief Collection Development Officer at the University of Southern California, can be reached at the e-mail Internet address lsipe@calvin.usc.edu.

28. Aspects such as marital status or sexual preference, career and current position of spouse or spouse-equivalent, children or intent to have children, age, national origin, or religious preference are irrelevant. However, should the candidate *require* information about child-care arrangements or the availability of assistance in placing a spouse or spouse-equivalent in employment nearby, such questions should be answered carefully, taking care not to use the candidate's question as an excuse to open an entire line of questioning on a forbidden topic. The candidate is the one who decides to make personal information available. It is wise of interviewing officials to take careful notes on conversations with candidates.

5

Recruiting Non-bibliocentric Collection Builders

Sheila S. Intner

Can a library be a library without books? Libraries have become identified as places that contain collections of books. The very names "library" and "librarian" incorporate the root of the Latin *libri*, meaning "books." Books, as handy, hardy, inexpensive, mobile vehicles for recording and transmitting our intellectual heritage, rightly occupy a central place in libraries, and none can or should dispute their importance. Yet books are not and have not been the sole carriers of humanity's intellectual records for a long time, although examination of library materials budgets might not show anything radically different.

For centuries, libraries have collected manuscripts and maps, pictorial representations, and even artifacts and pieces of laboratory equipment. Journals, which resemble little books or book parts, have been collected by libraries for more than 100 years, and librarians have grown accustomed to their idiosyncrasies even as they complain about them loudly and with much ado in public forums such as the "Worst Serial Titles of the Year" award ceremonies. Except for journals and other printed serials, however, nonbook materials have played so small and isolated a role in library collections that librarians have not recognized their true value and growing importance. To remedy this, Sheila Intner suggests recruiting non-bibliocentric collection development librarians.

In the chapter that follows, Intner asks that administrators and librarians recognize the barriers that prevent nonbook materials from being developed adequately and do something about it. The author explores the nature of non-bibliocentricity, the haunts of the non-bibliocentric, and methods of interesting them in collection development work. For the non-bibliocentric, the words on a computer monitor or the images on a video screen—with or without accompanying narratives and music—are as compelling as the words and pictures printed on paper pages and bound between two covers. The author sees the new breed of librarians reshaping library collections by acquiring materials in a different mix of carriers more closely resembling the hi-tech environment being built in the larger society.

What are non-bibliocentric collection builders and why should libraries want to recruit them? This chapter gives the author's answers to these two questions, plus ten suggestions about how to establish and implement a recruitment process that succeeds in obtaining people who fit the bill. Before proceeding to the task, it should be stated immediately that the author has a strongly held bias toward non-bibliocentricity and her chapter quite shamelessly advocates that libraries strive to achieve such a state.[1] Nevertheless, she has endeavored to be as objective as possible in interpreting her observations about libraries, library collections, and the librarians responsible for developing them.

BEYOND BOOKS: NON-BIBLIOCENTRIC COLLECTION BUILDERS

Taking an author's liberty, I define *bibliocentric* for the purposes of this chapter as "focused on books." Librarians have traditionally concerned themselves with books, so it is no surprise they have tended to be, generally, bibliocentric. Simply put, then, *non-bibliocentric* means "focused on non-books." I contend there are a great many factual, literary, and artistic expressions produced in physical manifestations other than books with which libraries and librarians might fruitfully be concerned. These include, but are not limited to, sound and video recordings, electronically transmitted data and other computer-based materials, maps and other cartographic representations, graphics of all kinds, three-dimensional objects, combinations of these, and others I have neglected to name. The list of physical formats in which intellectual and artistic expressions appear is long and getting longer, and humanity's technological ingenuity in inventing new ones seems to have few limits. Because old formats do not die when superseded by new ones, but continue to persist and be used along with their more advanced counterparts,[2] libraries that collect materials in old formats may be locked into maintaining and using them long past their vogue in the non-library world, especially if they include important, heavily used titles that prove difficult or costly to reformat.

Collection builders are librarians charged with special responsibility for adding items to and removing items from a library's stock of materials, a stock that is generally referred to as its *collections* (although in many circles it still is called *book stock*). To be a non-bibliocentric collection builder, a librarian must look beyond books to include intellectual and artistic expressions manifested in formats other than books. It sounds easy, but it is not. Libraries, particularly academic libraries in the United States, consist mainly of books,[3] but this status quo is not the sole factor underlying a dearth of non-bibliocentricity. Libraries operate within structures that contribute to the likelihood they will remain bibliocentric, and they are administered by staff who are not necessarily unhappy with the status quo.

Together, the nature of existing collections, administrative structures, and staff accustomed to them exert an enormous inertia with which non-bibliocentric librarians must contend.[4]

BIBLIOCENTRICITY IN LIBRARIES

The library budget is the principal administrative structure ensuring continuation of a status quo in which books continue to prevail. Usually, it is a line-item budget that divides materials into books (more formally designated "monographs"), continuing subscriptions to journals, annuals, irregularly issued titles, "serials," and "other." The proportion of dollars allotted to each category indicates its relative importance. I have observed few materials budgets that give the lion's share of the budget to "other." In most instances, the nonbook categories range between 1 percent and 10 percent of a library's materials budget, although some libraries spend more and some spend nothing.

In the 1970s, when I was in library school and the first years of practice, I read about the uncontrollable growth of serial subscription costs, consuming up to half—or sometimes more than half—of materials budgets. Later, in the 1980s and 1990s, I read about the devastating increases in serials costs, which threatened to swallow all allocations for materials and leave libraries with nothing to spend on monographs. Amidst all these papers addressing issues of budget allocations to books and printed serials, few pages of library literature since 1970 were devoted to raising the roof about allocations for films, videos, slides, photographs, maps, and other nonbooks, with one exception: electronic media. Reference departments responsible for the acquisition of computer-based products have been torn between continuing to buy the printed counterparts also or converting solely to online or CD-ROM versions. No matter what the decision, computer-based reference tools are costly to establish, and the papers written about them tend to complain that they consume the whole materials budget, squeezing the monies available for books. (Some reference departments do not have to fit the cost of computer-based products within their budgets because computer centers or automated systems departments handle these costs with allocations separated completely from those for reference books and serially issued printed reference books and materials. The question of integrating electronic and print media under one authority is an interesting one, but it lies beyond the scope of this chapter.)

The separate audiovisual department is a second kind of administrative structure that ensures the primacy of books and printed serials in the "main" library and among its staff. While the audiovisual department may have one or more librarians responsible for selection and collection development, the main library is likely to have numerous full-time and part-time subject bibliographers. The assumption seems clear that the main library's subject bibliographers are not responsible for nonbook materials in their subject areas. Under such a system, nonbook materials are not developed as much by subject area as by medium. Logic dictates that individual subject areas cannot be as well treated for nonbooks as for books unless audiovisual collection developers are, miraculously, equally expert on all subjects.

More distressing to this author than the separate nonbook media department in the library are separate nonbook media departments outside the library's aegis. I have heard of media/audiovisual departments that were entirely divorced from the library, organized instead under schools of continuing education, language departments, or schools of education.

Without regular interaction with non-books and responsibility for them and their equipment, mainstream librarians cannot help but fail to perceive books and non-books with equal familiarity and ease. Librarians' bibliocentricity is understandable and forgivable if they are responsible only for the ongoing selection, acquisition, organization, dissemination, and preservation of books, not of nonbooks.

To reiterate, my observations lead me to believe that in combination, the nature of current collections, the systems designed to accommodate them, and the librarians entrusted with their futures present a formidable set of barriers to achieving library non-bibliocentricity.

WHY SHOULD LIBRARIES WANT NONBOOKS?

For hundreds of years, books and booklike serials have been humanity's most important source of cultural, educational, and recreational material in most subject fields. Despite my strong non-bibliocentricity, I agree with pundits who believe books and printed serials will continue to dominate libraries for the foreseeable future.[5] Why make such a fuss about nonbooks? Why go to the trouble to seek out and employ non-bibliocentric collection builders? Four reasons justify it: (1) Nonbooks are there; (2) people want them; (3) certain formats have attributes that make them especially useful for libraries; (4) the foreseeable future is limited. We do not know what lies ahead, except that it is likely to include a larger role for nonbooks.

1. *Nonbook materials are there to be collected, and they surpass books in some ways.* Important materials needed to support research and study as well as other informational and recreational pursuits sometimes appear solely in nonbook formats. Even when the same materials are also available as books, the books are not always equal to the originals. Anyone who has read the book of a *Star Trek* episode knows that the book version is a poor substitute for the audiovisual experience, whether viewed as a video in one's living room or as a film shown on a wide screen in a movie theater. In fact, the relative merits of videos versus wide screen films is cause for an ongoing debate among the cognoscenti, who charge that home videos

spoil the impact and beauty of works originally intended to be seen on large screens in a theater. The choice of format impacts not only on aesthetics but, for other subjects and treatments, on the scientific utility or historical accuracy of the materials. Try convincing a medical student that reading a description of a surgical procedure in a book is as effective as viewing it in a carefully shot video recording designed for teaching purposes; or tell a historian that reading a transcript of Reverend Martin Luther King, Jr.'s "I Have a Dream" speech is the same as watching the living, breathing man deliver it, complete with the spontaneity of audience responses—all the interruptions, the clapping, and the shouting. Printed books may be substituted for the originals, but they fail to capture them completely.

The trend toward publication of materials in nonbook formats seems to be growing.[6] No one knows for sure whether electronic publishing will become the norm for particular types of materials, for example, for scientific papers or conference proceedings, but it is certain to expand as long as the infrastructure for its use—computers, communications networks, and so on—continues expanding. The speed and convenience of electronic document delivery for those already linked through networks to colleagues at remote sites, and the flexibility of electronic publications for use (one can print, download, edit, comment, forward to other colleagues, etc.) as well as their potential low cost make it difficult to imagine scholars giving all that up for more books, or even more printed journals.

2. *Consumers want to use nonbook materials.* Hundreds of public librarians surveyed in 1980–81 claimed sincerely that their clients preferred books over other types of materials.[7] Today, one wonders whether that view is still believable. Fifty years ago most people read newspapers to keep up with current events. Today reports of newspaper closings around the United States gravely document the fact that most people watch television to find out what went on in the world during the previous day. In fact, television news rarely goes back a full twenty-four hours, but tends to focus on happenings in the several hours that passed since the previous broadcast, usually no more than five or six hours. Only when a story has major importance or develops over a period of days will it remain in the news for longer than a single broadcast. As a result, television viewers are almost always aware of breaking news before it can be printed in the few newspapers left in business.

Nearly every library that collects videos reports far higher average circulation statistics for them than for comparable groups of books, although some of these differences might result from borrowing policies (e.g., videos may be loaned for two or three days, while books are loaned for two or three weeks).[8] Where fines for books are a few cents a day, they may be as high as several dollars a day for nonbooks such as videos and computer software. Similar policies and procedures typically govern the use of other nonbook materials, although some libraries have adopted uniform procedures for most media. One must believe that restrictive circulation policies are not capricious and would not be instituted unless they were necessary. What kind of necessity might warrant short loan periods and heavy overdue fines? Common sense says it is a combination of high demand for the materials and not enough of them to go around. It does not seem unfair to conclude that when relevant, interesting, useful, topical nonbook materials are made available, library clients want them and use them.

   3. *Certain nonbook formats are especially useful for libraries*. One of libraries' principal collection development challenges is the need to buy more materials than their budgets can cover. Sharing materials among groups of libraries is a simple, tried-and-true solution to the problem, which technological advances have made particularly attractive. Large computer-based bibliographic networks make it possible to locate desired materials in other library collections quickly and easily, while electronic communication systems make it child's play to transmit selected types of materials—anything already in electronic form or that can be converted to electronic form—to distant locations almost instantly. If a document is already in electronic form, it needs only to be addressed to the library or client who wants it before being transferred through the communication network to the recipient's mailbox. If a document is in a different form, it must first be transformed (electronified?) to be delivered electronically, or else it can be handled only the old-fashioned way by means of the U.S. Post Office or some other delivery service.

   Materials having the most flexibility for resource sharing are those already in or easily converted to electronic form. Books, which require character-by-character inputting or page-by-page scanning for hundreds of pages, are currently the least flexible type of material for such sharing. Journal articles are better solely because most of them have fewer pages than books to be converted. Books must be physically shipped to distant borrowers, which takes time, whereas computer-based files can be transmitted with little delay over the same networks used for bibliographic searching, and videos can be disseminated for viewing over cable networks and satellite hookups. Copyright issues aside for a moment, both types of transmission can be downloaded or copied for subsequent use by the distant borrower.

   To be fair, it must be pointed out that all nonbook formats do not have the same capabilities for electronic transmission. If a library does not have access to a cable network, then video recordings require delivery exactly like books, and so do sound recordings and other non-electronic nonbook materials. Sound and video recordings have different advantages over books, however, in that they can be copied easily and inexpensively. This enables a library sending a sound recording or video off to another part of the country to retain an archival copy in the event the original is damaged or not returned. (Some libraries send the copy and retain the original. Although copyright infringement might be a possibility, I am not aware that such activities are not considered "fair use" provided the copies are destroyed when originals are safely returned.)

The advantages for resource sharing of readily transmitted nonbook materials ought to make them especially valuable to libraries as materials budgets, space limitations, and staff shortages make it increasingly difficult to expand collecting activities to the degree librarians would wish.

4. *The foreseeable future is limited*. Libraries, being dynamic institutions, must be positioned for the future even though librarians cannot see beyond a very limited foreseeable future. No one knows how long what is perceived as the foreseeable future at this writing in 1993 might hold. Current trends, however, indicate substantive changes are occurring in the production, distribution, and dissemination of information, even if librarians do not yet know precisely when they will happen or exactly what form they will take.

Taking a lesson from recent history, librarians might reflect for a moment on technological change and its consequences in a somewhat different context—the music recording world. In the 1940s and 1950s, when classical music lovers bought symphony albums, each album consisted of several breakable disks, then called, simply, "records." At first, each record had to be turned over, one at a time, as each disk was played. Then, the addition of automatic record changers to turntables made it more convenient to organize the disks so that a whole stack could be loaded onto the automatic changer, and sides 1, 2, 3, and so on, played before the stack was flipped for the balance of the recording. In a three-record set, for example, side 1 would have side 6, not side 2, on its verso, side 2 would be paired with side 5, and only sides 3 and 4 would be back to back on one disk.

Before long, unbreakable disks were developed. Although they looked very similar to their breakable cousins, they played at less than half the speed and recorded much more music in the same physical space. The same symphony that required five or six sides of old-fashioned disks could be stored on the two sides of a new-style disk of the same size. The term *album*, which had been used to indicate a multiple-disk recording, came to mean something with similar amounts of recorded material, whether on one disk or more.

More recently, cassette tape and compact disk technologies are replacing the long-playing disks, providing music lovers with greater convenience, durability, and quality. With compact disks, the same symphony that occupied both sides of a twelve-inch long-playing disk can be recorded on one side of a disk less than half that size having greater sound reproduction capabilities; with cassette tapes, the symphony is telescoped into one tiny little box, although some sound fidelity is sacrificed with this technology. What happened to the old breakable disks? They have all but disappeared from the scene, except for those stored in archives and historical collections of recorded sound. What about unbreakable long-playing disks? They are in the process of disappearing, occupying relatively small sections of record shops and direct-mail catalog listings (compared with their allotted space twenty years ago) that decrease in size with each passing year.

These same changes affected the popular music recording market, but in that environment they were even more complex. Popular music recordings were typically issued in two ways—as individual songs or short pieces (singles) and as albums containing many songs or short pieces. Different disk technologies were employed for singles than for albums, such as the use of different playback speeds and disk sizes. (For a number of years, popular album tape recordings were issued in cartridges as well as in cassettes, but cartridges seem to have gone the way of the breakable disk.) Today, however, popular singles are also issued as short inexpensive videos, for which there is a huge market.

Music librarians are painfully aware of these inexorable changes brought about by technological progress. I can sympathize. In 1978, I was a music librarian administering a collection of approximately 25,000 long-playing record albums to which I was adding about 4,000 titles a year. It would seem unconscionable to discard them all. But no matter how hard or how long they resist the change, it is only a matter of time until libraries still holding on to their long-playing disk collections give them up and move on to newer formats. It is not a matter of choice but necessity. Increasingly, music library clients have given up on old-style stereo systems with their temperamental needles, fragile disks, and endless array of cleaners and disk-wipers and replaced them with tape decks and compact disk players. These people want to borrow materials they can use with their equipment. And librarians who make the switch are pleased with the hardiness and space economy of the new media.

Similarly, libraries and librarians cannot stop society from changing but must make changes that keep them in tune with the times. One thing is clear: Any vision for libraries based solely on what can be seen at the moment cannot help but be far from visionary. If librarians believe that nonbooks will have an expanded role in the library of the future, it is time to position ourselves for that future. It is time librarians begin establishing both the collections and the expertise needed to exploit nonbooks as fully as possible.

TEN SUGGESTIONS FOR SUCCESSFUL RECRUITING

The suggestions below follow a familiar pattern of operation that works well when applied to most of life's problems: Identify clear goals, design methods to reach them, allocate sufficient resources for the methods to work, and implement the methods. In practice, however, it is very difficult for librarians to create goals that differ sharply from whatever was done in their libraries previously and to agree to work toward them with sufficient resolve to enable planning to proceed. Furthermore, once beyond that point, the process does not become easier. Allocating enough money to make it possible for plans to take shape is no less difficult in these times of financial stringency, nor is it easy to motivate the people who must actually perform various roles and activities in the plan to do their work well enough for it to succeed. The carrot of reward and encouragement needs to be combined with the stick of requirement and obligation every step of the way.

1. *Suggest library careers to student aides and pages who display familiarity with nonbook formats and who show aptitudes for electronics, computers, and other mechanical devices.* In my capacity as a library school faculty member routinely interviewing prospective applicants to our program, I have observed that many believe their best credential for pursuing a career in librarianship is that they love to read books. Some even go so far as to profess they have chosen library work because they dislike machines, especially computers. I hasten to inform these reader-applicants that they are quite mistaken about librarianship if they think they will be paid to sit around and read books, and I assure them that much of their time will be spent dealing intimately with computers one way or another. I hope my advice will persuade the incorrigibles to give up on a career that requires a great deal of work they dislike, although I have never suggested our school should not admit them on this account. Perhaps I have been wrong. It might be easier and safer to avoid such people altogether than to allow them to enter the profession with their warped viewpoints. While it might be unfair to generalize, these people are probably the sort who turn into librarians for whom only books count, who must stretch their imaginations to include printed serials and microform copies of books and journals.

More effective than filtering undesirables out of the field, which is a purely reactive position, librarians can operate proactively by warming up to young people who exhibit a love for rock videos and computer games, and an aptitude for machinery—especially computers—and encouraging them to opt for a library career. Librarians can promise truthfully that library work will provide opportunities to utilize their skills and contribute knowledgeably to valuable collection building.

2. *Urge library schools to include knowledge of nonbook producers, publishers, and distributors in courses dealing with selection and other collection-related functions.* Library school curricula usually include courses on the selection of materials, how to develop policies and procedures for collection development, and other collection-related activities and functions. It is very easy to design such courses with only books in mind, or books and printed journals, justifying it on the grounds that books (or books and printed journals) are the bulk of library stock and, thus, the main work of collection

development, or because they are the simplest types of materials, nonbook formats requiring special tools, special knowledge, and special routines. Sometimes, one lecture of a semester-long course will be spent discussing nonbook materials, or one reading will cover non-book materials.[9] In some places—including my own school—this is the way cataloging is handled: The beginning course treats books; advanced courses treat nonbooks. One need not be a genius to realize that nonbooks are always oddballs if the basic assumption on which all library functions and services are taught is that books are the norm.

3. *Make knowledge of nonbook materials an essential credential for the position of collection development librarian.* Job advertisements for library collection development officers nearly always ask for a library degree, several years of experience in a similar setting, and a host of administrative skills, including "demonstrated" communication skills; ability to interface with institutional administrators, faculty, other librarians, and people from other institutions; and ability to manage budgets and supervise personnel. Often, they ask also for doctoral degrees, second master's degrees in a discipline, and knowledge of one or more foreign languages. I cannot recall any advertisement that asked specifically for the ability to work comfortably with materials in all physical formats, although there may be some out there.

In one respect, librarians are no different than other people: If they are required to do something, they will usually do it; if they are not required to do something, they won't. If collection development officers are not required to be able to develop collections of nonbook materials, they probably won't be able to do it, any more than they could be expected to deal successfully with Chinese language materials if that capability was not identified and required. It seems a simple, logical step, then, to require knowledge of nonbooks right up front, in the job descriptions and adver-tisements for collection development positions.

Ideally, all librarians having collection development responsibilities should be required to deal successfully with nonbooks. In the less-than-ideal world in which people function, however, that may be difficult to accomplish. Therefore, since collection development as defined in this book covers a broad range of activities constituting the equivalent of strategic planning for collections, knowledge of nonbooks is especially important to require for its top administrators. If the highest-level collection develop-ment officer does not know nonbooks, hiring a nonbook selector to work under him or her will not accomplish the same thing. The person respon-sible for formulating policies and allotting resources must be the one who understands nonbooks in order for these materials to be regarded as carefully as books when decisions are made.

4. *Mainstream nonbook materials in library functions and expect all librarians to use them comfortably.* Ideally, all librarians should be equally capable of

handling books and nonbooks,[10] and one way to ensure the universality of this expertise is to integrate materials in various physical formats within all library functions. Library functions such as cataloging, reference, or selection can be done for all materials instead of having separate operations for nonbooks. When a library has a large selection operation, it is natural to divide it into a number of subordinate units, each having a specialty focus. It is tempting to use physical format as the critical distinction, but it is just as practical to use subject, language, or audience in dividing the whole.

Separating materials by physical form has its advantages. It utilizes space more efficiently and economically. It does not require that every librarian work to keep up with developments in many industries and multiple reference tools. It allows the library to control security for nonbook materials and their associated equipment more effectively. It enables a library client with a particular format in mind to go directly to that type of material without having to contend with other formats. The issue for effective library service, however, should not be whether such people are more satisfied with separate nonbook libraries—clearly they are—but whether all or most of the people who use libraries are more concerned with the form of the materials they seek than their contents.

If they had the choice, would people prefer that librarians with medical expertise select sound recordings, videos, and multimedia materials for a medical library collection, or would they want librarians having sound, video, or multimedia expertise select them? This author's decision is clear—I would opt for the former   but in many well-respected institutions of higher learning librarians opt for the latter. My rationale is not complicated: I believe content is more important than physical form, and I want someone to evaluate materials according to the quality of their contents, not their form. I would rather buy a poor-quality video with good content than a high-quality video with poor or inaccurate content.

The value for recruiting non-bibliocentric librarians for integrating nonbooks into library functions is the attraction of being part of the mainstream, able to interact with all one's colleagues, and compete with them on an equal basis, not being isolated from the rest of the library.

5. *Allocate sufficient funds for nonbook material acquisitions to make selectors believe they are a high-priority material.* "Money talks" is an old saying, and, perhaps, a true one. Libraries that wish to attract staff who can develop nonbook collections ought to be willing and able to show their strength of purpose by committing funds to them. Why bother to seek this special expertise if a library is not serious about its non-book collections? It is simple arithmetic to figure out how many titles can be purchased given the total dollars available and average costs per title. If selectors have little to spend on nonbook materials, this action speaks louder than words in identifying the true priority the library accords them.

Allocations for various materials also function as a tangible measure of recognition and stature, which has psychological effects on the staff members who handle the materials. While it might be presumptuous to think that librarians would jump to be responsible for nonbooks if as much money was allocated to nonbooks as to books, it is common sense to recognize that librarians with nonbook expertise would be rightfully disappointed if funding for nonbooks lagged significantly behind books.

The ability to "do your stuff" and accomplish something deemed to be worthwhile by one's colleagues and superiors is a powerful recruitment tool. Strong budget support for nonbook materials is, to borrow a phrase used often in other contexts, the bottom line for non-bibliocentric collection developers.

6. *Provide librarians with reference tools needed to develop their expertise in nonbook industries as well as to select and acquire nonbook titles.* Books are a uniform medium that has developed over hundreds of years. In the process, reference tools that document book production and furnish bibliographic control for books also have developed. Nonbooks are really many diverse types of material, some of which have long histories (e.g., maps) and some which have been in existence for only a few decades (e.g., computer software). Some media groups that appear to be relatively uniform, such as sound recordings, can actually take many shapes and sizes, none of which are interchangeable. Under the circumstances, it is no surprise there is no *Nonbooks in Print* or *Producers' Trade List Annual* or any other reference tools comparable to the ones librarians use for books. Instead, a library must acquire many reference tools to support nonbook collecting, some covering several media, some only one.[11] Recruits for a job as a non-bibliocentric collection development librarian can be impressed by seeing a well-stocked professional reference shelf that demonstrated the library's understanding of the complexity of nonbooks, or they should receive assurances that support will be forthcoming for its development.

7. *Provide librarians with ongoing professional development opportunities to improve their skills in using nonbook materials.* One of the hallmarks of nonbook formats is rapid ongoing change, as illustrated by the brief description of the music-recording world, above. In particular, computer-based materials, fueled by intense industry competition, are undergoing changes virtually all the time, as are the computers and communication systems that support them. As a result, non-bibliocentricity requires ongoing education and training to keep up with new technologies. While it is as much the non-bibliocentric librarian's responsibility to obtain the requisite knowledge as it is the non-bibliocentric library's responsibility to provide it, opportunities to attend seminars, institutes, and training sessions, to visit new installations, experiment with new materials, and acquire new skills, can be extended willingly or grudgingly, depending on the way the library's staff development obligations are perceived by institutional lead-

ership. Encouragement does not mean perpetually subsidizing staff development, although money is an important measure of support. Encouragement can mean making it easy for a librarian to take leave without pay, or providing a backup while someone is attending a seminar, or doing away with complicated application forms, long lead times, and other administrative red tape involved in staff development activities. Evidence that ongoing staff development is viewed positively and supported to the extent possible is and should be important to potential recruits to the library's staff.

8. *Reward librarians whose skills with nonbook materials aid the library's public in utilizing them fully and effectively.* We all know people who take jobs that involve cuts in pay but promise greater rewards in intangible areas such as personal challenges and satisfactions. There is little that makes people feel more rewarded than recognition from their peers and colleagues. Recognition can take many forms, from things with obvious value, such as a special bonus or holiday, to those whose value lies solely in the mind of the beholder, such as a certificate bearing the name of a person given a special acknowledgment.

Rewards affect more than the people receiving them. They can also motivate others to strive for similar achievements because they bear witness to the esteem in which the institution holds their work. Appreciation of one's work, even when it does not mean more money in a staff member's pocket, is a strong force enabling one to derive satisfaction from the workplace. The recruitment process can and should exploit to the maximum a library's atmosphere of staff appreciation and emphasize its reward system, both in terms of the accomplishments deemed worthy of recognition and the recognitions themselves.

9. *Ask bibliographers to prepare mediagraphies of all book and nonbook acquisitions for users, not just bibliographies of new books.* One method frequently employed to promote and market library materials is production of bibliographies of new acquisitions. Sometimes such lists can be generated automatically from the library's acquisition or cataloging system, and sophisticated programming in the system may even enable the list to be routed automatically to major users of the materials. Personally, I have encountered these lists in nearly all the places I have taught, but nearly every one has listed solely the books acquired. The reason for excluding nonbooks, even new serial subscriptions, from these new acquisition lists could be that the systems generating them handled only books. Nevertheless, it sent a message to the faculties, loud and clear, that books counted for more than nonbooks.

Non-bibliocentric collection development recruits would probably not be satisfied with procedures that informed library clients solely about new book titles. They would expect, and rightly so, to include on their lists the titles of all new materials, not just the books, and, also, by placing all new materials—both book and nonbook—for brief periods on new materials shelves located in areas equipped with appropriate hardware, to invite faculty to browse through them.

10. *Incorporate hardware for browsing nonbook materials into reading and work areas of the library both for staff and users.* Being able to browse nonbooks as easily as books and do so in a convenient location is an asset both for library staff and members of the public. Moreover, the lack of sufficient hardware for staff to browse shipments of titles sent on approval or in demonstration versions could make it difficult for staff to do a good job no matter how willing they might be. Hardware is part of the infrastructure that certain kinds of nonbooks require, and its absence from the library's reading and work areas should make a potential nonbook collection developer beware. Libraries that have adequate hardware conveniently deployed have a distinct edge over those that do not, and they are entitled to exploit it for all it is worth.

Collection development recruits would do well to take a lesson from the environment in which nonbook catalogers operate. Nonbook catalogers are often faced with the prospect of describing, classifying, and indexing nonbook titles they cannot view, hear, or run. Elaborate rules providing substitutes for bibliographic data normally found by viewing the titles screens of a video or computer file have been devised to accommodate them. These conditions are part of the bibliocentric library environment that needs change. Catalogers seem not to have made the acquisition of adequate hardware a major issue; their rules and tools accept it and permit it to continue unchallenged. But collection development recruits have an opportunity to press for change as a condition of their employment. If they are willing to move into an inferior environment without protest, it is a good bet that they, too, will have trouble changing it.

CONCLUSIONS

Clearly, the best way for libraries to recruit non-bibliocentric collection developers is to be non-bibliocentric in the first place. Any library that follows the ten suggestions presented in this chapter could not be called bibliocentric, regardless of how many book versus nonbook titles were stored on its shelves. Bibliocentricity—or lack of it—is an attitude, a posture, a way of thinking about library materials and their use, more than it is a measure of the size of collections.

It is difficult to imagine a library that treats nonbooks equally and integratively with books failing to fund them more fully and utilize them more effectively than the traditionally bibliocentric libraries that isolate nonbooks and accord them "other" status. In the 1960s, in times when budgets were healthy, research activity was high, and interest in nonbooks was intense, bibliocentricity did not engender the development of nonbooks to any great extent. There were always more good books to buy and shelve, even if they were not used very often. Certainly, in times of financial scarcity, shrinking academic enrollments, and cutbacks in educational and community programs such as libraries are experiencing in the 1990s, bibliocentricity cannot be expected to give way to development of nonbooks without a struggle.

Changing the library's image from a storehouse of books to an interactive source of all sorts of materials takes time and effort, and it will consume no small amount of resources. Once the goal is accepted, however, the path is straightforward, and the result is an opening outward of the walls of the storehouse to incorporate a much larger universe of factual, literary, and artistic expression. If experts are correct, books will remain an important source for research and so will printed journals. But they will not be the only important and highly valued sources. Nonbooks will assume a hard-won position alongside these worthy formats to enable the library to serve its users more completely and more conveniently than ever before.

NOTES

1. My opinions are expressed at some length in Sheila S. Intner, *Access to Media* (New York: Neal-Schuman Press, 1984), 243–269.

2. Communication theorists freely admit this. See, for example, Marshall McLuhan, *Understanding Media: The Extensions of Man* (New York: McGraw-Hill, 1964), 7–21.

3. A glance through the statistics in any recent edition of the *American Library Directory* will confirm this claim. I used the 44th edition (New York: Bowker, 1991), 2 vols.

4. These issues are not new and were noted by Lester Asheim in his introduction to a theme issue of *Library Quarterly*, titled "Differentiating the Media: A Focus on Library Selection and Use of Communication Content," 45 (January 1975): 2.

5. Some experts, such as F. W. Lancaster of the University of Illinois (see his *Libraries and Librarians in an Age of Electronics* [Arlington, Va.: Information Resources Press, 1982] and subsequent writings on electronic publishing), predict electronic publications will capture the lion's share of scholars' attention, while others, such as Michael Gorman of California State University, Fresno (see his "Academic Library in the Year 2001: Dream or Nightmare or Something in Between?" *Journal of Academic Librarianship* 17 [March 1991]: 4–9), believe books and printed journals will not lose their primacy. An interesting discussion about the fate of the scholarly monograph can be found in Ross Atkinson, "The Acquisitions Librarian as Change Agent in the Transition to the Electronic Library," *Library Resources & Technical Services* 36 (January 1992): 9–10.

6. For a thorough discussion of electronic publications, see Barbara Buckner Higginbotham and Sally Bowdoin, *Access Versus Assets: A Comprehensive Guide to Resource Sharing for Academic Librarians* (Chicago: American Library Association, 1993), chapter 9.

7. Documented in *Access to Media*, 136–138.

8. Documented in Sheila S. Intner, *Circulation Policy in Academic, Public, and School Libraries* (Westport, Conn.: Greenwood Press, 1987).

9. In lecturing to my collection development classes, I am particularly sensitive to the need to be media-inclusive and always use media-neutral vocabulary; yet my students, absorbing the practices of the libraries in which they work or study and the coverage in their textbooks, typically focus heavily, if not exclusively, on books and journals when formulating collecting goals for their term projects.

10. This is not a new idea, nor did it originate with me. See Wesley A. Doak, "Administrative Problems and Their Solutions," *Library Quarterly* 45 (January 1975): 60.

11. An excellent source for information about non-book media reference sources is available in Carolyn O. Frost's *Media Access and Organization: A Cataloging and Reference Sources Guide for Nonbook Materials* (Englewood, Colo.: Libraries Unlimited, 1989).

Part III

EDUCATING FOR COLLECTION DEVELOPMENT

6

Collection Development in the Library and Information Science Curriculum

Paul Metz

When collection development officers gather at conferences and institutes or through electronic discussion groups, one of the recurring topics is the ideal composition of a course on collection development. They lament what was missing when they went to library school and the gaps in knowledge, both practical and theoretical, they see in new graduates. Each has suggestions for essential topics and for areas that need more emphasis. Paul Metz begins the section of this book devoted to educating librarians for collection development by examining the typical content of current courses in collection development and how that has changed in the last ten years. His analysis of changing content suggests that the curriculum is responsive to changes in the practice of collection development. He notes the addition of course components addressing resource sharing and fund allocation.

Metz expresses concern, however, that no course explicitly addresses two current areas of critical interest to collection development librarians—the issues of access versus ownership and the place of electronic media in library collections. Both are constantly before practitioners as they seek to balance meeting the needs of today's library users with those of the future. Metz offers a list of critical questions associated with the access-versus-ownership debate and suggests these issues can be productively explored in a collection development course. The second area, electronic media, is broader than the issues of selecting and budgeting for new information technologies. Electronic media cannot be addressed in isolation in the collection development course; decisions about this medium require increasing interdependence among collection development, reference, and automation units.

The trend toward increasing interdependence in library planning and decisions leads Metz to his conclusion: Library schools' primary responsibility in preparing students for collection development responsibilities is to develop a broad understanding of the library and an appreciation of the wider professional issues. Librarians who can understand the "big picture" are those best prepared to make collection management decisions in today's complex environment.

To many library users, there is little if any distinction between a library and its collection. Listening to conversations in which frequent library users compare perspectives on the various libraries they have used, one could easily be seduced by the belief that libraries are their collections, no more and no less. In the academic setting, the old saw that the collection *is* the library is nearly as common as the truism that the library is the heart of the university. University faculty almost never support cuts in library materials budgets, and they are usually indifferent to cuts anywhere else.

Experienced librarians and library educators know better. They understand that libraries differ in many critical ways and that the best collections can be hidden away by delayed, partial, or poor cataloging, by user-hostile catalogs, and by indifferent or uninformed reference staff. Experienced professionals understand that the ownership of library collections is becoming less salient every day, with ease of access to remote databases and collections offering a critical advantage to libraries aggressive enough to exploit them.

And yet it is possible to know too much. Library patrons come to libraries to acquire information, and in the most cases they come with the hope that what they seek will be available locally. Many decisions about information resources to which they have remote access will have been made by collection development staff. This suggests that the "customer's perspective," or naive point of view about what distinguishes a strong from a weak library, should still receive our considerable respect.

If the collection is the heart of the traditional library, if most of what librarians do deals with acquiring, describing, promoting the use of, and sharing collections, then the process of building library collections should have a prominent, if not a central, place in professional education. Is this the case?

THE CURRENT CURRICULUM

To document the place of collection development in the library and information science curriculum fully, one would have to attend every accredited library school. Since this is impossible, a substitute methodology might be to inspect the catalogs of each library school, or at least the catalogs of the schools that purport to lead the way in library education.

In order to gain something of an impression of the top schools of library and information science, I studied the most recent catalogs I could obtain of about half the schools generally considered in the top twenty. This survey, while admittedly unscientific, provided a useful sense of the priorities prevailing in education for collection development.

My inspection of the course catalogs of a selection of highly rated library schools revealed a mixed pattern. A course on the topic of collection development, or on collection development and acquisitions, is required in a slim majority. Most of the library schools not requiring such a course give explicit attention to collection development in other required courses, such as core courses dealing with philosophical issues or with the information universe.

Not all library schools go even this far, and thus there are leading library schools from which one can obtain the M.L.S. without attending a single course in which collection development is sufficiently prominent to warrant mention in the catalog. This conclusion is buttressed by Margaret Stieg's recent, more systematic, inspection of library and information science catalogs, in which she found that the only constants among required courses were an introductory survey and courses in reference and cataloging.[1]

The place of collection development in the library school curriculum may not have eroded as badly as that of other areas, but it was probably not possible to receive a degree without having explicitly studied collection development in the time of the Williamson report, when each of the eleven library schools then extant gave collection development significant attention and the topic trailed only cataloging in the mean number of hours of classroom instruction.[2]

Curriculums of the library schools studied are about evenly divided, with half offering two courses explicitly devoted to collection development, and half offering only one. Collection development issues surface in several other courses. Courses devoted to particular types of libraries provide a good forum for the discussion of collection development issues, since collection development differs so much from one kind of library to another, and indeed the topic is frequently an important part of "type of library" courses. Collection development is also explicitly or implicitly addressed whenever curriculums include such commonly offered courses as rare books, nonprint media, serials, technical services, intellectual freedom, and contemporary book publishing.

Equally important as the question of whether collection development is taught is the question of just what is studied in collection development courses. In the mid-1980s, Richard Krzys laid out the fundamental elements of a basic course in collection development as found then in the typical library and information science curriculum.[3] According to Krzys, the traditional course syllabus in collection development looks like that shown in Table 6.1.

Table 6.1
Traditional Collection Development Course

Course Introduction
    Description   Outline
    Objectives   Requirements

Historical Background of Books and Libraries

Types of Libraries and Their Communities

Library Material   Use
    Nature   *Organization and
    Categories   Arrangement

Publishers and Publishing
    Nature   Functions
    *History and Development   Types

Selection of Material
    Purpose   Selection Aids
    Community Analysis   Format
    Principles   Subjects
    Policies   Censorship

Acquisition of Material
    *Principles   *Annotation Writing
      Examination and Evaluation of Material   *Book Talks

Collection Evaluation
    Storage   Preservation
    Weeding   *Replacement

Conclusions of Course Participants

*Elements of the traditional curriculum that seem to have disappeared or to have become less
    prominent.

WHAT HAS CHANGED

Today's curriculums focus on many of the same topics, but there are differences. An admittedly unscientific effort to code the topics mentioned in library school catalogs descriptions of collection development courses suggested a wide range of topics. These are arrayed below in the frequency of their occurrence in the catalogs I was able to inspect.

Topics in Contemporary Collection Development Courses

(most frequently   Evaluation and selection
occurring)   Collection development policies
                        Publishing and distribution

Censorship/intellectual freedom

Resource sharing

Community analysis/needs

Acquisitions organization and processes

Collection evaluation

Fund allocation

Preservation

Alternative formats

(least frequently   Storage alternatives

occurring)   Selection tools

While one would not want to put too much emphasis on one person's prescription for library and information science in 1983 or on the results of a small sample of catalogs reviewed ten years later, comparisons between the Krzys agenda and the typical offerings of today's courses are suggestive.

The first question to be answered is, What has disappeared from the curriculum? The areas indicated by asterisks in Krzys's list seem to have disappeared, or to have been given much less prominence in contemporary library and information science courses on collection development. "Organization and arrangement" of collections is now generally assumed to be a classification issue, and a solved one at that, but this may be an unfortunate assumption. The many possibilities for the physical groupings of collections, including the structure of branch library systems, are at bottom a collection management problem, and if we do not consider these in collection development courses, where will they be studied?

The history and development of publishing and the distribution infrastructure is now generally given little attention, as the press of new information technologies has probably claimed historical considerations as its chief victim to be supplanted in the library and information science curriculum.[4]

Book talks? Were we really doing this even ten years ago? Annotation writing? In "library hand," perhaps? These topics stand as startling evidence of how quickly things have changed. Finally, the issue of "replacement" has dropped away, presumably because it is simply a special case of more general decisions bibliographers make every day.

What topics have been added? Looking at the ranking of topics taught in today's collection development courses, we see a prominent position for "resource sharing," a topic not included in Krzys's list. Further down the list we find "fund allocation," also not mentioned by Krzys. Both topics reflect the harsh financial realities of contemporary collection development, as well as the spectacular success of interlibrary loan networks, which are now reliable and efficient enough to allow collection development officers to make cost avoidance decisions with faith that they have not denied their clients ultimate access to desired materials.

It seems fair to say that the addition of resource sharing and fund allocation to collection development courses represents a realistic and perceptive effort by educators to prepare students for the library world as they will find it. Ultimately, we should always expect the library schools to adapt to changes in professional realities, of course. The historic shift from "book selection" to "materials selection" and then to "collection development" in course naming reflects this reality.[5]

What is the dog that is not barking in all of this? That is, what important elements have library and information science educators failed to add to the collection development curriculum that they should have added?

Of all the elements that might be added to the curriculum for collection development today, none seems more pressing than the issue of access versus ownership. It is probably fair to assume that this issue is currently being addressed more than the catalogs reflect. Certainly it is impossible to tell the extent to which instruction in resource sharing, which holds a relatively high rank in the listing of frequently occurring topics, deals with the ownership-versus-access issue. Nevertheless, the implications for local collection-building efforts of resource-sharing opportunities have taken some time to become clear even to the best practicing collection managers, and the implications of the more recent surge of electronically available information resources or the possible role of commercial document providers have been the slowest to become clear.

It would be difficult to find an issue of greater concern to today's chief collection development officers, as they try to spread scarce resources for today's clientele while worrying about the implications of their actions for future users. The point has been well made that ownership is the ultimate form of access, but ownership is less and less a realistic choice for many kinds of materials.[6]

The need for future librarians to appreciate the means by which local collections can be extended is so pressing that Sheila Intner has called for the library schools to educate "access librarians" as a specialty subsuming, but going beyond, traditional circulation and document delivery. Intner lists computer expertise, a penchant for risk taking, and skills in communications, research, problem solving, and leadership as critical to the success of access librarians.[7]

The access-versus-ownership dilemma raises several questions that should stimulate the minds of library science students, while preparing them for career-long active concerns. The following are only examples of the broad questions raised by this trend:

- To the degree that all libraries move in the direction of access, what remains distinctive about each?

- If everyone moves toward access, who will still own the materials on which everyone else plans to rely?

- At what point does copyright limit the access model?
- How much of a disadvantage is it to patrons to have deferred access to materials that might once have been near at hand?
- How serious is the loss of the ability to browse, and can satisfactory electronic alternatives to browsing be designed?
- Can the library afford to extend the access model to all its clients, or does the model imply differential strata of privilege, as for example faculty versus students or fee-paying local companies versus private citizens?
- How does the library limit costs if it puts the ability to order documents in its users' hands?
- Can the access model rest on the backbone of traditional interlibrary loan, or does it require a new reliance on a growing industry of document providers?

Each of these questions provides sufficient meat for a lecture, a classroom debate, or a term paper. While the access-versus-ownership issue has become prominent only in recent years, most of the issues it raises relate to classical philosophical problems that have characterized librarianship from the beginning. Library schools could therefore address the issue without being vulnerable to the charge that they were excessively short-sighted and vocational in their training. Moreover, though in some ways the access-versus-ownership question has a short history, it is likely to have a long future.

A second issue deserving additional attention in the library and information science curriculum for collection development is the place of electronic media in library collections. Digital technologies have obviously recast all manner of traditional tools, transforming the nature of reference services, making many phonograph collections obsolescent and, increasingly, beginning to compete with the printed text itself.

More fundamental from a policy point of view, electronic media are competing for ever-larger proportions of library materials budgets and are therefore of direct concern to collection development librarians. Successful collection development officers can no longer ignore reference decisions or decisions about library automation. To do so would abrogate responsibility over too large a share of their budgets. Thus we see an increasing interconnectedness of reference, automation, and collection development. The implications of these shifts should be examined for, and by, library and information science students.

Related to the interdependence of reference, automation, and collection development is an increasing tendency for collection development responsibilities to become diffuse throughout the library. Formerly contained within acquisitions departments or sequestered in the offices of a cadre of academically inclined specialists, collection development is now nearly ubiquitous in the modern library. This is partly true because decisions about which electronic information resources to acquire are difficult to extricate from issues of software, hardware, and the nature and goals of reference service. It is also true because of the slow decline of the full-time bibliographer, an increased interest in job enrichment, and the recognition that libraries contain remarkable assortments of on-staff skills and areas of knowledge. As a result, there is a tendency to assign collection development responsibilities to a greater number of librarians.

The diffusion of collection development throughout the library raises several questions worthy of attention in the library and information science curriculum. What is the best organizational structure for collection development? Can matrix, or dual reporting, structures provide a balance of accountability and flexibility? Can a consistent picture of where a collection is and should be headed be maintained when so many hands are involved?

The many questions listed above have in common a concern for global perspectives on collection development. They show a recognition that collection development cannot be extricated from the major strategic choices a library must make in charting its identity. Issues of purpose, audience, budget, and goals, of the articulation together of collection development, reference, technical services, and automation cannot be evaded by a narrow focus on collection development. This is especially true when we reflect on the high percentage of library and information science students who will ultimately be responsible for library systems or branches.

The broader intellectual understandings that successful collection development librarians must possess have been usefully cataloged by Charles Osburn:

The most fundamental knowledge and capabilities required in collection development can be summarized as follows: knowledge of the information and publication universe, ability to control that information bibliographically, knowledge of the community related to publication and information, understanding of the likely causes of change in the information universe, understanding of the likely causes of change in the community, ability to monitor the information universe and community, knowledge of signs of change in each, ability to adjust policy and procedures, knowledge of quality control methods, ability to effectively integrate collection development policy and procedures into library operation.[8]

Some might question whether all librarians who will ultimately be responsible for selecting materials and managing collections, often as a small part of their jobs, require some of the more general levels of understanding Osburn cites. The argument that such preparation is essential rests on three considerations: (1) that many of today's students will at some point in their careers be responsible for entire libraries, if only at the branch level; (2) that one of the worst, and hardest to eradicate, faults of new bibliographers is a tendency to think parochially about their assigned collection areas; and (3) that the skills necessary for careful selection can, with practice, be acquired by one who understands the big picture, but that the reverse process of induction, of comprehending global collection development concerns based on experience at the microscopic level of collection management, never seems to happen.

Clearly, success in collection development requires a broad understanding of the library itself, of the publications universe, of management and budgeting, all within a broader appreciation of professional values. It is interesting that the responses to Karen Schmidt's survey of practicing acquisitions librarians identified knowledge of the publishing business and personnel management as key areas in which their library schools should have been expected to provide a significant portion of their knowledge base.[9] These needs are shared by collection development librarians.

The library schools are the place where an appreciation of these broad professional concerns and a strong initial knowledge base about them should be acquired. Certainly it is vain to hope that students will have such an opportunity once they are at work, fighting the daily demands that make it so difficult ever to clear one's desk or "to do" list.

Can we teach collection development on a high plane, hoping that what future bibliographers and managers learn about the sociology of communications, about scholarship and science, and about an information society will make them better practitioners? Shouldn't we also ground them in some of the more basic topics we find on Krzys's list?

The problem, of course, is that all these elements of knowledge are important. No library should have to teach a recent graduate the difference between a firm order and a blanket order, or the difference between acquisitions and collection development. No library should have to inform recent graduates about the standard tools selectors use in evaluating materials, or to sensitize them to the semi-intuitive means by which bibliographers use very partial information to help them assess the likely utility of a book to their collections.

There are ways to resolve the tension between macro-level intellectual understanding and practical knowledge and skills, both of which library and information science education must convey to future collection development librarians. Various approaches to the problem are currently in practice in our library schools.

A key approach is to make sure that the content of the core courses in which all students participate includes the larger questions that all librarians must think about, but that are especially relevant in collection development. How can we tell who our community is so that we can serve their needs? How do we ensure that information and expression are not stifled? What is the current nature of the information and publishing industry, and how is it changing? How do I run my library in an effective and responsible manner? How do I manage resources?

It is critical that core courses never consider the library and its collection as a given in the equation of library management. No course, indeed, should assume that the collection grew under a cabbage leaf or was delivered by storks and need now only be managed or described. The choices that collections represent, the distinction between the macro choices that set policies and place subscriptions or write approval profiles, and the micro choices of daily selection and management that Hendrik Edelman described should be clear even to future catalogers and systems analysts.[10]

Once these understandings are established in the core, special courses in collection development can deepen and review them while moving into more detailed and technical areas pertinent to the selection and management of collections, ordering, preservation, community outreach, and the like.

The case study method has great potential for the teaching of collection development principles. Many collection development courses already incorporate the technique to a small degree in that students typically perform an exercise in which they are given a fictitious budget with which to select materials in a given area for a hypothetical library clientele. Many librarians fondly remember this exercise years after graduation.

The potential of the case study approach may be even greater, however. Many basic tenets of professional philosophy and many management principles appropriate to core courses can be given tangible reality and application via the case technique. A fuller elaboration of the host library could expose students to management dilemmas while sensitizing them, as selectors, to what Ross Atkinson has called the "archival context" of selection. Fuller elaboration of the imagined host institution or client community could teach community analysis techniques while sensitizing potential selectors to the "community context" within which selection takes place. Studies of the sociology of science and scholarship, of citation analysis and similar techniques, could strengthen students' appreciation of the "thematic context," or the literatures within which potential new selections reside.[11]

Susan Sommer has reported success in teaching students how to write a collection development policy, how to select materials, and how to initiate orders within the context of a "model library" dreamed up by student teams. She notes, "By teaching collection development as part of an overall pattern shaped by the purpose and function of the library I hope that . . . theoretical principles will emerge from the contextual reality."[12] Sommer's success in teaching collection development in a broader "type of library" course may have implications for all library educators trying to wrestle with the dilemma of balancing broader professional values and understandings with the inculcation of specific knowledge and skills.

Whether the creative integration of core and specialized courses, greater use of the case study technique, or another approach is taken, it is clear that to give students the philosophical perspectives they need, to teach them sufficiently about the information universe, and yet also to convey the sheer technical information a bibliographer should know, and to encompass all this in one part of an ever-expanding curriculum will be the special challenge of library and information science faculty with an interest in collection development for the foreseeable future.

NOTES

1. Margaret F. Stieg, *Change and Challenge in Library and Information Science Education* (Chicago: American Library Association, 1992), 109.

2. Charles C. Williamson, *Training for Library Service: A Report Prepared for the Carnegie Corporation of New York* (New York: D. B. Updike, 1923), 22.

3. Richard Kryzs, "Collection Development Courses," in *Internationalizing Library and Information Science Education: A Handbook of Policies and Procedures in Administration and Curriculum*, ed. by John F. Harvey and Frances Laverne Carroll (New York: Greenwood Press, 1987), 203.

4. Stieg, *Change and Challenge*, 110.

5. Kryzs, "Collection Development Courses," 201.

6. Aqueduct Conference [on Serials Acquisition and Scholarly Communication], *Aqueduct Action Agenda* (point 1), unpublished report Chapel Hill, 1992.

7. Sheila S. Intner, "Education for the Dual Role Responsibilities of the Access Services Librarian," *Reference Librarian* 32 (1991): 73–94.

8. Charles B. Osburn, "Education for Collection Development," in *Collection Development in Libraries: A Treatise*, ed. by Robert D. Stueart and George B. Miller, Jr., 565, Foundations in Library and Information Science, vol. 26 (Greenwich, Conn.: JAI Press, 1980).

9. Karen A. Schmidt, "The Education of the Acquisitions Librarian: A Survey of ARL Acquisitions Librarians," *Library Resources & Technical Services* 35 (January 1991): 7–22.

10. Hendrik Edelman, "Selection Methodology in Academic Libraries," *Library Resources & Technical Services* 23 (Winter 1979): 33–38.

11. Ross Atkinson, "The Citation as Intertext: Toward a Theory of the Selection Process," *Library Resources & Technical Services* 28 (April/June 1984): 109–119.

12. Susan T. Sommer, "Teaching Collection Development in Context," *Fontes Artis Musicae* 35 (July-September 1988): 197.

7

Among the Disciplines: The Bibliographer in the I World

Michael T. Ryan

Ask any librarian for a list of the hot topics among their users and many will list some, if not all, of the following social and political concerns: ecology and the environment, bioethics, public policy, biotechnology and genetic engineering, AIDS, international relations, diversity and multiculturalism. What do these subjects have in common? They cross disciplinary and subject divisions, they are controversial, they are of interest to many people (regardless of professional or academic home), and they are highly fluid.

No one is more sensitive and aware of these topics than the person trying to select materials for the library. Michael T. Ryan writes about bibliographers who build and manage research collections in the new interdisciplinary, or "I," world. He begins by describing the library's responsibilities in the I world and then suggests ways in which bibliographers can be prepared to perform their tasks better. This is not a simple matter of adding a new area of responsibility or combining two or three existing subject responsibilities. Each new hybrid or interdisciplinary field of research and study is more than the sum of its parts.

Ryan counsels resocialization of bibliographers into new working groups that emphasize coordination and interaction. While new bibliographic specialists may be appropriate in some areas, a collaborative model of collection development that parallels the workings of the I world is essential. Making connections across fields is as important in the library as it is in the academy. In addition, the developing, fluid nature of the I world requires constant monitoring of issues and topics. The rapid rate of change makes continuing education, both formal and informal, imperative.

Automated information delivery is particularly crucial to work in new hybrid areas because of its immediacy and responsiveness to current concerns. Online options not only affect the delivery of information but also shape the nature, character, and agenda of research itself. Bibliographers need new skills to work effectively with new forms of information. They must have the ability to identify, evaluate, and work with disparate types of sources and materials.

Ryan concludes by examining ways in which library schools can prepare graduates to work in the I world. M.L.S. programs should emphasis the disciplinary breadth of collection development, stressing the instability and fluidity of literatures. All future librarians must understand the increasingly collaborative nature of knowledge, along with its dynamic character. Bibliographers must come to their work realizing that no fixed boundaries exist between disciplines within the research setting, nor should they exist between colleagues in the library.

THE I WORLD

That we live and work in an age of academic interdisciplinarity is an observation that has surely attained cliche status. The *Oxford English Dictionary* tells us that the word *interdisciplinary* has been around since at least 1937, though doubtless the notion and its practices have a much older genealogy. The "I word" is all-pervasive; its consequences are everywhere: in the curriculum, in hiring decisions, in research, in the organization of institutions. It is a subject in its own right. A search of the ERIC (Educational Resources Information Center) thesaurus will turn up over 10,000 citation for "interdisciplinary approaches."

No area or subject constellation is immune: Interdisciplinarity plays shaping roles in the sciences, the social sciences, and the humanities. Moreover, the cross-fertilizations are not only within but among the broad groups: Methodologies and concerns of the sciences, for example, metastasize and mingle with those of the humanities. The professional schools— law, business, medicine, and engineering—are often key players, teaming up with colleagues from various academic disciplines to create new programs. The I word has created an "I world" in universities. Courses and degree bulletins are full of these new species, from bioethics, earth systems, and various "textualizations" of science to the theory and practice of computer music. Many of these programs reflect contemporary social and political concerns and the availability of funding to support teaching and research in them: the environment, public policy, genetic engineering, medical technologies, the politics of race and gender, and standards of professional conduct. The emergence of the multicultural campus and increasingly explicit institutional commitments to diversity and an expanded multicultural curriculum have brought with them new interdisciplinary agendas and challenges. Moreover, most newcomers want ancestors to validate their legitimacy; thus, pedigrees are researched, histories written, new texts exhumed and examined, new canons formed. Another piece of the past is "recovered," dusted off, and made to serve the needs of the present.

The dominance of the I world today is evidence of a healthy ferment in higher education, an openness to the new, the different, the once-marginal. The life of the mind is, if nothing else, livelier. Much of this work implicitly involves an epistemological shift: The isolated Cartesian investigator has been socialized; groups, *equipes*, and workshops are more prominent in all areas. Universities are congested with centers, institutes, and programs that allow faculty and students to come together from across the institution to participate in new research and learning contexts. Electronic communication networks, bulletin boards, and online information sources have served to promote as well as support the evolving I world.[1]

Simultaneously, traditional academic departments remain in place and seem as strong as ever, while the disciplines they represent continue to play dominant roles in training, hiring, and promoting faculty. There appears no rush to dis-establish departments or abandon the disciplines. For what would take their places? The relative stability of departments and disciplines, in fact, seems a necessary condition for the flourishing of the I world. Professional and institutional business gets done as the quest for new knowledge proceeds in its own quirky and unpredictable ways. The persistence of the department alongside the proliferation of the program and the center documents well James March's classic characterization of universities as "organized anarchies."[2]

THE LIBRARY AND THE I WORLD

No one on campus is probably more sensitive to and aware of the implications of the I word and its world than the subject or area specialist in the library. The multiplication of new literatures and new information formats generated in part by the I world seem to require a Cerberus-like capacity for vision and the stamina of the long-distance runner to monitor adequately. New research vocabularies must be learned, new methods of investigation assimilated. If the bibliographer works in a branch collection, he or she will confront not only a primary school or departmental constituency but faculty and students from many different units on campus engaged in interdisciplinary projects. The I world not only spawns new literature, it makes older literatures once peripheral to scholarship now central and so increases pressures on the selector not only to master the new but remaster the old. It may also bring with it new pressures to duplicate collections to meet service needs. Collection development and management issues, of course, are only part of the agenda before the bibliographer: Teaching clients how to navigate the ocean of bibliographical and informational resources used for research in the I world requires a daunting range of competencies dimly perceived even a decade ago.

Like faculty colleagues, the bibliographer probably also works in an organizational context structured to match the formal academic organization of institutions as a whole, with selection responsibilities and selection policies keyed to established departments and disciplines. Like academic colleagues, too, the bibliographer has probably been trained in a discipline and understands well the need and claims for disciplinary integrity. The contemporary bibliographer is both a specialist and an inveterate transgressor of specialization, working within and among disciplines and fields, literate in a variety of methodologies, and competent in a multitude of research vocabularies. Just as clients may stretch across the university, so, too, the staff with whom he or she must increasingly collaborate connect the bibliographer with many selection programs in the system. He or she knows well the limits of personal expertise and appreciates the need to tap that of fellow selectors in adjacent fields. In short, the bibliographer has become adept in the ways of the I world.

How, then, does one prepare for this? To what extent can librarians be educated and trained for the I world? Are there curricular options? Do we need new cadres of experts and expertise? These are but a few of the questions posed for academic librarianship by the fragmented nature of the contemporary intellectual scene. There are no ready or pat answers to any of them; they rest astride a seismically active fault zone. Nevertheless, some generalities are possible. For if the earth is moving beneath our feet, at least we should know *how*, if not *where*, to stand.

SPECIALISTS NEW AND OLD

Do new fields require new specialists? For senior library managers even posing this question can conjure up a Pandora's box full of unwanted staffing increments and budget-busting program costs. There is no easy yes or no answer to the question that does not in turn beg a multitude of qualifying issues and considerations. Some of these are local and political; others relate to the nature of the new field, its knowledge and information requirements, and the structure of the literature or literatures on which it draws. Among local issues are those such as the prominence of the program and of its advocates, its position within the institution, the composition of the client group, and the budgetary consequences of program growth. If collection development and management are seen as integral to academic planning, many of these questions will answer themselves. More often than not, though, academic planning is a retrospective exercise, with the knowledge and information needs of new programs at best an interesting afterthought left to the library to negotiate on its own. Some new programs carry with them politically charged baggage that requires adroit handling. Client groups may have more than information needs to be acknowledged and met, and these will contribute to shaping decisions about adding new bibliographic expertise to the staff. This may be the case especially in fields such as ethnic and women's studies, where institutional agendas tend to be more volatile than in other fields. Similarly, hybrid programs may embody singular institutional aspirations that, because of their definitional potency, demand a dedicated expertise as part of the library's acknowledgment of their role and importance.

The nature of the program is also key to understanding and assessing its needs and their potential impact. Is it a degree-granting program? If so, at what level? Undergraduate? Master's? Doctoral? Is it a program with a curriculum but no degree? Does it represent a federation of existing faculty, fields, and courses? Or does it bring with it new billets and new fields? Depending on how these questions are answered, the bibliographer may be looking at either considerable adjustments in collections and services, policies and procedures, or business more-or-less as usual. The possible life cycle of the hybrid also needs to be evaluated and considered. Is it here for the long haul? Or is it an epiphenomenon of something else? Is it a passing trend, or will it root and take hold? Hybrid programs too dependent on a single faculty member or laboratory may be as transient as the players themselves and their interests. Dedicating staff to them may be myopic on the part of the library.

On the other hand, several new enterprises seem to have found homes in the academy and in the library. Women's studies, various fields of ethnic studies, international studies, and environmental studies, for example, speak to abiding concerns that are both intellectual and public; their places in the academy appear secure. These may form new specialties requiring, if not deserving, new, dedicated library experts. To the extent that the new hybrid constitutes a separate field with a definable identity, dedicated expertise will surely be in order. Thus, the case for women's studies made by Susan Searing and Joan Ariel:

In most settings, women's studies collection development is best accomplished by a single selector with a commitment to the integrity of the discipline, someone in a position to monitor holdings across other disciplines, to guarantee a balance within the collection, and to acquire the more specific and often elusive materials generated by feminist scholars and activists.[3]

The coalescence and concentration of a variety of disciplines, subjects, topics, and enquiries into a single hybrid field can create a whole that is more than the sum of its parts. The history of science is also a good example of a broad, interdisciplinary field that has, over time, evolved into a mature and identifiable professional profile and literature structure; it has thus become a whole that is more than and different from the sum of its parts. As far as new hybrids comprise such wholes, they also may require a matching expertise in the library to see and understand the integrity of the hybrid. Searing and Ariel emphasize the need to get inside the hybrid, adopt its identity, understand its point of view; in other words, to approach it as a practitioner.

How best to meet the bibliographical requirements of the new hybrids is the bottom-line issue, and it is not clear that breaching the walls of the establishment brings with it the need for dedicated expertise concentrated in a single person. Thus, new programs offering terminal degrees at the bachelor's or even master's level will not typically generate the new materials or service needs that doctoral programs can. While new centers and new programs will often bring with them new service needs, their impact on collection development policy may be marginal, since the literatures they use and to which they in turn contribute already exist somewhere in the library. While a new program in earth systems or environmental studies may prompt some fine-tunings of collection development policy on the margins, it is probably also the case that large research libraries are already acquiring the necessary literatures for teaching and research in support of the array of separate disciplines and fields whose coalescence comprises the hybrid program. Here, as with the disciplinary configuration of the hybrid, the whole may be greater than the sum of its parts. This concentration of disparate scholars into a program or center, on the one hand, and the dispersal of "their" literature around the system, on the other, will present the library with important access, service, and coordination issues. These test the ability of the library as an organization to appreciate and respond to the wholeness of hybrid programs in sympathetic yet practical ways.

Often the I world spawns programs whose collection needs can best be met by existing expertise functioning in more self-consciously collaborative modes. Just as these new programs assemble faculty and affinity groups from across the campus under one tent, so, too, teams of selectors will coalesce to sift, sort, and define collection needs and selection responsibilities. In this scenario, the library whose collection development program is formally organized to match the constellation of academic departments and schools operates in much the same way as the client groups it serves. Formally grounded in disciplines and departments, selectors come together in new ways to explore and meet the needs of faculty doing something similar. In both cases, that of the faculty and that of the collection development staff, individuals are in effect being resocialized to work in new, frequently ad hoc groups. In both cases, the success of the effort will relate directly to the coherence and cohesiveness of the community created. For selectors, then, the issue may be as much social as intellectual: the effective reconfiguration and redeployment of existing expertise. At the management and policy level, the issue becomes one of coordination and the creation of workplace contexts that discourage turf and encourage easy staff interactions. The new knowledge represented by hybrid programs also reflects new relationships among scholars and a new sociology of knowledge. Meeting the bibliographic need of these new hybrids also may

require a new sociology of collection development and new patterns of
socialization among selectors.

Some new hybrid programs will require new bibliographic specialists
with particular training in the programs they are supposed to serve. Someone will need to understand and interpret the relative integrity of hybrid
programs into collection development and management policy. There are
certain to be curricular options of which selectors can avail themselves. If
experience offers any guide to praxis here, its counsel urges at least equal
attention to the resocialization of specialists and the facilitation of new
communities of interdisciplinary collaboration within collection development programs. How this is done will depend much on local custom and
culture; it is the importance of the larger conceptual issue that is being
asserted here. Library managers and collection development officers can
do much to create an infrastructure that encourages collaboration and
cooperation without having to redraw the organization chart yet another
time. This may involve creating informal teams or working groups, spon-
soring intraprogram seminars and colloquia, requiring firm linkages with
new academic programs, and ensuring that selectors have the workstation
environment that eases communication and the sharing of information.
Whatever the mechanisms, however, the overarching objective is the
achievement of a highly social, collaborative model of collection development that to some extent parallels the working milieux of the I world.

ACADEMIC GROUNDINGS

The best preparation for successfully negotiating the I world is that
which the faculty themselves bring with them: a firm grounding in their
primary discipline or field. As important as professional education and
certification are, there is no substitute for advanced work on the graduate
level in providing the selector with the methodological and conceptual
basics necessary for meeting the knowledge and information needs of the
primary client group and those of its extended family. Understanding the
range of research possible under a disciplinary umbrella and the methodologies that undergird that range will give the selector a good sense of
who and where the "kin" may be outside the department and thus of
those fellow selectors with whom he or she ought to be prepared to
collaborate.

Collection development work is a form of enforced "continuing education" in which selectors are routinely exposed to the new and the
different in addition to the established and the familiar. Selectors who
bring with them a solid disciplinary grounding will be better positioned
to take advantage of these daily refresher courses and to move with
confidence among faculty and graduate students. Ideally, this should
involve some type of participation in or affiliation with the hybrid pro-

grams that make up the topography of the selector's client groups. In short, making the relevant connections in the I world depends in no small measure on establishing one's credentials within a primary disciplinary community.

Viewed from another angle, the I world does not so much generate new areas of specialization as it blurs and melds older ones. In promoting relationships among fields, it challenges the viability of investing too heavily in specialization and narrow forms of expertise. It privileges and rewards discourses among fields rather than conversations within them. It values synthetic as opposed to merely technical skills. It defines excellence more in terms of ability to make connections across the field of play than the persistence needed to excavate a deep hole. Centers and institutes provide valuable interstitial space. Sometimes that space is programmatic and has a discernable shape; sometimes it is deliberately amorphous, defined solely by those who choose to come together in it. Thus the right question to ask may not be, "What is international studies, anyway?" but "What is it *not?*" The medieval scholastic preference for defining by the negative may be the more helpful way of coming to grips with the loose affiliations of fields, subjects, and disciplines that make up woolly hybrids such as public policy, population studies, urban studies, popular culture centers, bioengineering, organization studies, and so on. The case of environmental studies illustrates the point well. As Bill Robnett observes:

The disparate nature of information sources resulting from our attempt to understand the ecosystem requires the selector in environmental studies to monitor scientific, technical, social, historical, political, economic, and legal publishing. Environmental studies also has generated its own literature with the development of research in environmental engineering, environmental toxicology, environmental history, environmental policy, environmental geology, etc.[4]

If graduate training can prepare a selector for working in these broader, fuzzier contexts, it probably should involve the broadest possible selection of dishes offered on the disciplinary menu. The attainment of expertise and the mastery of method and technique are crucial, but they do not preclude recognizing the potential relevance of cognate approaches, methods, and expertise. Graduate training allows scholars to find their niches, but in the I world it should also equip them to move beyond the niche. Even from within the scholarly bunker or foxhole, wide-angle vision has become *de rigueur*. In collection development programs, it is increasingly the case that bibliographers as well as managers must "think globally" while acting locally. This is also true in the I world, where graduate training develops expertise alongside the capacity to take that broader view of the intellectual terrain that has the potential for bridging fields and linking niches.

INFORMATION EXPERTISE

If interdisciplinary research and training programs have been part of the academic scene for the better part of this century, what is truly new about them at present is not only their pervasiveness but the information tributaries and channels that feed them. Although there is no hard evidence, it is reasonable to suggest that the increasing availability of information online has played a considerable role in buoying and promoting the re-alignment of disciplines. Online databases, indices, and texts have not only made certain research procedures easier and more convenient, they appear to have the potential to transform the fundamental nature, character, and agenda of research itself. They are opening up new lines of interrogation, new fields to plow. Their role in shaping the I world has been subtle but real, as any bibliographer or reference librarian working in an academic research library can amply confirm. The "library without walls" seems an appropriate partner for those centers, programs, and institutes sheltering scholarship without boundaries.

There has been much written in recent years about the library of the future and the ways in which the nature and constellation of services it offers will have changed by the end of the millennium.[5] These changes depend largely on the pervasiveness and relative transparency of online information sources, and in the view of some prognosticators they herald basic transformations in the ways in which the library fulfills its mission of supporting scholarship. As the library becomes less important as a set of places for staff, patrons, and materials, the argument goes, so it becomes more prominent as a set of distributed functions and expertise providing specialized access and information services. Conspicuous in the new landscape is the collection development specialist who comes increasingly into focus as an information as well as a library materials specialist, though no one is willing to pen a requiem for collection development—yet. The bibliographer cum information navigator appears the direction in which we are headed, and whatever its exaggerations, this scenario seems appropriate to the evolving I world and its diffuse needs.

Insofar as the availability of information online suggests a future even as its presence is felt today, and to the extent that future is intimately linked to the hybridization of disciplines and the relative permeability of fields, the bibliographer will need to develop new sets of skills to be able to work effectively with a diverse array of clients and their heterogeneous needs. Electronic information formats do not so much encourage the dissolution of disciplines as development beyond them in new ways, through access to knowledge and sources until now remote, inaccessible, invisible. Facilitated access paths expand the universe of the potentially relevant, making it increasingly important for subject specialists to understand and to master the growing inventory of available databases, indices, and text files.[6]

The challenge here for subject specialists is clear. Developing and maintaining expertise in a subject area requires the ability to negotiate broad, disparate ranges of sources and materials. To "select" in political science may require some level of competency in sources and methodologies embracing business, engineering, geophysics, and medicine. Science and engineering bibliographers will need to feel comfortable with a variety of social science and government document sources. And what field is, literally, untouched by the earth, the environment, by "life" in its broadest sense? Selectors are not required to have the topic-specific expertise that the scholar brings to a field, but they do need basic methodological and reference literacy at a certain level of generality to be able to work usefully with scholars involved in interdisciplinary research projects.

While printed sources will remain the dominant medium of scholarly discourse for the foreseeable future, their vitality will depend in part on the ways in which new information sources make them visible and accessible as tools in the scholar's workshop. Ironically, electronic information seems to fuel the appetite for print. Selecting a corpus of printed materials for library collections will remain at the core of a bibliographer's responsibilities, and this function will continue to require firm disciplinary grounding as well as good peripheral vision. This expertise will increasingly need to be complemented by the honing of skills appropriate to the age of electronic information and interdisciplinary research. Together, these sets of skills comprise a matrix at once dense and broad, practical and visionary.

NEW ROLES FOR LIBRARY SCHOOLS

Library schools seem well positioned to play a key role in preparing librarians for collection development and management in the era of interdisciplinarity. Few professions or disciplines are more the product of and better adjusted to the realities of the I world than librarianship and information studies. A collection development curriculum that emphasizes not only the functional but the disciplinary breadth of the activity could go a long way toward creating an appropriate mindset for new bibliographers. Particularly for those who come to library school with advanced graduate training on their curriculum vitae, library schools can broaden horizons and allow specialists to appreciate the interrelatedness and connectedness of academic fields and disciplines. If it is true that contemporary intellectual cultures are more information-dependent than ever, information studies can help reconceptualize and refine key issues in collection development and management today such as "access to information." In short, library schools can do this and much more; they can contribute in important ways to acculturating librarians to the I world—but they need to be self-conscious and explicit about it. Library schools need to approach interdisciplinarity and its implications in terms of articulated curriculum goals and objectives. That is what, for this librarian anyway, seems crucial at the present.

A collection development curriculum that tacitly rests on the assumption that literatures are stable and well defined, that selection tools map easily to disciplines and fields, and that selection fields comprise coherent wholes will not adequately equip librarians for the realities of collection building and access in the 1990s and beyond. At the introductory and orientational level, library school curriculums need to remain in touch with and sensitive to the boundaryless as well as the bounded in the contemporary scholarly scene. They can achieve this in at least three related ways. One would be emphasizing practicums that force students to work outside their fields of expertise and competence. It will be important for the engineering bibliographer, for example, to appreciate at the outset the extent to which "engineering" intersects with and is intersected by other professions and disciplines. The "integrity" of engineering as a self-evident, clearly defined field may not be as obvious as it once was. Therefore, a curriculum that orients students to the permeability of disciplinary boundaries could contribute significantly to preparing discipline-based librarians for multidisciplinary collection development careers.

Equally important, library school curriculums need to pay attention to the diverse information requirements of the I world and the ways in which access needs parallel, but do not displace, ongoing collection-building functions. For interdisciplinary research, access to heterogeneous information sources online may be as important as access to material on-site. While much of the current literature on the subject is too fond of pitting "access" against "ownership," as if the matter were a simple case of either/or, both are necessary for the I world and its denizens.[7] Bibliographers need to be prepared to handle both, and thoughtful conceptual orientation to overlapping reference and collections functions in library school could give the novice a refreshingly mature perspective to bring to bear on the academic workplace.

Finally, library school curriculums should be sensitive to the new, collaborative cultures of knowledge and provide ways in which potential bibliographers can experiment with and adapt to more social modes of selection, access, and collections management. Here, too, practicums that define objectives in terms of group or team efforts would be useful in acclimatizing selectors to the contexts in which they will doubtless soon find themselves. Although much bibliographical work will remain a matter of individual application, the lone-wolf bibliographer is increasingly anomalous in contemporary librarianship. Placing the nature of bibliographical work in a more collaborative light will help better position both the professional and the profession for more active and productive involvements with scholars and their research.

Beyond the master's level, though, library schools have another series of opportunities presented to them by the I world and its legion of hybrid fields. Collaborating with academic departments, schools, and centers in doctoral and post-doctoral programs seems a logical and timely way of engaging librarianship with the academy in the new age of information. While library schools have long participated in co-sponsored degree programs with other units in their host institutions, the proliferation of interdisciplinary ventures on campuses provides a richer than ever reservoir of partners for post-graduate training programs. The centrality of information needs and electronic communication paths to much contemporary research, especially in new hybrid areas, has the potential for generating creative joint programs—degree and non-degree—in which the librarian is more than a silent partner but actually brings something important to the seminar room. Such programs could be of great value not only to librarians but to graduate students in the hybrid field desiring some firmer grounding in the array of sources making up the field.

If anything, library schools should be well served by the complex network of specialties clustered around campuses today. At the very latest, library schools could offer a perch from which to take a broad view of the ways in which these networks behave and interact. They could also play a role in defining and shaping new hybrids and their information requirements—and that *is* exciting.

CONCLUSION

Collection development is an art or, rather, several arts. It requires creativity and imagination as much as it does technical knowledge and sets of practical skills. Like many arts, it is not something that can be readily taught, though it can be learned—through experience, praxis, and reflection. Synthesizing academic programs, mapping disciplinary trends, interpreting research needs to the marketplace, shaping collections and services, all demand sensitive judgment and a plastic intelligence able to bring coherence and form to a broad array of activities. Nowhere is the artfulness of collection development more apparent or better tested than in interdisciplinary work. Idiosyncratic and eclectic, interdisciplinary research is a sort of proving ground on which bibliographers can measure and refine their art. New hybrid programs by definition challenge the established, the conventional, the formal. Their creativity is subversive but not destructive. They reimagine the intellectual landscape, they redraw the scholarly terrain. They are vital and inventive, the energy of the institution. They are also a formidable set of challenges to the bibliographer's art. Collection development in the I world requires deep pockets of knowledge, to be sure, but it also insists on relational and integrating skills that allow selectors to give shape and coherence to the programs they support and their diverse needs.

In the stress and press of daily business, selectors can often feel that they have the opportunity to see the world only from the trenches. But selectors must also climb the mountain occasionally and survey the scene as a whole, so that life in the trenches is more than a series of random interactions. If the accelerated pace of disciplinary hybridization brings with it something new for bibliographers, it is, at the bottom, more than additional workshops and courses or broader curricular preparation. It is renewed emphasis on the art and craft of collection development and the mental agility it presupposes.

NOTES

1. An excellent set of surveys that document current research patterns and trends as well as their knowledge and information requirements has been prepared by the Research Libraries Group under the general editorial supervision of Constance C. Gould: *Information Needs in the Humanities: An Assessment* (Stanford, Calif.: Research Libraries Group, 1988); Constance C. Gould and Mark Handler, *Information Needs in the Social Sciences: An Assessment* (Mountain View, Calif.: Research Libraries Group, 1989); and Constance C. Gould and Karla Pearce, *Information Needs in the Sciences: An Assessment* (Mountain View, Calif.: Research Libraries Group, 1991). Though focused chiefly on the humanities, the brief summary of the 1990 Conference on Research Trends and Library Resources held at Harvard is also useful: *Harvard Library Bulletin* NS 1: 2 (Summer 1990): 3–14. In addition, see Michael F. Winter, "Specialization and Interdisciplinary Growth in the Social Sciences," *Behavioral and Social Sciences Librarian* 10:2 (1991): 1–7.

2. Michael D. Cohen and James G. March, *Leadership and Ambiguity*, 2nd ed. (Boston: Harvard Business School Press, 1986), chapters 3 and 9 especially.

3. Susan Searing and Joan Ariel, "Women's Studies," in *Selection of Library Materials in Applied and Interdisciplinary Fields*, ed. by Beth J. Shapiro and John Whaley (Chicago: American Library Association, 1987), 252. With chapters on "Race and Ethnic Studies," "Environmental Studies," and "Urban Planning," among others, this volume is probably the best practical introduction to the topic at hand in a single volume. It complements the earlier and equally fine American Library Association publication edited by Patricia A. McClung, *Selection of Library Materials in the Humanities, Social Sciences, and Sciences* (Chicago: American Library Association, 1985). The article by Paul Metz and Bela Foltin, Jr., "A Social History of Madness: Or, Who's Buying This Round? Anticipating and Avoiding Gaps in Collection Development," *College & Research Libraries* 51 (January 1990): 33–39, is also worth consulting.

4. Bill Robnett, "Environmental Studies," in *Selection of Library Materials in Applied and Interdisciplinary Fields*, 97.

5. Among many, see Anne Woodsworth, Nancy Allen, and Irene Hoadley, "The Model Research Library: Planning for the Future," *Journal of Academic Librarianship* 15:3 (July 1989): 132–138; Pat Moholt, "The Future of Reference III: A Paradigm for Information Services," *College & Research Libraries News* 51:11 (De-

cember 1990): 1045–1051; and Peter Lyman, "The Library of the (Not-So-Distant) Future," *Change* 23:1 (January-February 1991): 34–41. For a different—and valuable—perspective, see also Richard D. Hacken, "Tomorrow's Research Library: Vigor or Rigor Mortis?" *College & Research Libraries* 49:6 (November 1988): 485–492.

6. Sarah M. Pritchard has written a good case study here: "Linking Research, Policy, and Activism: Library Services in Women's Studies," *Reference Librarian* 20 (1987): 89–103.

7. The *locus classicus* of this appears to be Richard M. Dougherty's provocative piece: "Research Libraries Must Abandon the Idea That 'Bigger Is Better,' " *Chronicle of Higher Education* (June 19, 1991), A32.

8

Collection Development Is More Than Selecting a Title: Educating for a Variety of Responsibilities

Peggy Johnson

In the earlier, simpler days before collection development became a euphemism for any activity relating to acquiring materials for libraries, from filling out an order slip to fund raising for new computer systems, selection—still a central task for line collection development librarians—was the name people used. It still comes as a shock to many of them to learn that selection isn't the only thing that collection development librarians do, and that they need to be educated for tasks other than weighing the value of titles in a particular subject area. Peggy Johnson explores the areas in which collection development managers—an important subset of the group now known as collection development librarians—need to explore and acquire basic knowledge before they move into the real world.

Johnson suggests lessons in a sweeping variety of areas: communication, finance, negotiation, persuasion, research. These are exactly the things speakers at conferences jest (or, sometimes, complain) "they never taught us in library school." But why not? To judge from current collection development textbooks, educators recognize the need to cover more topics than simple selection. They include chapters on most, or at least some, of Johnson's suggested areas. Perhaps it is more difficult than faculties realize to make paradigm shifts in curriculum. Certainly, the contrast between what Johnson suggests and what the traditional selector was thought to need is vast.

The discrepancy may lie in one's definition of "collection development librarian." The professional in Johnson's scenario is a high-level manager, competing for budget dollars with other units of the institution, making the hard decisions over collection goals and priorities, allocating funds that have been obtained from a variety of sources among a plethora of worthy disciplines and interdisciplinary groups, and solving the eternal problems of monetary shortfalls, overlapping interests, and administrative red tape. The collection development officer is responsible for all these tasks and more—directing and supervising and, possibly, recruiting, hiring, and training a corps of selectors, but rarely having the luxury of spending the major proportion of his or her time making title-by-title recommendations for purchase. This change in the territory that libraries now call collection development may not be identical in everyone's vocabulary, but the concept of a collection development manager should be—and who other than library educators are in a position to shoulder the burden of preparing students for the job? Johnson's chapter sheds light on what the real world expects; students and teachers should take note.

Collection development has been defined and redefined extensively over the last twenty-five years. We find agreement in the professional literature that this term encompasses the functions of materials selection, deselection, bibliography, and collection analysis. In addition, planning and policy making, preservation decisions, user liaison, resource sharing, program evaluation, and fiscal management are now commonly recognized as collection development responsibilities.

Library schools have concentrated on teaching collection development as skills and expertise that are based on collections, materials, and information resources. The more effective programs also explore the history of collection development as a specialty and place it within the context of other library operations. This approach, which focuses on selection, acquisition, and collection analysis, is too narrow because it fails to recognize the myriad of responsibilities performed by most collection development librarians today and the proficiency required in their execution. Subject expertise, literary background, and knowing how to make good selection decisions are no longer sufficient educational preparation for collection development librarians.

Hendrik Edelman described the collection development function as threefold: policy formation, selection, and acquisition, each growing out of and dependent on the others.[1] Charles Osburn built on this view when he defined collection development as "a process of establishing priorities that will allow the most effective use of a budget in achieving predetermined goals, both long-term and short-term."[2] Dennis Carrigan stressed the priority setting nature of collection development when he wrote that "the essence of collection development is choice."[3] Other writers on collection development have made clear that choices are not limited to selecting a title here and a title there. Choices are necessary to accomplish any of the functions that are part of collection development: planning and policy making, preservation decisions, user liaison, resource sharing, program evaluation, and fiscal management.

Informed and prepared collection librarians make effective choices. They develop consistent policies and practices for selecting and providing access to materials. They have learned productive processes for developing priorities, planning, implementing, and evaluating. They know and understand their community and environment in order to define a library's plan for meeting the service needs of its constituents. They have studied organizations and behavior to work within the library and to span its boundaries. They have mastered the basics of financial management, fund accounting, statistical analysis, and needs analysis. They know something about development and encouraging donors. They have mastered various modes and strategies for communication in different situations and types of organizations. The rest of this chapter will explore these competencies as they should be taught in library schools to prepare students to become successful collection development librarians.

FINANCIAL SKILLS

A collection development librarian is usually allocated a specified amount of money to spend within a specified period and within specified guidelines about subject, format, language, and so on. Financial skills are essential to execute these functions responsibly. Few collection development librarians will serve as their library's accountant, but they likely will work with an accountant or the accountant's financial reports. They will need to understand accounting terms and interpret financial reports. They will manage fund allocations, balancing expenditures against available funds. They will plan budgets and make funding requests.

Yet most librarians graduate knowing only that library budgets are seldom large enough and that the bigger the budget, the better the position of the library. Professional library schools should do more to prepare students for their financial responsibilities. Financial skills are particularly central for executing collection development responsibilities, since the competent management of fiscal resources is one measure of success.

Ideally, professional library schools should provide a course on library finances, which would address all aspects of budgets from salaries to operating expenses to materials budgets. At a minimum, each collection development course should introduce students to basic financial concepts, terminology, and responsibilities. Collection development librarians require a fundamental understanding of budgetary processes both to execute their responsibilities and to affect the process.

A financial module should begin by exploring budgeting as a management concept. Students should understand that budgeting is different from accounting—that it serves to relate goals to the specific means for achieving them. Students should learn that budgeting provides a control function as one seeks to learn whether goals are being met and if they are not, what can be done. What changes might be made so that existing goals are still achievable? Should the existing goals be modified? Implicit in the control process is performance evaluation—managers reviewing the results of work done by others in the library.

A financial module should examine budgeting in not-for-profit entities and explore the difference between budgeting on the basis of cash flows (expenditures and receipts) as opposed to revenues and expenses. Students need not be drilled in accounting principles, but they should be familiar with financial terms such as allocation, commitment, encumbrance, free balance, fund accounting, line budgets, incremental budgeting, zero-based budgeting, and accountability. They should know how to interpret accounting data, financial statements and their source documents, and have seen samples of periodic materials budget reports produced by manual and automated systems.

Collection development courses should teach the importance of monitoring the financial environment external to the library and relating this to the library's budget. Graduates should know how to obtain information about materials price increases (foreign and domestic) and how to follow the value of the dollar on the international market. They should be able to make reasonable materials costs projections based on this information, while realizing much of this will be educated guessing. They should be knowledgeable about serials pricing trends and the implications of serials to monograph expenditure ratios. They should know how to prepare and analyze a variety of reports that track allocations and expenditures by categories, including fund, subject, format, language, and country of publication.

Collection development librarians should be taught several models for allocating funds, so they will understand the process in their library and be aware of alternatives. They should have experience in presenting a materials budget funding proposal that combines local needs analysis and cost projections. They should also recognize that most funding requests succeed because of political acceptance as well as a defensible theoretical framework.

Financial expertise prepares the collection development student to analyze, defend, and justify budgets. He or she will understand the available fiscal information and how to monitor expenditures and balances. Adequate competencies will equip the new collection development librarian to make informed decisions and effective plans for good budgeting.

STATISTICAL SKILLS

Many graduate programs require a course in statistics as a prerequisite for admission. This is because graduate programs often expect students to conduct statistical analyses as part of research projects. Collection development librarians will continue to need statistical skills throughout their careers. They analyze financial data provided by internal and external sources. They evaluate circulation statistics and user populations. They use statistical information to prepare reports and graphs.

A collection development course should relate the basic concepts and techniques in statistical analysis to the data with which collection development librarians work. Students should master methods of summarizing and presenting statistical data. They should understand the normal curve and probability sampling, regression analysis, measures of correlation, dispersion, reliability, and validity, and methods of interpretation. Learning standard practices in data analysis will increase understanding of the evidentiary uses of data for budget and cost analysis, for user needs assessment, and for collection evaluation.

ORGANIZATIONAL BEHAVIOR

Every professional graduate program, whatever the field, should provide its students with an introduction to organizational behavior and an understanding of interpersonal relations. These terms describe an array of theories that help individuals comprehend the motivations and behaviors of the people with whom they interact on a daily and occasional basis. The goal is to empower the student to function as effectively as possible. No collection development librarian works in isolation. Collection development librarians work with upper-level administrators who may not have direct contact with or immediate understanding of collection development activities. They work with department managers, who supervise their work or that of other units in the library. They work with colleagues and subordinates. They have responsibilities as liaisons with their constituents, whether academic departments or community groups. They build relationships with other libraries. They serve on committees that often cross departmental lines.

Library schools should ensure that graduates are familiar with theories of management and organizational behavior. Students should understand how these relate to strategies and techniques for managing people in organizations. They should know Abraham Maslow's framework for human needs and understand the theories of human behavior in organizations proposed by such behavioral scientists as Douglas McGregor, Rensis Likert, and Frederick Herzberg. They should read in the literature on leadership and management theory. Graduates should be familiar with concepts about organizational culture, group dynamics, change processes, and conflict resolution.

Well-prepared collection development librarians will understand the nature and uses of organizational power, both within and outside the formal organizational structure. They will understand that power and authority are not necessarily the same. They will be able to identify the administrative structures in their libraries and parent institutions. They will be familiar with Max Weber's and Henri Fayol's bureaucratic models and the pros and cons of function- and goal-based organizational structure. They will have read Peter Drucker's works on management and the changing organizational structure. They will have read about professionalism and be aware of the discussions on this issue in the library world.

An effective introduction to organizational behavior should introduce students to theories about organizational politics. Pfeffer defines organizational politics as those "actions taken in organizations to acquire, develop and use power and other resources to obtain a preferred outcome in situations in which there is uncertainty or dissensus about choices."[4] The ability to operate politically should not have the negative connotations traditionally associated with "politics." Politics, as understood by behavioral theorists, is the ability to function successfully in complex organizations. Richard De Gennaro has said that "a library operates in a political environment and nearly all the really important decisions that are made at the highest levels have an overriding political component."[5]

Collection development librarians need to understand the positive implications of acting politically. They need to recognize that political skills are those skills used consciously to overcome opposition and enlist support to achieve the library's goals. To be successful politically, a collection development librarian must be prepared to learn about the library's culture, its structure, and its power base, as well as that of the parent organization. The librarian also should understand the importance of knowing about the individuals in the organization. Understanding backgrounds, experiences, and biases of those with whom one works is practical information for mustering support and overcoming opposition.

Once collection development students understand the major influences on job behaviors, they will be better prepared to identify, analyze, and solve problems. They will know more about themselves and begin to understand those around them. They will be able to enhance their productivity and satisfaction and that of those with whom they work. They will begin developing interpersonal skills and finesse that will help in accomplishing their complex responsibilities.

ETHICAL CONSIDERATIONS

Ethics pertains to the rightness or wrongness of selected behavior according to certain standards of behavior. These standards can be legal or moral and deal with what is right or wrong, good or bad. Collection development librarians face ethical considerations in their dealings with individuals and with groups, with materials suppliers, with confidentiality of information, and with selection decisions.

The most familiar ethical decisions associated with collection development responsibilities are choosing which materials to add, retain, or preserve. Value decisions are made on a daily basis. Collection development policies provide guidelines, but collection development librarians apply discretion with each choice they make. Ethical considerations also influence how the collection development librarian interacts with materials sellers and suppliers. Do free meals and hospitality hours obligate the librarian to use the services of a particular vendor? Is it ethical to send title notification slips provided by one vendor to another vendor as orders? Is it ethical to reduce the cost of a journal subscription by identifying it as a personal subscription instead of paying the higher institutional rate?

Professional library schools should prepare students for the ethical decisions they will make regularly. This instruction should explore the sources of ethics and assist students in preparing for the decisions they will face. A personal code of ethics may develop out of civic and religious convictions. Collection development librarians should be warned about letting a self-imposed code of morality affect professional decisions. The result can be censorship when decisions about feminist, radical, gay, or ethnic publications are made according to a personal moral stand. Collection development students should explore their own ethical codes so they know the personal values that will guide their behavior.

A collection development course should identify professional and organizational ethics as additional sources affecting choices. Organizational ethics are the standards of behavior to which the librarian should conform within his or her library. These may vary from library to library. For example, all materials budget information may be confidential in one library, yet a matter of public record in others and widely shared with other libraries. Professional ethics are the behavior standards set forth, either formally or informally, by the profession of librarianship. Students should be referred to the American Library Association's various documents that address professional ethics,[6] as well as to discussions on this topic in the library literature.

A library school course that explores ethics cannot be prescriptive. It should, however, lead students to an understanding of the basis of ethical decisions and of their pervasiveness. A collection development student should be prepared to ask appropriate questions about the sources of each choice made. Is it ethical? Is it balanced? What leads me to make this decision? Can I live with my conscience?

COMMUNICATION SKILLS

Elaine Sloan has written that collection development is a "boundary spanning activity . . . an activity that requires many transactions across interorganizational and intraorganization boundaries."[7] Communication skills are essential tools for collection development librarians, who must gather and share information within their libraries and with groups and individuals outside their organizational boundaries. They must be able to write and speak effectively to convey this information persuasively to a variety of audiences. Most library school students have experience writing research papers, but few have studied professional communication techniques. Creating handouts, designing overhead transparencies, and crafting a presentation on the impact of electronic information resources on the library's budget for a faculty committee is significantly different from preparing a paper on the same topic for a course.

Communication is the process of sharing an understanding between two or more persons. Collection development librarians are expected to communicate well in many forums and formats. They will be asked to speak to classes, community groups, and committees outside the library. They will write requests for more funds, more staff, more space. They will serve in working groups and write reports. They will write memos and annual reports. They will attend and chair meetings. They will prepare agendas. They will develop and revise collection policies. They will meet with faculty and donors. They will write professional papers and give presentations. They will work with colleagues and individuals above and below them in the organizational hierarchy. They will prepare user surveys and circulation studies. They will represent the collection development program to user groups and governing agencies.

Many librarians have learned their communication skills from the poor speakers, the flawed documents, and the incomprehensible memos they have suffered. Library schools can aid future collection development librarians by equipping them with the skills to write and speak effectively in the workplace. Education for collection development should include a module on managerial communications that not only teaches competencies but also explains the communication process.

The communication module should introduce dyadic and small-group communication models, as well as techniques for effective skills in groups. It should cover verbal and non-verbal communication. The module should teach how to identify and eliminate barriers that affect communication. It should cover various modes and strategies for communication in different types of organizations. It should address the nature of listening, since more time is spent listening than speaking, reading, or writing. The communication module should present skills for negotiation and conflict resolution.

Students should gain experience and skill in task-oriented group communication processes. They should understand work groups, committees, and task forces, plus the types of communication behaviors that individuals exhibit. They should learn how effective communication relates to team building and leadership. Graduates should be introduced to techniques for conducting a good meeting and keeping a working group on task.

Collection development librarians are required to be informative, argumentative, or persuasive—and often all three—as the need arises. They continually seek to increase understanding between two or more persons. Sometimes the medium is written, sometimes spoken. A graduate school communication module should explain the differences between reports and proposals, memos and letters. It should offer practical information about spoken communication processes and sharpen the student's skills in all areas ranging from one-on-one meetings to presentations to telephone conversations.

According to Osburn, collection development should be seen as the "communication process driving an integral system of library, information universe, and community."[8] Good communication skills provide the framework through which the collection development librarian achieves organizational and personal professional objectives. A good graduate library program should improve students' abilities to use appropriate communication devices and strategies to achieve these objectives.

MARKETING AND FUND RAISING

Funding for libraries has not kept pace with the increased amount of information available nor the library services necessary to obtain that information in a variety of formats. Many libraries are turning to funding sources beyond their traditional parent agencies. Collection development librarians often participate in library efforts to increase community support and secure additional dollars for special projects and ongoing programs. They meet with prospective donors and friends groups, prepare grant proposals, and seek community endorsement. Collection development librarians need to understand the potential of obtaining additional support to maximize the opportunities, as well as the processes for doing so.

Library schools should introduce students to techniques for and the benefits of development, marketing, and fund raising. Marketing, like politics, is not necessarily a grimy activity. Philip Kotler defines marketing as the effective management of the relationship of an organization with its various publics.[9] Marketing seeks to evaluate constituent attitudes (needs and wants), to match the library's activities with the interests of its constituents, and to plan and execute a program that results in constituent understanding and support. This view means that every contact between a collection development librarian and a member of the public has marketing potential.

A collection development student should be introduced to practical information about developing and maintaining positive community relations. They should learn techniques for gaining and retaining support of others. This can be both formal programs for liaisons with individuals and groups and informal contacts that occur as the result of routine activities. Osburn stresses that collection development must be a very outward looking process: high profile and proactive.[10] It requires continuing communication between the library and those who have the power to affect its operations. While stressing the service orientation of librarianship, library schools must ensure that their graduates will be proactive in their relationships with their communities.

Fund raising often requires professional expertise, and some libraries may have an individual who serves as grants coordinator or development officer.

Nevertheless, library schools should acquaint students with sources of funding, that is, with foundations, individuals, corporate sector, and state and federal groups. They should learn about proposal writing, endowments, development campaigns, capital funding, and methods of building volunteers and friends groups. A well-prepared collection development graduate will be able to work with the development initiatives under way in his or her new library and, in time, to propose additional sources for support.

DECISION MAKING

At the beginning of this chapter, collection development was described as a process of making choices. Collection development librarians are continually faced with situations that require decisions. They must seek good alternative courses of action, evaluate them, and predict the outcomes of these plans. Effective decisions depend on consciously choosing the best alternative from among those available—that is, choosing the one that seems most likely to resolve the immediate situation and further the library's objectives.

Collection development librarians make decisions while evaluating collections, selecting new materials, monitoring and reviewing gifts and exchanges, selecting retrospectively, and selecting for preservation treatment. They make decisions when preparing and revising collection development policy statements. They make decisions about budgets, cooperative collection development, and resource sharing. They make decisions as they participate in planning processes. They make decisions every time they interact with others in their libraries and with their constituents.

Graduate library school programs should include a segment that introduces students to theories and models for effective decision making. Besides teaching students how to obtain, understand, analyze, and evaluate quantitative and qualitative information from a variety of sources, the program should introduce techniques for identifying issues, problems, and opportunities. Students should be prepared to analyze internal library resources and the external economic, political, legal, and cultural environment to make strategic choices. They should know how to identify the philosophy and goals of their libraries and to derive objectives from them. They should be able to develop and implement a plan of action that will integrate with the activities of the various parts of the library.

The best decisions are made through a successful combination of creative and analytical thinking. Analytic thinking is the ability to organize and evaluate information in a logical and systematic manner. It is cognitive, linear, and associated with left-brain thinking. Creative thinking is sometimes described as intuitive or right-brain thinking. Creative thinking is unstructured and unpredictable; it is necessary for innovation and progress.[11] The most effective decisions draw from both creative and analytical thinking. This is the decision making that can solve problems and have the solutions accepted. It produces a combination of credibility and clout. It calls on knowledge and experience, plus interpersonal skills. Students should understand that effective decision making is problem solving by analysis, interaction, and intuition.

A successful graduate library program should enable students to make intelligent decisions and provide experience in working together toward a common goal. Students should be well informed about the interrelated nature of libraries as complex organizations in a complex society and the importance of viewing individual solutions in a larger context. They should be alerted to the ease with which some solutions create new problems.

Students should also be prepared to deal with the problems that complicate decisions: unavailability of data; not knowing what to look for; premature evaluation; effects of personal values; limits of the situation and individuals. They should know that librarians must often accept the less-than-ideal situation as it is. Most decisions are made amid uncertainties, inconsistencies, and incompleteness. Students should become comfortable with less-than-perfect decisions and know that the real life library is seldom as tidy as the textbook variety.

A graduate program segment on decision making should introduce the positive aspects of risk taking, particularly as it relates to change. Risk taking is taking action when the outcome is unknown. Rapid change is a reality in libraries, as it is in society, and risk taking is a crucial element in coping with change. People differ in their comfort with risk taking. Well reasoned risk taking requires careful decision making. The value of the risk is in the potential payoff, not in taking the risk. The process of risk taking involves both making the decision to take the risk and developing a strategy that minimizes the risk. While making a decision to take a risk, the individual considers the library's expectations, potential rewards, supports, available resources, his or her feelings about taking the risk, and experiences. Librarians who understand risk taking as part of change are prepared to be innovative: to try new tasks, skills, and work methods, to move in new directions to make the change work well for themselves and the library.

The informed collection development graduate will understand that decisions are the product of common sense and intuition, supported by education and intellect. Several writers on the practice of collection development have called it an art form instead of a science. They stress that conventional formulas and comparative guidelines are never sufficient; collection development is not a mechanistic process. Logical, intuitive, thoughtful decisions can be made only by informed, prepared, and confident librarians.

CONCLUSION

The competencies recommended in this chapter are appropriate for all librarians and critical for librarians with collection development responsibilities. An effective professional library school will prepare its students to carry on varied, complex, evolving responsibilities. This education should be grounded in the traditional skills for and knowledge about the practice of librarianship, but it must include course work that transcends the customary understanding of library specialties such as reference, cataloging, and collection development.

Graduate library schools should educate students for diverse responsibilities that call for expertise in finance and statistics, organizational behavior, ethical considerations, communication skills, marketing and fund raising, risk taking, and decision making. Besides a theoretical introduction to these topics, students will have been given practical applications of the information covered. They will be able to relate the concepts to daily performance of their responsibilities. The best-equipped library school graduates will be able to collect and analyze information, manage budgets, encourage library support, communicate successfully, operate effectively in complex environments and situations, and make considered, ethical decisions. They will be able to envision the future of the library and contribute creatively to the process of innovation.

NOTES

1. Hendrik Edelman, "Selection Methodology in Academic Libraries, *Library Resources & Technical Services* 23 (Winter 1979): 33–38.

2. Charles B. Osburn, "Toward a Reconceptualization of Collection Development," *Advances in Library Administration and Organization* 2 (1983): 176.

3. Dennis P. Carrigan, "Librarians and the 'Dismal Science,' " *Library Journal* 113 (June 15, 1988): 22.

4. Jeffrey Pfeffer, *Power in Organizations* (Marshfield, Mass.: Pitman, 1981), 7.

5. Richard De Gennaro, "Library Administration and New Management Systems," *Library Journal* 103 (December 1978): 2480.

6. These include the American Library Association's Statement on Profesional Ethics, the Library Bill of Rights, and the Freedom to Read policy. A more in-depth examination of issues associated with freedom to read can be found in the *Intellectual Freedom Manual*, 4th ed. (Chicago: Office for Intellectual Freedom, American Library Association, 1992)

7. Elaine F. Sloan, "The Organization of Collection Development in Large University Research Libraries," Ph.D. dissertation, University of Maryland, 1973, 48.

8. Osburn, "Toward a Reconceptualization of Collection Development," 196.

9. Philip Kotler, *Marketing for Nonprofit Organizations* (Englewood Cliffs, N.J.: Prentice-Hall, 1975).

10. Osburn, "Toward a Reconceptualization of Collection Development," 183.

11. G. Edward Evans, *Management Techniques for Librarians*, 2d ed. (New York: Academic Press, 1984), 74.

SUGGESTED READINGS

Works in this list have been selected because they are recognized land-mark works, they are particularly cogent discussions of the topics, or they are representative of contemporary theories. Works cited in the chapter are not included.

Bennis, Warren G., Kenneth D. Benne, and Robert Chin. *The Planning of Change*. 4th ed. New York: Holt, 1985.

Blau, Peter M. *Exchange and Power in Social Life*. New Brunswick: Transaction Books, 1986.

Blanchard, Kenneth H. *The Power of Ethical Management*. New York: W. Morrow, 1988.

Bradford, Leland P., ed. *Group Development*. 2nd ed. La Jolla, Calif.: University Associates, 1978.

De Bono, Edward. *Six Thinking Hats*. Boston: Little, Brown, 1985.

Drucker, Peter F. *Management: Tasks, Responsibilities, Practices*. New York: Harper & Row, 1974.

_____. *Managing in Turbulent Times*. New York: Harper & Row, 1980.

Fayol, Henri. *General and Industrial Administration*. London: Sir Isaac Pitman and Sons, 1949.

Galbraith, Jay R. *Organization Design*. Reading, Mass.: Addison-Wesley, 1977.

Richard H. Hall. "Professionalization and Bureaucratization." *American Journal of Sociology* 33 (February 1968): 92–104.

Herzberg, Frederick. *Work and the Nature of Man*. Cleveland: World Publishing Co., 1966.

Howell, William S. *The Empathic Communicator*. Belmont, Calif.: Wadsworth Publishing Co., 1982.

Kanter, Rosabeth Moss. *The Change Masters: Innovation for Productivity in the American Corporation*. New York: Simon & Schuster, 1983.

_____. *When Giants Learn to Dance: Mastering the Art of Strategy, Management and Careers in the 1990s*. New York: Simon & Schuster, 1989.

Keen, Peter G. W. "Information Systems and Organizational Change." *Communications of the Association for Computing Machinery* 24 (January 1981): 24–33.

Katz, Daniel, and Robert L. Kahn. *The Social Psychology of Organizations*. 2nd ed. New York: Wiley, 1978.

Kotler, Philip. *Marketing Decision Making: A Model Building Approach*. New York: Holt, Rinehart & Winston, 1971.

Likert, Rensis. *The Human Organization: Its Management and Values*. New York: McGraw-Hill, 1967.

Lynden, Frederick C. "Financial Planning for Collection Management." *Journal of Library Administration* 3 (Fall/Winter 1982): 109–120.

McGregor, Douglas. *Human Side of Enterprise: 25th Anniversary Printing*. New York: McGraw-Hill, 1985. (First published in 1960.)

Maslow, Abraham H. *Motivation and Personality*. 3rd ed. New York: Harper & Row, 1954.

Massie, Joseph L. *Essentials of Management*. 4th ed. Englewood Cliffs, N.J.: Prentice-Hall, 1987.

Mintzberg, Henry. *The Nature of Managerial Work*. New York: Harper & Row, 1973.

Munter, Mary. *Guide to Managerial Communication*. 2nd ed. Englewood Cliffs, N.J.: Prentice-Hall, 1987.

Osburn, Charles B., and Ross Atkinson. *Collection Management: A New Treatise*. 2 vols. Foundations in Library and Information Sciences, vols. 26A-B. Greenwich, Conn.: JAI Press, 1991.

Peters, Tom. *Thriving on Chaos: Handbook for a Management Revolution*. New York: Knopf, 1987.

Peters, Tom, and Nancy Austin. *A Passion for Excellence: The Leadership Difference*. New York: Random House, 1985.

Pfeffer, Jeffrey. *Organizations and Organization Theory*. Marshfield, Mass.: Pittman, 1982.

Riggs, Donald E., ed. *Library Communication: The Language of Leadership*. Chicago: American Library Association, 1991.

Rogers, Carl R. *On Becoming a Person*. Boston: Houghton Mifflin, 1961.

Sheldon, Alan. "Organizational Paradigms: A Theory of Organizational Change." *Organizational Dynamics* 8 (Winter 1980): 61–80.

Skinner, B. F. *Beyond Freedom and Dignity*. New York: Knopf, 1971.

Tichy, Noel T. "Managing Change Strategically: The Technical, Political, and Cultural Keys." *Organizational Dynamics* 11 (Autumn 1982): 59–80.

Weber, Max. "Bureaucracy." In *From Max Weber: Essays in Sociology*, translated by H. H. Gerth and C. Wright Mills, 196–244. New York: Oxford University Press, 1962.

Weingand, Darlene E. *Marketing for Libraries and Information Agencies*. Norwood, N.J.: Ablex Publishing Corp., 1984.

Zuboff, Shoshana. *In the Age of the Smart Machine: The Future of Work and Power*. New York: Basic Books, 1988.

9

Should Courses in Acquisitions and Collection Development Be Combined or Separate?

Thomas E. Nisonger

Thomas Nisonger explores the complex issues involved in the design of library school curriculums in general and, more specifically, in alternatives for courses in acquisitions and collection development. He begins where Paul Metz leaves off, taking the reader into a logical analysis of the relationships, alliances, and conflicts between education for acquisitions work and education for collection development work.

Nisonger's analysis of curricular components and the experience of different combinations provides an array of models that library schools might adopt. The temptation for library educators is to be prescriptive. Instead, Nisonger takes a neutral stance, arguing persuasively for a large measure of objectivity, and urges the reader to make his or her evaluation of the alternative models based on a particular institution's mission and focus, stated program goals, and the individual needs and talents of its faculty and students.

Clearly, practitioners and educators must find areas of agreement on certain essential issues in order for curriculum to fulfill its expected function. Nisonger calls for a meeting of minds over these fundamental issues in order that library school faculties may proceed with their right business, namely, designing and implementing relevant programs that prepare graduates to enter and succeed in the practice of either or both of these professional specialties.

This is an age of exciting challenge for library and information science educators. Many students entering our programs today will not finish their careers until thirty or forty years from now. Thus, we must teach students the fundamentals of present-day librarianship while simultaneously preparing them to manage unforeseen, and perhaps unimaginable, change: in technology, in the paradigm of our discipline, and in the economic and social fabric of the world at large—to name only the most obvious changes that will affect libraries well into the twenty-first century.

One of the most important mechanisms for molding a prospective librarian's education is the library school curriculum, along with the faculty and their research interests: not only what courses are offered, but the substance of those courses. Consequently, questions of curricular design are of vital significance not only to library educators but also to the entire library profession.

This chapter's topic can be addressed at two levels. First, due to their intrinsic nature, are collection development (used as a synonym for collection management throughout this chapter) and acquisitions best covered in a single course or two separate courses? Second, since contemporary American library education programs commonly include a collection development course that contains an acquisitions component but not an acquisitions course, should library school curricula add a separate course devoted to acquisitions?

The author will not take a strong evangelistic position on either side of these questions. Instead, this chapter's objective is to examine the major issues and place them in an analytical framework. No attempt is made to review the pertinent literature systematically or present original research findings, although several previous studies that help clarify the issues will be noted. The author's personal perspective as a former collection development and acquisitions librarian as well as a current library and information science educator also will be incorporated into the discussion. The focus will be on Masters of Library Science (M.L.S.) education, not library technician training. The analysis will be limited to the North American context. (References to international collection development and acquisitions education are included in the recommended reading list appended at the chapter's end.)

ARE ACQUISITIONS AND COLLECTION DEVELOPMENT BEST TAUGHT TOGETHER OR SEPARATELY?

To answer this question the following issues must be addressed: What is the intellectual relationship between acquisitions and collection development? What is the knowledge domain of each? Is the total academic content appropriate for one course or two? Who, in terms of career interests, would be the audience for each course?

The Intellectual Relationships

At the most fundamental level, the issue of intellectual relationships may be reduced to a definition of terms. Considerable ambiguity and misunderstanding exist concerning the terms *collection development* and *acquisitions*.

In fact, *acquisitions* has sometimes been used in library literature to refer to the entire collection development process, especially several decades ago before collection development was explicitly recognized as a specific library function. What is now considered the acquisitions function was, then, often called order work. Yet miscomprehension concerning these terms continues to exist. Hendrik Edelman's selection process model helps clarify the relationship. He outlines a three-level hierarchy consisting of (1) collection development, which is "a planning function"; (2) selection, which is "the decision-making process"; and (3) acquisitions, which "implements . . . the selection decision."[1] For this chapter's analysis, levels 1 and 2 of Edelman's hierarchy, the planning function plus the intellectual process of deciding what items to add to the collection (selection), are considered collection development, while level 3, the technical procedures involved in placing and receiving the order, constitutes acquisitions.

The Knowledge Domains

The collection development domain typically includes community analysis, planning for collection building, collection development policies, selection, selection tools, publishing, intellectual freedom and censorship, weeding, and collection evaluation. Preservation is often considered part of collection development.

Based partially on lists of acquisitions "components" compiled by Nancy Williamson and on topics enumerated by William Fisher, one can conclude that the exclusive domain of acquisitions encompasses order files and routines, receiving, claiming, invoice processing and payment, bibliographic searching, the out-of-print market, the acquisition department's organization and structure, personnel, ethical and legal issues in acquisitions, processing special and nonprint materials, acquisitions automation, and vendor selection and evaluation.[2]

Although acquisition and collection development may be analytically distinct in theory, in actual practice the two are often closely interconnected, as, for example, in the handling of gifts and approval plans. Quite a few topics are therefore relevant to both, including publishing and the book trade, international publishing and the foreign book trade, national and trade bibliography, budgeting, networking, and online databases.

Collection development represents basic knowledge and skills that will be used in more than one functional area of librarianship, including reference, media, government documents, serials, children's librarianship, archives, special collections, and administration. Acquisitions is considerably more specialized. In a large or medium-sized library most professionals will not be directly involved in the acquisitions process.

Nevertheless, neither function is performed in isolation from the other. Collection development and acquisitions librarians both will sometimes be indirectly involved in the other function. Certainly they will interact with each other and therefore require some knowledge of the other's problems and procedures. In some libraries, tension may exist between the two areas. Henry Yaple refers to "war stories" between acquisitions and collection development.[3] On the other hand, many positions explicitly combine both collection development and acquisitions. Gail Kennedy has noted the "wide variety of organizational approaches among libraries to acquisitions and collection development . . . and . . . the overlap or close contact of functions" between the two no matter which organizational approach is used.[4]

Summary

The chapter's primary question may be analyzed in terms of the major issues outlined at this discussion's beginning.

Intellectual relationship between and knowledge domains of collection development and acquisitions. The two functions are closely enough related to be taught in a combined course, yet they are sufficiently distinct to warrant separate courses. Some might argue that acquisitions and collection development are so inextricably intertwined that they cannot be taught separately, although this seems a dubious contention. Thus, this criterion does not offer a definitive answer. The intellectual relationship could be used to justify either approach (which probably explains why the question is asked in the first place).

Course purpose or audience. At least two major objectives for library education courses exist: (1) exposing students who will be working in other functional areas to general concepts all librarians should know or (2) educating students who will be employed in the course area. It is possible, of course, for a course to fulfill both purposes. On initial impression, it seems that a combined collection development and acquisitions course would best meet the first objective, whereas separate courses would be most appropriate to the second purpose. However, a course to meet the second objective may not be realistic. A single course will not be sufficient to prepare a student adequately for a career in a particular area. Moreover, research by Herbert White and Sarah Mort reveals that most students end up in specializations different than those in which they initially planned to work. For example, in their survey of library school graduates, only fourteen of thirty-seven respondents whose first professional position was in technical services had originally planned to work in that area.[5] Advocates of a separate acquisitions course, such as Joyce Ogburn, have justified the separation by claiming that all librarians need to know about the acquisitions function.[6]

Amount of material to be covered. Given the amount of material to be covered, two separate courses would be preferable. The author has the impression that in combined collection development and acquisitions courses, it is acquisitions that assumes the minor role—a consideration that may help explain the deficiency of formal acquisitions education perceived by practitioners. Given the need for additional coverage of topics such as automation, networking, resource sharing, the Research Libraries Group Conspectus, and preservation, which have assumed greater importance during the last decade, there is certainly enough material pertinent to collection development and acquisitions to fill two courses.

In sum, there is no ideal or perfect answer. The combined and separate course approaches each offer advantages and disadvantages. Moreover, the question, as posed, may be artificial in that an either/or answer is assumed. Both options—inclusion of acquisitions as a unit within a collection development course (possibly a required course at an introductory level) along with a separate, perhaps more advanced, course devoted exclusively to acquisitions—are theoretically possible. Thus, the need for and desirability of establishing a separate acquisitions course will be explored in the remainder of this chapter.

SHOULD A SEPARATE ACQUISITIONS COURSE BE ADDED TO THE CURRICULUM?

The issue of adding an acquisitions course relates to several broader questions. To what extent do the course offerings of U.S. library schools fulfill the need for acquisitions education? What are the educational experiences and expectations of contemporary acquisitions librarians? What is the purpose of library and information science education? What type of work do professional acquisitions librarians actually do? Is there a professional knowledge domain for acquisitions? What impact will automation have on acquisitions?

The Coverage of Acquisitions in Formal Library Education

Karen Schmidt's history of acquisitions education showed that from the late nineteenth century until the 1930s, "training for acquisitions work was a fundamental part of any librarian's education."[7] The leading library schools of that era, including Columbia, Pratt, Drexel, Illinois, and Chicago, offered acquisitions courses. Over a period of years these separate courses were eliminated.[8] By 1966, W. Royce Butler deplored the fact that "library schools are doing little to train potential acquisitions librarians."[9] In the late 1970s, Sara Heitshu noted that acquisitions librarians were "ready to joke about our lack of education in acquisitions."[10]

Williamson's survey of the sixty-four accredited library schools in the spring of 1978 revealed that only two of twenty-seven responding schools offered a separate acquisitions course. Nevertheless, acquisitions was often a "module" within other courses. It was a component of sixteen collection-building courses, eight technical services courses, three "foundations" or introductory courses, and two library automation courses. Acquisitions was also included in varying degrees in government documents, serials, media, and rare books courses, leading Williamson to conclude that "it is probable that there is 'hidden' coverage of some aspects of acquisitions in courses of most library schools."[11]

Schmidt's 1988 survey of Association of Research Libraries (ARL) acquisitions librarians showed that acquisitions courses had previously been taught at nine institutions.[12] In the spring of 1990 Cohen surveyed the deans of the sixty American Library Association (ALA)–accredited library education programs (fifty-two responded) concerning the role of acquisitions in their curriculum. Her findings revealed that seven schools offered courses "characterized by the respondents as devoted primarily to acquisitions." However, there may have been a definitional misunderstanding concerning what makes up "acquisitions," as Donna Cohen notes some courses were entitled "Collection Development" or "Collections Management."[13]

This author conducted his own survey by examining the course listings section in the most recently available catalog for fifty-eight of the fifty-nine ALA-accredited library education programs, as of October 1990. (The University of Puerto Rico catalog was not available.) Two of these institutions (Brigham Young and Columbia) have recently closed their library education programs. A catalog survey approach may not produce one hundred percent accurate findings for a variety of reasons, for example, because courses can be listed that are no longer offered, the course descriptions may be incomplete or ambiguous, and in a few instances the catalog's most recent version was not available. Nevertheless, the findings should be helpful for the purposes of this discussion.

Not a single course devoted exclusively to acquisitions was found! Fifty-one of the fifty-eight programs offered at least one course devoted entirely to collection development or collection development in combination with acquisitions. Of the seven programs without a full collection development course, one offered a course entitled "Acquisitions and Organization" that appeared to cover collection development and cataloging (but not acquisitions) under a single umbrella. Another school combined collection development with foundations. As nine programs offered two general collection development or collection development/acquisitions courses, a total of sixty such courses were identified. A breakdown between required and elective courses was not attempted because this information was often not contained in the course listings. The figure does not include literature or information resources courses that are obviously relevant to collection development.

Eight of the sixty courses contained the word *acquisitions* in the title, while the course descriptions for twenty-six others explicitly stated that acquisitions was included. Some other collection development courses may include acquisitions, though it is not mentioned in the course description. For example, acquisitions is not specified in the Indiana University School of Library and Information Science catalog course description, but the author knows it is included because he teaches the course. Nineteen technical services courses and ten automation courses listed acquisitions as an included topic. Acquisitions was specified as incorporated in a smattering of courses on government documents, serials, media, archives, music librarianship, legal materials, and Latin American publishing. There were seventeen courses on contemporary publishing and one on national and trade bibliography, topics that support both collection development and acquisitions.

Although the absence of a single course devoted exclusively to acquisitions is extremely noteworthy, apparently significant coverage of acquisitions occurs in many library school curricula.

The Educational Experience and Expectations of Acquisitions Librarians

Given the demonstrated paucity of separate acquisitions courses, it comes as no surprise that acquisitions librarians report having received little or no M.L.S. education in their specialty. Schmidt's survey of 141 ARL acquisitions librarians found that "fewer than 10%" had taken a separate acquisitions course during their M.L.S. program, but 56 percent "received some form of training in acquisitions in library school."[14] Thus, 44 percent apparently received no training at all.

Fisher's "informal" survey of twelve academic and public acquisitions librarians in California revealed that six of the ten who held an M.L.S. degree said that they had received no formal acquisitions education while in library school. Three had taken an acquisitions course as part of their M.L.S. degree, while one had received acquisitions education as part of another course.[15]

It is striking that several survey respondents report having taken an acquisitions course, whereas the author's own catalog survey suggests that no such course exists. The obvious explanation for this discrepancy is that respondents considered combination collection development and acquisitions courses to be an acquisitions course. A misunderstanding concerning the definition of acquisitions seems unlikely. After all, if acquisitions librarians do not know what *acquisitions* means, who would? Perhaps the fact that these combination courses were deemed to be acquisitions courses indicates they were perceived to be meeting a need for acquisitions education.

Survey evidence concerning acquisitions librarians' desire for coverage of their function in the M.L.S. curriculum is inconclusive. Eleven of Fisher's twelve respondents believed that acquisitions should be included in the

M.L.S. curriculum (the twelfth did not answer the question). Five felt it should be a required course; five, an elective course; while one stated that acquisitions should be introduced in a required course with an elective course entirely devoted to the topic.[16]

On the other hand, Schmidt found that responding ARL acquisitions librarians believed that most of their training should result from on-the-job experience, whereas only a quarter (26 percent, to be precise) should be provided by formal library school education.[17] She concluded that "library schools need to add a relatively small amount of information about acquisitions to the curriculum to satisfy their needs."[18] Also, Joe Hewitt's analysis of student essays from the University of North Carolina, Chapel Hill, library education program revealed that 54 percent (seven of thirteen) did not feel a separate three-hour acquisitions course was justified.[19]

Both Fisher's and Schmidt's surveys reveal the importance attached to on-the-job education. In Schmidt's study, ARL acquisitions librarians reported by a fifteen-to-one ratio that "acquisitions tasks were learned through on-the-job training rather than through library school education."[20] Fisher's survey respondents ranked on a 1 (low) to 5 (high) scale how well three educational mechanisms prepared them for their current acquisitions position: on-the-job experience was rated 4.9, the formal M.L.S. program scored 2.5, and continuing education was rated 2.4.[21]

It is thus clear that acquisitions librarians obtain more education from experience than from the M.L.S. curriculum. Unclear is whether this phenomenon is due to deficiencies in the M.L.S. curriculum or to the intrinsic nature of acquisitions work.

The Purpose of Library Science Education

Most library and information science educators agree that the purpose of library and information science education is, as the term logically implies, "to educate" rather than "to train." "Education" implies broadly focused, theoretically oriented knowledge, whereas "training" implies a more narrowly focused, practical approach concerning how a particular library performs a specific function. Collection development is thus often perceived as a higher-level intellectual function, requiring education, whereas acquisitions is seen as a lowly clerical routine, worthy only of training. Within this context, any acquisitions course must "educate" instead of "train" to justify its place in the curriculum.

Professional Acquisitions Work and Its Knowledge Domain

An M.L.S.-level acquisitions librarian is more likely to find himself or herself managing an acquisitions department than engaged in the clerical nitty-gritty usually handled by non-M.L.S. subordinates. Schmidt's 1985 survey of ARL acquisitions departments, although noting professionals' considerable involvement in "non-professional tasks," revealed that at least 75 percent of respondents "regularly handle" developing and setting policy, budget planning, and vendor analysis.[22] As stated cogently by Sheila Intner, "Professional roles are becoming largely managerial. Degreed librarians will be charged with directing others in performing technical service tasks and providing them with the training and the tools to do so, but not necessarily in doing such tasks themselves."[23]

Besides staff management, professional acquisitions librarians must handle exceptions to the routine workflow, calculate the overencumbrance necessary to avoid underspending or overspending the various funds, and negotiate with vendors concerning discount rates—to name only a few of many instances requiring expert judgment. Moreover, automation presents a host of challenges, discussed in the next section.

Thus, management of the acquisitions function requires a formidable array of diverse knowledge and skills. Foremost among these are staff direction, business practice, accounting procedures, implementation of automation, and publishing trends. Furthermore, acquisitions personnel must understand the realm of external agencies, such as vendors.

Is an acquisitions course the appropriate place to teach these skills? A closely related issue concerns whether a professional knowledge domain unique to acquisitions exists. Much of the required professional-level knowledge concerning management and automation arguably belongs in the domain of other courses, whereas many topics that are unique to acquisitions, such as processing orders, are non-professional. If a professional acquisitions knowledge domain cannot be identified, it would be difficult to justify a separate acquisitions course. Hewitt has suggested that publishing and the book trade, including pricing, mergers, business practice, and ethics, may constitute a professional knowledge domain for acquisitions.[24]

The Impact of Automation on Acquisitions

The 1980s trend toward integrated automated systems, which provide an online public access catalog, circulation, serials control, and acquisitions, has raised questions concerning whether the traditional technical services tripartite division into cataloging, serials, and acquisitions will continue. In an integrated system all basic functions can be performed (with the proper authorization codes) on any terminal, and thus are not restricted to the geographical area of a particular department. Already anecdotal accounts of "turf battles" between acquisitions departments and cataloging departments in libraries using the NOTIS integrated automation system are legend. Some libraries are discussing the possibility of allowing selectors to bypass the acquisitions department and electronically transmit orders directly to vendors. Thus, it is conceivable that in the future libraries will cease having separate acquisitions departments.

Nevertheless, as long as libraries continue to collect materials, the acquisitions function must still be performed, whether a separate department exists or not. As Ross Atkinson succinctly states, "The function of acquisitions is for the time being not at all in jeopardy, but the acquisitions department might be."[25] It must be remembered that collection development is taught as a function, although most libraries do not have a separate collection development department. Accordingly, the demise of the traditional acquisitions department—if it were to take place—would not eliminate the need for teaching the acquisitions function. In fact, one could argue that if libraries decentralize to the point where non-acquisitions librarians perform traditional acquisitions tasks, the result would be a greater need for acquisitions education.

Another related issue concerns whether automation professionalizes or deprofessionalizes technical service functions such as acquisitions. Detailed examination of the question is beyond this chapter's scope. It is clear, however, that automation requires a greater knowledge level on the part of acquisitions librarians. At the minimum, they will need to know how to perform ordering, receiving, and claiming on an automated system (although these tasks are directly handled by non-professionals). Probably the ability to evaluate and select among many automation options and vendors, manage departmental workflow in an automated environment, adapt to new relationships with other library units due to automation's impact, and understand how hardware, software, and humans synchronize to form an effective system will be required of professionals. Given the rapid advance of technology, it is likely that future acquisitions librarians will also need to know how to manage the migration from one automated system to another. In a subtle way, integrated automated acquisitions systems place more pressure on acquisitions librarians. This is through the obvious presence of perceived failures; for example, orders that have been unfilled for an extended period are advertised to the public in the online public access catalog.

In summary, while the acquisitions department's future structure or even its independent existence is undetermined, automation clearly increases the complexity of managing the acquisitions function, and this will continue into the future. Unclear is whether these considerations imply the necessity of a separate acquisitions course.

Proposed Outline for an Acquisitions Course

To evaluate the feasibility and value of a separate acquisitions course, a tentative course outline is presented here. For each topic, the emphasis would be on the broader theoretical issues.

- Introduction; Overview
- Workflow through Acquisitions: Orders, Claims, Receipts
- Budgeting and Fund Accounting
- Approval Plans; Standing Orders; Lease-Purchase Plans
- Gifts and Exchanges
- The Out-of-Print Market
- Vendor Selection and Evaluation
- U.S. Publishers, Publishing and the Book Trade
- The International Book Trade and Acquisition of Materials Published Abroad
- Acquisition of Non-print Materials
- Management of an Acquisitions Department
- The Ethics and Legalities of Acquisitions Work
- Automated Acquisitions Systems
- Acquisitions and the "Electronic Library"

Review of Arguments Pro and Con

Based on reviewing the literature, conversations with others, and the author's own analysis, the major arguments for and against a separate acquisitions course are recapitulated below. Both the theoretical and the pragmatic as well as the library practitioner and library educator perspectives are included. Some arguments in the pro and con sections may logically contradict each other, as they represent different interpretations of the same issues. The arguments are not enumerated in any priority order, nor do they necessarily represent the author's own opinion.

Arguments in Favor of a Separate Acquisitions Course

A gap in the curriculum would be filled. As previously stated, North American library education programs do not currently offer such a course.

The needs and wishes of important constituencies would be met. There is considerable evidence that both practicing acquisitions librarians and employers perceive a need for more acquisitions education in the library school curriculum. Representing the former, Karen Schmidt asserts, "There has been a growing feeling among acquisitions librarians that their educational needs have been ignored within the library science curriculum."[26] Louise Sherby, an employer, has stated, "Acquisitions and serials librarians are important positions in every academic library, yet increasingly it is difficult to recruit for such positions without having to be resigned to conducting intensive in-house training programs."[27]

Enhanced status for acquisitions work. Because acquisitions work is often perceived as a lowly clerical routine, a library school course could help enhance the acquisitions function's perceived status. Hewitt states, "For many librarians, the inclusion of content related to a function in academic curricula constitutes a kind of validation, or at least a recognition that the knowledge base of the specialization contains respectable academic content."[28]

Acquisitions coverage in non-acquisitions courses may be inadequate. Students report the perception that acquisitions topics that are covered as units within other courses do not receive the same in-depth treatment that a separate course would provide. Likewise, the acquisitions component in specialized courses, such as government documents or archives, would not cover general acquisitions work.

A professional knowledge base for acquisitions would be legitimized. As stated by Ogburn, "The library school curriculum may be the only place where a professional knowledge base is formally communicated."[29]

Requirements of the acquisitions function are complex and challenging enough to warrant a course. Beyond representing a clerical processing routine, acquisitions requires managerial, business, and political skills.

The recruitment of acquisitions librarians would be facilitated. Again Ogburn states, "Educational opportunities in acquisitions would give students some basis on which to decide whether they desire to work in acquisitions."[30]

Automation increases the complexity of acquisitions and the need for professional education. Librarians must understand the nature and functions of automated acquisitions systems to supervise the staff members who do the tasks. They will need to evaluate options, direct workflow, and manage change.

Arguments Against a Separate Acquisitions Course

The necessary content may presently be covered by other courses. Courses on collection development, technical services, and library automation often include an acquisitions component. Also, a motivated student could design his or her own acquisitions course within the context of a readings course or practicum. The real issue may be, not whether there is a separate course in acquisitions, but whether acquisitions receives adequate coverage in the curriculum.

It may not be a politically propitious time for library schools to introduce a new course dealing with a traditional library function. Library education programs are facing increasing pressure to demonstrate intellectual rigor and research productivity to their parent university. The introduction of a new course dealing with what is often perceived to be simply a library processing function may not be consistent with this goal. In fact, many library and information science schools may face an objective conflict between serving the library community's needs and securing their niche in a research-oriented university.

There may not be enough full-time acquisitions librarians to justify establishment of a separate course. Hewitt has stated, "It may be unrealistic to expect programs of library education to prepare students to practice a specialization for which there are so few professional positions."[31]

Alternative education methods may be more appropriate for acquisitions. A significant portion of the knowledge required for acquisitions work is either specific to a single library's procedures or best acquired through the experience of working with vendors. Consequently, in-house training or continuing education may be more appropriate than formal library courses.

Acquisitions is not a truly professional task worthy of significant coverage in a library school curriculum. The author personally rejects this perspective, but this argument must be listed because it is frequently voiced.

There would not be enough "academic content" to fill a course. Again, the author does not agree with this often-heard point. The complex and challenging managerial, business, political, and automation skills necessary for acquisitions work warrant academic attention at the course level.

It would "crowd" the curriculum to add yet another course. The persuasiveness of this argument will obviously vary among different library education programs.

A professional knowledge base unique to acquisitions may not exist. The author rejects this argument. Professional acquisitions librarians are required to exercise considerable management skills, including staff direction, business practice, and accounting and budgeting. They must be familiar with and monitor the publishing sector and understand the functions and services of a variety of vendors and service agents. Few of these proficiencies will be taught in other courses.

Automation may deprofessionalize acquisitions and result in the elimination of the acquisitions department. The author believes that automation makes acquisitions planning and managing responsibilities more complex; although a separate acquisitions department may disappear, acquisitions functions will continue and will require professional management.

CONCLUSIONS

There are four basic options for the coverage of the acquisitions function in a library education curriculum: (1) a separate required course on acquisitions; (2) a separate elective acquisitions course; (3) no separate course, but inclusion of acquisitions in other courses, either required or elective; and (4) no coverage of acquisitions at all. Options 1 and 4 may be rejected outright as unacceptable extremes. There can be no justification for requiring all M.L.S. candidates to complete a separate acquisitions course, but the failure to include some acquisitions education in the curriculum cannot be justified, either. Option 3 represents the *status quo* in most contemporary library education programs. Thus, finally, the choice boils down to options

2 or 3, and the question remains as originally posed in the chapter title: Should acquisitions be taught as a separate course or as a unit within other courses, such as collection development?

The author believes that in a perfect world in which all legitimate needs are met, library education programs should ideally include a separate acquisitions course. In the real world of financial and political constraints that library education confronts in the 1990s, a separate acquisitions course has not been demonstrated to be truly essential.

This question has been analyzed in the abstract. Whether a particular library education program should introduce an acquisitions course depends upon a variety of factors unique to that institution, including the needs of students, the coverage of acquisitions in the present curriculum, and the program's priorities. Thus, a uniform answer applicable to all programs would be unproductive and unwarranted.

NOTES

The author gratefully acknowledges useful input from colleagues Herbert S. White, Judith Serebnick, George Whitbeck, Margaret Johnson, Jay Wilkerson, Elizabeth Hanson, Anne McGreer, Dennis McGreer, and Jerome Conley. Judith Serebnick read the manuscript and provided valuable feedback. Thanks are also due Karen Fouchereaux, graduate assistant, who photocopied course listings of ALA-accredited library education programs.

1. Hendrik Edelman, "Selection Methodology in Academic Libraries," *Library Resources & Technical Services* 23 (Winter 1979): 33–34.

2. Nancy J. Williamson, "Education for Acquisitions Librarians: A State of the Art Review," *Library Acquisitions: Practice & Theory* 2:4 (1978): 202; William Fisher, "Education for Acquisitions: An Informal Survey," *Library Acquisitions: Practice & Theory* 15:1 (1991): 30–31.

3. Henry M. Yaple, "Gunfight at the O.K. Corral: Holding Your Own with Collection Development," *Library Acquisitions: Practice & Theory* 15:1 (1991): 33.

4. Gail A. Kennedy, "The Relationship between Acquisitions and Collection Development," *Library Acquisitions: Practice & Theory* 7:3 (1983): 225.

5. Herbert S. White and Sarah L. Mort, "The Accredited Library Education Program as Preparation for Professional Library Work," *Library Quarterly* 60 (July 1990): 204.

6. Joyce L. Ogburn, "Why We Need Acquisitions in the Library Science Curriculum," *Library Acquisitions: Practice & Theory* 15:4 (1991): 477–478.

7. Karen A. Schmidt, "Education for Acquisitions: A History," *Library Resources & Technical Services* 34 (April 1990): 159.

8. Ibid., 160–163.

9. W. Royce Butler, "The Missing Link in the Library School Curriculum? Acquisitions," *Library Journal* 91 (May 1, 1966): 2271.

10. Sara C. Heitshu, "On Formalizing Acquisitions Training," *Library Acquisitions: Practice & Theory* 2:4 (1978): 207.

11. Williamson, "Education for Acquisitions Librarians," 201.

12. Karen A. Schmidt, "The Education of the Acquisitions Librarian: A Survey of ARL Acquisitions Librarians," *Library Resources & Technical Services* 35 (January 1991): 10.

13. Donna K. Cohen, "The Present State of Education for Acquisitions Librarianship," *Library Acquisitions: Practice & Theory* 15:3 (1991): 359–360.

14. Schmidt, "The Education of the Acquisitions Librarian," 10, 18.

15. Fisher, "Education for Acquisitions," 29.

16. Ibid., 30.

17. Schmidt, "The Education of the Acquisitions Librarian," 21.

18. Ibid., 7.

19. Joe A. Hewitt, "Education for Acquisitions and Serials Librarianship: The Students' View," *Library Acquisitions: Practice & Theory* 11:3 (1987): 188.

20. Schmidt, "The Education of the Acquisitions Librarian," 19.

21. Fisher, "Education for Acquisitions," 30.

22. Karen A. Schmidt, "The Acquisitions Process in Research Libraries: A Survey of ARL Libraries' Acquisitions Departments," *Library Resources & Technical Services* 11:1 (1987): 41.

23. Sheila S. Intner, "For Technical Services: The Future Is Now, the Future Is Us," *Catholic Library World* 62 (May/June 1991): 424.

24. Joe A. Hewitt, "On the Nature of Acquisitions," *Library Resources & Technical Services* 33 (April 1989): 109–110.

25. Ross Atkinson, "The Acquisitions Librarian as Change Agent in the Transition to the Electronic Library," *Library Resources & Technical Services* 36 (January 1992): 8.

26. Karen A. Schmidt, "Highlights of the ALCTS/RS Acquisitions Administrators' Discussion Group, January 15, 1991," *Library Acquisitions: Practice & Theory* 15:4 (1991): 469.

27. Louise S. Sherby, "A Vision for Professional Education," in *Library Education and Leadership: Essays in Honor of Jane Anne Hannigan*, ed. by Sheila S. Intner and Kay E. Vandergrift (Metuchen, N.J.: Scarecrow Press, 1990), 168.

28. Hewitt, "On the Nature of Acquisitions," 108.

29. Ogburn, "Why We Need Acquisitions," 478.

30. Ibid., 476.

31. Hewitt, "On the Nature of Acquisitions," 108.

SUGGESTED READINGS

Alemna, A. Anaba. "Acquisitions and Collection Development Education in Ghana." *Library Acquisitions: Practice & Theory* 14:1 (1990): 53–59.

Anderson, Greg. "Complement or Contradiction: The Role of Acquisitions in the Access versus Ownership Dynamic." *The Acquisitions Librarian* no. 6 (1991): 3–14.

Atkinson, Ross. "The Acquisitions Librarian as Change Agent in the Transition to the Electronic Library." *Library Resources & Technical Services* 36 (January 1992): 7–20.

Biancofiore, Piera, and Lucilla Vespucci. "Acquisitions and Collection Development in Italy." *Library Acquisitions: Practice & Theory* 13:3 (1989): 303–313.

Brooks, Terrence A. "The Education of Collection Developers." In *Collection Management: A New Treatise*, ed. by Charles B. Osburn and Ross Atkinson, Pt. A, 145–58. Foundations in Library and Information Science, vol. 26. Greenwich, Conn.: JAI Press, 1991.

Butler, W. Royce. "The Missing Link in the Library School Curriculum? Acquisitions." *Library Journal* 91 (May 1, 1966): 2271–2274.

Cohen, Donna K. "The Present State of Education for Acquisitions Librarianship." *Library Acquisitions: Practice & Theory* 15:3 (1991): 359–364.

Cotsell, R. J. L. "Education for Acquisitions in Australian Library Schools." *Library Acquisitions: Practice & Theory* 9:4 (1985): 331–350.

Cronin, Blaise. *The Education of Library-Information Professionals: A Conflict of Objectives?* London: Aslib, 1982.

Evans, John. "Education for Acquisitions and Collection Development in Papua New Guinea, with Reference to Courses at the University of the South Pacific." *Library Acquisitions: Practice & Theory* 14:1 (1990): 43–52.

Fisher, William. "Education for Acquisitions: An Informal Survey." *Library Acquisitions: Practice & Theory* 15:1 (1991): 29–31.

Gorman, G. E. "Standing Still or Moving Forward? Demands and Directions in Australian Acquisitions Education." *Library Acquisitions: Practice & Theory* 14:4 (1990): 389–399.

Heitshu, Sara C. "On Formalizing Acquisitions Training." *Library Acquisitions: Practice & Theory* 2:3/4 (1978): 205–207.

Hewitt, Joe A. "Education for Acquisitions and Serials Librarianship: The Students' View." *Library Acquisitions: Practice & Theory* 11:3 (1987): 185–194.

––––––. "On the Nature of Acquisitions." *Library Resources & Technical Services* 33 (April 1989): 105–122.

Hollender, Henryk S. "Smart Guys Wanted: Education for Library Acquisitions in Poland." *Library Acquisitions: Practice & Theory* 14:2 (1990): 195–207.

Intner, Sheila S. "For Technical Services: The Future Is Now, the Future Is Us." *Catholic Library World* 62 (May/June 1991): 420–427.

Kennedy, Gail A. "The Relationship between Acquisitions and Collection Development." *Library Acquisitions: Practice & Theory* 7:3 (1983): 225–232.

Kent, Philip G. "Demands and Directions in Australian Acquisitions Education: Report of an Australian Workshop, July 1989." *Library Acquisitions: Practice & Theory* 14:4 (1990): 401–404.

Krzys, Richard. "Collection Development Courses." In *Internationalizing Library and Information Science Education: A Handbook of Policies and Procedures in Administration and Curriculum*, ed. by John F. Harvey and Frances Laverne Carroll, 201–214. Westport, Conn.: Greenwood Press, 1987.

Marcum, Deanna B. "Acquisitions in the Library School Curriculum." *Library Acquisitions: Practice & Theory* 15:4 (1991): 471–474.

Maxwell, Jan. "Whether It Is Better to Be Loved or Feared: Acquisitions Librarianship as Machiavelli Might Have Described It." *Library Acquisitions: Practice & Theory* 16:2 (1992): 113–117.

Mosher, Paul H. "Collection Development to Collection Management: Toward Stewardship of Library Resources." *Collection Management* 4 (Winter 1982): 41–48.

Myrick, William J. "The Education of Mr. X." *Library Acquisitions: Practice & Theory* 2:3/4 (1978): 195–198.

Nassimbeni, Mary. "Professional Education for Library Acquisitions in South African Library Schools." *Library Acquisitions: Practice & Theory* 14:1 (1990): 73–99.

Ogburn, Joyce L. "Why We Need Acquisitions in the Library Science Curriculum." *Library Acquisitions: Practice & Theory* 15:4 (1991): 475–479.

O'Neill, Ann L. "Evaluating the Success of Acquisitions Departments: A Literature Review." *Library Acquisitions: Practice & Theory* 16:3 (1992): 209–219.

Osburn, Charles B. "Education for Collection Development." In *Collection Development in Libraries: A Treatise*, ed. by Robert D. Stueart and George B. Miller, Jr., Pt. B, 559–583. Foundation in Library and Information Science, vol. 26. Greenwich, Conn.: JAI Press, 1980.

Pors, Niels Ole, and Leif Kajberg. "Education for Acquisitions: Problems at the Danish Library School." *Library Acquisitions: Practice & Theory* 10:2 (1986): 141–149.

Rahman, Afifa. "Acquisitions and Collection Development Education in Bangladesh." *Library Acquisitions: Practice & Theory* 12:1 (1988): 43–51.

Schmidt, Karen A. "The Acquisitions Process in Research Libraries: A Survey of ARL Libraries' Acquisitions Departments." *Library Acquisitions: Practice & Theory* 11:1 (1987): 35–44.

―――. "Education for Acquisitions: A History." *Library Resources & Technical Services* 34 (April 1990): 159–169.

―――. "The Education of the Acquisitions Librarian: A Survey of ARL Acquisitions Librarians." *Library Resources & Technical Services* 35 (January 1991): 7–22.

―――. "Highlights of the ALCTS/RS Acquisitions Administrators' Discussion Group, January 15, 1991." *Library Acquisitions: Practice & Theory* 15:4 (1991): 469.

Serebnick, Judith. "Are Library Schools Educating Acquisitions Librarians?" *Library Acquisitions: Practice & Theory* 2:3/4 (1978): 209–211.

Sherby, Louise S. "A Vision for Professional Education." In *Library Education and Leadership: Essays in Honor of Jane Anne Hannigan*, ed. by Sheila S. Intner and Kay E. Vandergrift, 167–174. Metuchen, N.J.: Scarecrow Press, 1990.

Stieg, Margaret F. *Change and Challenge in Library and Information Science Education.* Chicago: American Library Association, 1992.

Tóth, Gyula, and Beáta Bobok. "Education and Training for Library Collection Development in Hungary." *Library Acquisitions: Practice & Theory* 12:3/4 (1988): 313–323.

White, Herbert, and Sarah L. Mort. "The Accredited Library Education Program as Preparation for Professional Library Work." *Library Quarterly* 60 (July 1990): 187–215.

White, Herbert S., and Marion Paris. "Employer Preferences and the Library Education Curriculum." *Library Quarterly* 55 (January 1985): 1–33.

Williamson, Nancy J. "Education for Acquisitions Librarians: A State of the Art Review." *Library Acquisitions: Practice & Theory* 2:3/4 (1978): 199–208.

Yaple, Henry M. "Gunfight at the O.K. Corral: Holding Your Own with Collection Development." *Library Acquisitions: Practice & Theory* 15:1 (1991): 33–37.

10

The Practicum in Collection Development: A Debate

Elizabeth Futas

Theory versus practice is another of the Great Debates in library education, involving both educators and practitioners in sometimes acrimonious stand-offs that defy resolution. Practitioners bemoan the fact that library school students are not prepared to be effective practitioners the day after they are hired and berate educators for stuffing their heads with useless theories instead of practical knowledge that can be put to use immediately upon going to work in a real library. On their part, educators suffer Excedrin headaches trying to arm students with enough practical information to land jobs, but not to the exclusion of imparting to them knowledge that has lasting value, which, by definition, is not specific to any particular library, system, or vendor. A few years ago, an exasperated library educator said in conversation:

> I only have time to teach my students one or two systems. Suppose I teach them NOTIS and CLSI, but they get hired by a GEAC library? They'll think what I taught them was worthless. But if I spend my little bit of time with them teaching them the basic theory of how automated bibliographic systems work they can go into any one of those libraries and learn how to function fairly quickly, because they understand the basics. Libraries ought to be willing to train them in VTLS, or INNO-VACQ, or DRA, or whatever they happen to have.

Yet library schools still try to integrate some practical experiences for students in the context of their academic programs, usually in the form of a brief practicum, internship, or fieldwork course. In her chapter, Elizabeth Futas explores the terminology of the practice course and its history in American library education. Once the definitions and context are clearly identified, she describes both sides of the debate, explaining the advantages and disadvantages ascribed to practicums by educators and practitioners, before drawing conclusions from her analysis.

Although she may not have resolved the Great Debate, Elizabeth Futas presents scenarios for success and failure that may be helpful to individual libraries and library schools wishing to reexamine their current implementations of practice courses and breathe new life into this time-honored method of conveying something beyond textbook learning to the pre-professional librarian.

INTRODUCTION

A traditional method of conveying education, especially in a professional field, is the internship or practicum. Every field from medicine to teaching has some form of "practice work" in the curriculum for their students. The profession of librarianship is no exception. For years we have placed our students in courses with titles such as fieldwork, practice work, internship, or practicums. Yet very little has been researched about the efficacy of this form of teaching. In almost every faculty there have been debates about the wisdom of relying on this form of coursework. Sometimes it is mandated beyond the school's control; that is, the state's education department requires school library media practicums for students planning to become certified school librarians. Sometimes it is not available at all for students. Most library schools, however, attempt to offer it within the context of an already crowded one- or two-year degree program, and they do so with more or less success.

Definitions

To debate the issue of the feasibility of this form of teaching, it is necessary to start with some definitions. The Association for Library and Information Science Education (ALISE) has recently worked on developing definitions for practicums. For the purposes of this chapter, their definitions (while not formally approved) will be used:[1]

- *Internship* and *Field Experience*
  the structured pre-professional work experience which takes place during graduate coursework or after coursework but preceding the degree, usually for a short amount of time
- *Residency*
  the post-degree work experience designed as an entry level program for professionals who have recently received the M.L.S. degree from a program accredited by the American Library Association (ALA)
- *Mid-Career Fellowship*
  the experience, often referred to as a middle management internship, designed to assist librarians who already have some professional experience to develop a specialty or to improve management skills

Although the ALISE definitions seek to standardize the wording of the "practice work" in the curriculum for library science education, it remains to be seen whether their definitions will be adopted and used by the schools and faculty who teach in them.

Several years ago, in an effort to standardize our own terminology in the field, the University of Rhode Island's Graduate School of Library and Information Studies searched through its collection of library school catalogs to decide what to call our practice course. What we found was a plethora of titles, all meaning, we believed, the same thing. The choices were the following:

Practicum in Librarianship

Library Practicum

Field Problems

Professional Field Experience and Seminar

Internship in Librarianship

Internship in Libraries

Library Practice Work

Directed Field Work

Cooperative Education

We chose to call our course "Professional Field Experience."

Since the term *practicum* is used in the title of this chapter, it will be used to encompass all forms of "practice work" in the field of library and information studies, whether it be internship, fieldwork, or practicum. The debate, therefore, will cover all three types of work as long as the work takes place within the graduate curriculum of library schools and in conjunction with the field of collection development.

Historical Overview

The value of the practicum in library education was first noted in C. C. Williamson's classic study *Training for Library Service: A Report Prepared for the Carnegie Corporation of New York* published in 1923. In the study, he discussed the value of the "underlying pedagogical principles" of practicum or fieldwork as part of a regular library service curriculum.[2] A second early study, that of Ernest J. Reece in 1936 commented on the lack of control and direction exhibited by faculty toward field coursework that was then relatively popular in library education.[3]

Samuel Rothstein's study in the late 1960s found very little changed from the time of the Williamson and Reece studies, and he noted that practicums were far more important in Great Britain's library schools than they were in schools in the United States.[4] A survey of practicum opportunities in the late 1960s–early 1970s by Laurel Grotzinger revealed a complete turnaround in the number of schools offering fieldwork. In the original survey in 1969, seventeen schools reported that they never had a practicum as part of the graduate curriculum, while an additional eleven said that they had discontinued that offering. Only fourteen months later, nearly 71 percent of ALA-accredited programs had a practicum provision as part of their curriculum.[5]

By 1975, although most the library schools offered some sort of practicum,[6] only two schools required it for preparation for the degree.[7] In 1981, Margaret Monroe's paper on field experience in library school curriculums suggested that the practicum was back in vogue. She also stated that "only the education of school librarians has sustained a requirement of field experience (practicum or internship) over the years, and this has been reinforced by state law in most parts of the United States."[8]

Two recent studies have again turned in similar results indicating that little has changed in the area of practicum offerings. In 1988, J. Gordon Coleman, Jr., surveyed the then sixty ALA-accredited library school programs as to the prevalence of the practicum, its administrative aspects, including coordination by faculty, its funding, and its requirements. He discovered that 93.2 percent of the schools reported that their curriculums included a practicum option.[9] Researchers Josette Anne Lyders and Patricia Jane Wilson published the results of a national survey of all accredited and non-accredited library education programs studying the school library media practicum as to the nature of the internship, involvement of university faculty supervisors, student involvement, field supervisor's involvement, and finally, faculty evaluation of the experience. They found that 75 percent of the programs *require* the internship experience.[10]

At this time there still has been only one study published based on a dissertation that surveyed the students' evaluation of their practicum experience, done in South Africa.[11] The results of this study point to the fact that fieldwork, or the practicum, gets very mixed reactions from both those who administer it and those who take it.

Practicum Value for the Student

Before beginning a debate on the value of the practicum, it is necessary to explain the reasons why professional education is so much enamored of the idea. What exactly does the practicum add to library and information studies education? For each experience there are a set of expectations upon which to judge the efficacy of the time and effort spent in the field by the student. According to Mary Nassimbeni, there are theoretical, practical, philosophical, and ethical reasons related to practicums upon which the field experience can be evaluated. According to her study, the following nineteen aims, listed in rank order from most to least important, are possible:

1. To provide the link between theory and practice
2. To familiarize students with tools and routines of library and information work
3. To learn about the organization of libraries/information centres

4. To expose students to various working environments
5. To perform basic skills
6. To illustrate material taught in class
7. To learn about user needs and behaviour
8. To instill confidence
9. To instill professional attitudes
10. To practice communication skills
11. To observe good practice
12. To develop problem-solving skills
13. To observe good librarians and information workers at work
14. To develop independent learning
15. To test students' suitability for the profession
16. To provide students with professional contacts
17. To test students' practical ability
18. To vary teaching methods
19. To provide a break from formal class[12]

Although it may be impossible for a single practicum, no matter how well done or how well received, to accomplish all of the above possible aims, certainly this gives us a point to begin interpreting what the value of an experience might be.

Practicum Value for the Supervisors

Besides contemplating what a student might find valuable within the practicum experience, there are two other parties connected to this experience whose opinions and ideas must be factored into any evaluation: the faculty supervisor and the field supervisor. Since the practicum is usually done within the context of a course with credit received and entails working at a library or information agency location, what kind and amount of time and energy does the preparation of the faculty and field supervisors take? In addition, how do the faculty benefit in terms of their own workloads, and how does the field supervisor and, by extension, the practicum site agency benefit?

The possible payoffs that the faculty supervisor could get from a student's practicum include counting the program as part of the coursework load, and through it recognizing new applied research topics, gaining help in promotion and tenure decisions, and for the school, making linkages with their own or other institutions of learning or other public, corporate, or governmental collections. On the other hand, if the supervision of the field experience mitigates against any of these benefits, junior faculty should at least be leery of spending the time and energy required in being involved in them.

For the field supervisor and the library providing the site of the practicum, some of the same payoffs enumerated above may be in place: preparation for and training of new personnel (after all, what else are these students but constantly changing personnel?) may be part of the job description for the field supervisor; development of possible publication topics with practicum student and faculty supervisor may help the supervisor with job security and promotion; and for the supervisor's library or the individual some sort of reward system from the placing agency, for example, money or tuition remission. For the field site location, benefits include the addition of almost professional support for special projects, an extra hand to work during rush times, and cheap or free labor for a specific length of time.

Collection Development Definitions

Since the debate revolves around the value of the practicum in the field of collection development, perhaps a working definition of that term might be in order. Since collection development is a subject taught in most library and information science schools, the easiest place to get a definition is in a textbook ordinarily used in these classes. Two of the most popular texts respectively define collection development as the following:

all planning for the systematic and rational building of a collection.[13]

the process of identifying the strengths and weaknesses of a library's materials collection in terms of patron needs and community resources and attempting to correct the weaknesses, if any. Collection Development is the process of making certain the information needs of the people using the collection are met in a timely and economical manner, using information resources produced both inside and outside of the organization.[14]

For the sake of this debate, collection development will not include acquisitions of the material, but its selection, evaluation, maintenance, preservation, and weeding. The purely technical function of acquisitions is not part of these definitions and for the sake of this debate will not be counted as such.

Collection Development in Different Types of Libraries

Collection development may be differently administered in different types of information agencies. Within the context of the larger academic library, with a full department known as collection development, there may be many selectors, and even one or more administrators building the collections of a university library. Within a school media center, collection development is one of the many jobs of the person who, frequently, will be the only professional in the library. In large school districts, the process of collection development may be handled at an administrative center apart from any of the actual libraries in the system. In the public library, depending on the size and complexity of the organization and community, collection development may be handled by one professional or several, or a committee representing branches in different types of neighborhoods. In corporate, governmental, or any other type of special library or information agency, collection development may consist more of the acquisitions of materials needed by individuals in the firm or organization rather than any planned process of building a self-contained "library." Different types of agencies require different types of models of collection development. Each produces differences in the practicum experience for a student. For the purposes of this debate, the practicum will be one that takes place in the library, with professionals who are building a collection for the present and the future, with their unique community in mind.

What a Collection Developer Does

Since we know what collection development librarians do not do (i.e., acquisitions), we should now decide just what they do. Besides knowledge of the publishing world, both print and audiovisual in the broadest interpretation of that word, a collection development officer (or that part of the librarian's job that calls for the development of his or her collection) selects, protects, maintains, preserves, acquires (in the non-technical sense of the word), evaluates, and weeds all of the materials that are to be part of the library's ongoing collection. All these different processes are part of the job of the modern collection development officer and are part of every librarian's professional responsibility if the building of the collection is under his or her jurisdiction. Anything to do with the collection from finding it to getting rid of it is fair game for the collection development librarian.

THE DEBATE

Given the importance and the necessity for a practicum in the educational experience of students in master's degree programs, is such an experience in the area of collection development going to give the student the sense of a real-life experience? Is the translation of the theoretical into the practical going to work with a collection development practicum? As in all things there are many sides to that question. Presented next is the pro side, which gives the benefits of such an internship, followed by the anti or con side, which gives the drawbacks and the frustrations that may occur.

The Pro Side

Although the classroom is an excellent place to learn the more theoretical aspects of the process of collection development, it is an uneasy and cumbersome place to try to learn, or to teach, the practical aspects of collection development. No professional does collection development in a vacuum. Collection development is a process that needs to have a community at its root. When determining what to buy for an information agency, it is necessary to consider several outside influences: individuals to whom the collection is directed, other resources available outside, library goals and objectives, as well as publishing in the areas of purchase. In addition, what types of materials, what subjects, and what formats also come under consideration in the collection development process.

From within the institution there is also the problem of what has already been purchased and what the existing collection looks like. Some evaluation of the current offerings helps to decide the policies and processes of what comes next. Nothing but experience can teach you how the process works, no matter how much you talk and discuss it. Therefore, a practicum in collection development seems an obvious way in which to introduce reality into the realm of the theoretical.

Much as we might like to think that teaching helps the student know how a library or information agency works in any given situation, it is only with the routines of practice that such objectives can be achieved. The day-to-day living of a process is a better teacher than any explanation of such a process within the confines of a classroom. No matter what types of assignments may be given to mimic or represent the real experience, in the end, only being there and participating will ensure that the student receives what he or she needs to know.

The parts of collection development for which a student is eminently qualified to contribute are in the area of maintenance and evaluation. These labor-intensive processes need to be designed by the resident librarian (the field supervisor), but once set up, they could be carried out entirely by a practicum student. The decisions of what needs to be stored, weeded, or replaced are ones that, with guidelines established, might easily be done by a student in an internship capacity. A practicum student might supervise student aides in the completion of such jobs and learn the administrative role of the collection developer as well.

One of the most difficult things in collection development to explain in a classroom situation is how to select materials. The reason this is so difficult is that no one can really select in a vacuum. Whom you select for and what you select from are questions that face a selector in a real-life situation. That type of situation is impossible to create within the classroom, so a practicum would give students experience and simultaneously allow them to practice with tools they have looked at and learned about but not necessarily used in the classroom. In addition, such experience will instill a sense of confidence that no assignment will do for them. Within certain parameters and given the necessary professional guidance, students charged with helping to create a collection could learn quite a lot about selection criteria, principles, and types of problems to be faced.

The iterative process of creating a collection development policy and writing it down is the area in which a practicum student might be of most value to a field supervisor and the information agency. It is most important for an information agency, especially a traditional library, to have a written working collection development policy. The tendency is to have the person in charge of collection development write the policy and then pass it around to others. This gives only one person's ideas room to be represented in the policy and limits the value and usefulness to the library. A library and information studies student, new to the literature of the field through classroom exposure, might add to the process of writing the policy and simultaneously bring fresh eyes to the unwritten and traditional mores of the agency. When seen through these eyes, a valuable service of uncovering areas of weakness might be found. In this respect, use of a practicum student would be extremely valuable to the library.

Although what a student learns in class is of great importance, the instructor's practical knowledge of what is actually going on is limited. Many professors have not been active in their fields for several decades.[15] New technology introduced within the recent past is something that they know about theoretically, but not on a practical level. The student needs to have experience with hands-on tools in addition to classroom assignments. The practicum's value doubles when the understanding of the rapid technological changes that are difficult for the practitioner to master are set against the library school faculty's lack of recent experience. Good grounding in all processes is important because without theory, when changes, even technological ones, are introduced, the professional who does not know and understand the theory will be lost. Practice, however, makes theory intelligible and understandable. It also helps train students for first positions, especially if the practicum comes at the end of their program. With the increasing use of large automated circulation and acquisition modules and the array of statistical data that they can produce providing all kinds of information for decision making, a collection development practicum becomes not only important but imperative.

Although acquisitions is not necessarily part of collection development in many libraries, having a practical knowledge of the steps involved in acquiring material once it has been selected should be included for anyone wishing to work in the area of collection development. A practicum in one adjunct area, such as acquisitions, would be of value to the student.

The Con Side

The process of collection development requires knowledge of specific information about the agency, its clientele, and its environment. Some information required to grasp the knowledge so important to the process requires expenditure of much time and energy by the individual who seeks to build the collection. A professional whose job it is to build this collection learns about both in time—and time is something that practicum students and the agency at which they work do not have. Most practicums are set up in the semester before they begin. Although some last for a year or even more, most consist of half that time, usually four months or, in a summer semester, as little as five weeks. Some knowledge of the community and the environment in which the library functions can certainly be learned through policy statements, interviews with professionals who work in the environment, and even direct observation for a time. But the requirements of collection development are such that in the shorter practicum experiences, students could spend almost all of their time learning how to do the jobs that the practicum consisted of without ever getting a chance to do them. In fact, they would be consuming the time of the field supervisor and the host library or information agency without ever giving any payback in terms of work accomplished for that agency. Of what value would that be for the field supervisor?

In order for a practicum experience to be valuable, it must work not only for the student but for the host agency as well. If the agency spends its time only training a student to do a job, and then the experience ends before the student can accomplish anything, the practicum becomes a frustrating exercise for everyone concerned. In some areas the use of fieldwork or internships can be very valuable. This is especially true if the education received in the classroom has direct bearing on the process to be accomplished in the library. But in the area of selection, knowledge of the community for whom the selection is being done is necessary for any part of the process. Unless students come in with knowledge of that particular library's clientele, the entire practicum will be spent learning about the audiences for whom they are selecting instead of how to select for them. The purpose of a practicum is to achieve "a balance between theory and practice; . . . instruction in theory to the exclusion of practice leaves the student without the competence to perform successfully on the job."[16] Therefore, the *practice* in a practicum, not just learning how to do the job, is the mark of a useful experience. That can be accomplished within the classroom and need not take up a field supervisor's or a host agency's time, energy, or money.

If the process of selection of materials for a particular library is not likely to be accomplished within the collection development practicum, how valuable would it be to spend the time to set one up? Since the student might never get to experience the central process within collection development, that is, the selection of material for clientele in context, the value of the entire experience is called into question. Can we ask a host library or information agency to take on a practicum student with very little chance of being able to expect any real work from that student? Probably not. Should we ask a faculty member to take on the administration of a practicum that is not likely to add the element of "practice" to what that faculty member provides in a classroom situation? The answer to these three questions appears to be no. Therefore, the practicum experience in the area of collection development is perhaps not often the best use of the student's, field supervisor's, or faculty supervisor's time and energy.

Other parts of the collection development process may also not yield the type and kind of experience necessary for a successful practicum. Although some of collection development is very practical, for example, maintenance, inventory, and some parts of the weeding and storage decisions, much of collection development, instead of being product oriented, is a long and arduous learning process. Collection development is successful when the entire process is accomplished, including those parts that are entirely, or mainly, process driven. A very practical experience is difficult or impossible to provide in this context.

CONCLUSION

As technology plays a more important role in the area of collection development and as more library and information agencies become interested in writing collection policy documents, students can play a successful role through practicums. Until that time, this analysis suggests that collection development practicums should focus on areas in which student contributions can be made within the timeframe available and should exclude those areas in which it is not possible to provide a meaningful experience in the context of a library school course.

NOTES

1. Association for Library and Information Science Education, unpublished paper, 1990–91.

2. Charles C. Williamson, *Training for Library Service: A Report Prepared for the Carnegie Corporation of New York* (New York: Merrymount Press, 1923), 54.

3. Ernest J. Reece, *The Curriculum in Library School* (New York: Columbia University Press, 1936), 127.

4. Samuel Rothstein, "A Forgotten Issue: Practice Work in American Library Education," in *Library Education: An International Survey*, ed. by Larry Earl Bone (Champaign/Urbana: University of Illinois Graduate School of Library Service, 1968), 197–219.

5. Laurel Grotzinger, "The Status of the 'Practicum' in Graduate Library School," *Journal of Education for Librarianship* 11 (Spring 1971): 332–339.

6. R. C. Palmer, "Internships and Practicums," in *The Administrative Aspects of Education for Librarianship: A Symposium*, ed. by M. B. Cassata and Herman Totten (Metuchen, N.J.: Scarecrow Press, 1975), 239–263.

7. Virginia Witucke, "Library School Policies toward Professional Work Experience," *Journal of Education for Librarianship* 16 (Winter 1976): 162–172.

8. Margaret E. Monroe, "Issues in Field Experience as an Element in the Library School Curriculum: A Background Paper," *Educational Resources Information Center*, ERIC Number: ED 200231:8 (1981).

9. J. Gordon Coleman, Jr., "The Role of the Practicum in Library Schools," *Journal of Education for Library and Information Science* 30:1 (Summer 1989): 19–27.

10. Josette Anne Lyders and Patricia Jane Wilson, "A National Survey: Field Experience in Library Education," *School Library Journal* 37:1 (January 1991): 31–35.

11. Mary Nassimbeni, "Role and Value of Fieldwork in Education for Library and Information Science: A Cross-Site Comparison of Two Case Studies," *South African Journal of Library and Information Science* 58:1 (March 1990): 75–86.

12. Ibid., 77.

13. Rose Mary Magrill and John Corbin, *Acquisitions Management and Collection Development in Libraries*, 2nd ed. (Chicago: American Library Association, 1989), 1.

14. Edward G. Evans, *Developing Library and Information Center Collections*, 2nd ed. (Littleton, Colo.: Libraries Unlimited, 1989), 13.

15. Robert Brundin, "Field Experience and the Library Educator," *Journal of Education for Library and Information Science* 31:4 (Spring 1991): 365–368.

16. Ibid., 366.

SUGGESTED READINGS

Brundin, Robert E. "Field Experience and the Library Educator." *Journal of Education for Library and Information Science* 31 (Spring 1991): 365–368.

Clemons, Bonnie J., and Melissa Trevvett. "Integrating New Professionals into Large Academic Libraries: A Symposium." *Journal of Academic Librarianship* 17 (May 1991): 68–78.

Coleman, J. Gordon, Jr. "The Role of the Practicum in Library Schools." *Journal of Education for Library and Information Science* 30 (Summer 1989): 19–27.

Evans, G. Edward. *Developing Library and Information Center Collections*. 2nd ed. Littleton, Colo.: Libraries Unlimited, 1987.

Genovese, Robert. "The Use of Library School Students for Technical Services Projects." *Technical Services Quarterly* 8 (1991): 63–69.

Lyders, Josette Anne, and Patricia Jane Wilson. "A National Survey: Field Experience in Library Education." *School Library Journal* 37 (January 1991): 31–35.

Magrill, Rose Mary, and John Corbin. *Acquisitions Management and Collection Development in Libraries*. 2nd ed. Chicago: American Library Association, 1989.

Malesky, Christine Shields. "All Things Researched: Internship at National Public Radio's Library." *Special Libraries* 76 (Summer 1985): 183–186.

Nassimbeni, Mary. "Role and Value of Fieldwork in Education for Library and Information Science: A Cross-Site Comparison of Two Case Studies." *South African Journal of Library and Information Science* 58 (March 1990): 75–86.

Part IV

TRAINING FOR COLLECTION DEVELOPMENT

11

Training for Success: Integrating the New Bibliographer into the Library

George J. Soete

The start of a new job is a tension-filled time. The newly hired librarian may not be aware that this period is also stressful for the supervisor. Both want a positive outcome—successful performance, satisfaction with the choice made, and pleasant working environment—yet often neither is sure of the best way to assure accomplishment. George J. Soete offers a blueprint for achieving success that can be followed in all types of libraries.

Soete directs his chapter to the collections officer, coordinator, or other supervisor, who will find it exceedingly useful as a practical checklist for a training program. New librarians will benefit also; they can use the information presented here as a benchmark against which to measure the training they are offered and as a source for questions that should be answered and areas that should be covered. Soete states that training should result in integration—comprehensive effectiveness in the job. He identifies the critical factors that will assure that the organization, the trainee, and the training program are ready.

From the beginning, Soete stresses the importance of careful planning in designing and executing training. He outlines five steps in a general training program, focusing on outcomes or major competency areas to be mastered—the knowledge, skills, and abilities necessary to do an effective job. Potential trainers and new librarians alike will find Soete's training needs checklist of lasting value, both as a practical tool and as a conceptual framework for understanding competencies.

THE IMPORTANCE OF A TRAINING PROGRAM FOR NEW BIBLIOGRAPHERS

Bringing a new bibliographer onto the staff is both a wonderful opportunity and a daunting challenge for the academic research library. The first six months or so are the best time in the newcomer's tenure to set the direction and establish the context that will lead to success. Enthusiasm is high; motivation to learn is especially strong; and learning, whether structured or not, occurs at a very fast rate. Simultaneously, both the newcomer and the collections officer are keenly aware of the mass of new information that must be taken in so that the new person can be successful. Typically, new bibliographers in the 1990s face such added challenges as dual appointments, budgets in chronic decline, an explosion of information and publishing in their areas of selection responsibility, and a crazy quilt of interdisciplinary university programs to discover. Moreover, the collections officer is faced with the challenge of portraying an increasingly complex environment in which selecting materials for the collection, the traditional core activity for the bibliographer, may be but a fraction of the newcomer's responsibility. For both the new librarian and the organization, there are key underlying questions: How can the newcomer most effectively spend these first few months? What is urgent? What can be deferred and incorporated into the ongoing educational process? What will lead most expeditiously to success?

Preparing the new bibliographer for success is essentially a training process. Here, however, the focus will be broader than traditional training programs; it will encompass a program of *integration*, the goal of which is to bring the new person to comprehensive effectiveness in the job. The intention is to provide detailed guidance for the collections officer, coordinator, or other supervisor (the trainer) in the development of a program that will lead to success for every new bibliographer (the trainee).

READINESS: CRITICAL FACTORS

The effectiveness of any training program is dependent on the readiness of (1) the organization, (2) the trainee, and (3) the training program. *Organizational readiness* focuses on *what* the new person is being integrated into. Is the organization relatively sophisticated, with clearly articulated vision and values? Is planning, through long-range, strategic efforts and goal setting, part of the fabric of organizational life? Is there a lively, open and multidirectional communication system? Do staff have enough information to be successful in their jobs? Are collections policies and priorities clear? Are there systems in place for documenting plans, policies, and priorities? Does the organization promote creativity and risk taking, tolerate failure, and empower staff through appropriate delegation? Or is the organization somewhat "primitive" in some or all these respects? Newcomers can be successfully integrated into virtually any type of organization, but answering these questions candidly at the beginning will help the trainer design the integration program best suited to the organizational setting.

A serious obstacle can occur, for example, in the library organization where there is insufficient understanding and appreciation of collections work. An attitude sometimes encountered is that anyone can be a bibliog-

rapher and that collections work does not require much training or attention.[1] Another view is that collection development is an art that simply
cannot be taught.[2] In fact, in no previous era have on-the-job training and
the overall process of integration been so important as they are today; if we
choose one dimension of the current library scene, chronic and sharp de-
clines in budgetary buying power, it would argue strongly for a structured
approach to training the new bibliographer—if only in basic coping skills.[3]
Fortunately, no small part of organizational readiness, of course, resides in
the very collections officer who is planning the training program. Even
within a mediocre setting, a committed collections officer can develop and
implement a highly successful integration program by supplying within the
collections program what is lacking in the organization as a whole.

Trainee readiness focuses on *who* will be integrated—the knowledge,
skills, and abilities brought to the job by the trainee. Newly hired librarians
can range from the recent library school graduate with little subject preparation to the veteran who has a doctorate in the subject, years of successful
experience, and a well-deserved national reputation. There are risks
throughout the range. At the extremes, brand new librarians may be
overwhelmed by everything they have to learn and uncomfortable with
decision making, and veterans may assume they have nothing to learn and
be especially impatient with local priorities, policies, and constraints.

Program readiness focuses on the *how*. The need for flexibility of approach
is strongly suggested by the wide range of librarian readiness. Such a large
number of possible variables argues strongly for tailoring the orientation
program to each librarian's specific needs. Simultaneously, the trainer
needs to develop a "core curriculum": What is it that everyone needs to
learn, from veteran to neophyte? Time spent on assessing resources also
can be useful. Is there money for outside training—coursework, workshops? Do key people in the organization have the skills and time to help
orient the trainee to aspects of the new job? Are there up-to-date, clearly
written manuals and policies? Judith Paquette wisely counsels not waiting
until everything is in place to begin an in-house training program for new
selectors.[4] However, a quick inventory of resources can help in planning
even the most rudimentary program.

DEVELOPING A TRAINING PROGRAM

Following is an outline of how a general training program might be
developed, with five steps that parallel, for the most part, the classic stages
of planning and implementing a new program. This general outline forms
a basis for the individual program tailored to each trainee's needs.

1. *Needs assessment.* Absolutely critical to the planning process is identifying training needs by learning where trainees are and where they should
be. Needs emerge in two ways: The trainer identifies the core information

all bibliographers need to do their jobs, and the competency "gaps" that need to be filled for an individual trainee are identified. The first should be relatively easy. Obviously, the collections officer can develop a list of most core needs, but other bibliographers on the staff, as well as key staff in other departments (acquisitions, special collections), can supply ideas as well.

Identifying gaps in individual competence is more difficult; the best approach is to work very closely with the trainee in identifying needs in specific competency areas from the beginning. Establishing a supportive climate is important in needs assessment of this sort: The goal is not to catalog weaknesses and focus on inadequacies but to identify specific strategies for maximizing success. The new person needs to understand this goal. One approach is to emphasize that the newcomer has joined a "learning organization," in which it is not only acceptable to identify areas for development but expected.

The most effective technique for identifying the training needs of newcomers is to invite them to assess their needs using a formal competencies list such as the one outlined below. A self-assessment of this sort provides very useful material for discussion with the trainer. It also establishes the expectation that newcomers will have a major role in their performance planning throughout their tenure in the organization. After this initial assessment, the trainer remains alert during regular conversations with trainees to discover indications of other needs and adds these to the list; for example, a new librarian might not understand the need for additional training before joining a major weeding project in progress. A critical part of the identification process is to sort needs by degree of importance and urgency. What should be addressed right away, and what can wait a while? Without such priorities, trainees are likely to be overwhelmed by a long list of undifferentiated needs.

2. *Development of training objectives.* Needs are the raw data; objectives organize needs into a plan. The best training objectives are clear and specific expressions of what we want someone to know or be able to do under certain conditions in a way that meets specific criteria. Although such a tight conceptual structure might sound daunting, effective written objectives can be generated very quickly once the needs are known. Thus the need to know order procedures might translate into this objective: After four weeks, the bibliographer will be able to initiate direct-order requests and make approval selections following prescribed Acquisitions Department procedures without assistance. And the need to learn about campus programs might become this: After three months, bibliographers will have an understanding of campus programs in their areas of responsibility such that they can make well-informed selection decisions; ability to summarize programs extemporaneously, for example, in a bibliographers' meeting, will be a useful measure.

Objectives need not be so formally structured. Indeed, needs in some areas (e.g., organizational culture) cannot be converted into objectives easily. Yet it is valuable even in such areas to work through the objectives-formulation process, which enables both trainer and trainee to understand clearly the direction and hoped-for results of the training program. Finally, a key piece of the planning process is deciding priorities. Thus one approach is to address only the most urgent needs first, moving on to others later and developing objectives over time as each new phase of the training program starts.

3. *Identification of methods and activities.* The training methods that one is likely to use with the new bibliographer include the following: *reading* (e.g., manuals, policies, journal articles); *lectures* (e.g., orientation presentations by heads of library units); *guided discussions* (e.g., periodic sessions with the trainer); *demonstrations* (e.g., performing a search on the online public access catalog); *supervised practice* (e.g., reviewing approval receipts while the trainer looks on); *hands-on participation* (e.g., drafting a collection profile for an area not yet covered); *attendance at workshops*; *formal course work*; *field trips*; and *mentoring*. Very creative trainers might experiment with other methods, such as simulations and role playing, but most are likely to stay within this menu.

Choice of methods is important, since clearly some methods work better than others with individual learners. The more actively adult learners participate in an experience, the more effective and long-lasting the learning. The contrast is clearly visible in two very disparate activities focused on the same topic: *reading* existing policies versus *writing* a new policy. Both are valid, but the gain from the second is likely to be more profound and lasting. If there is a rule of thumb, it is to prefer active, participatory experiences over passive ones. This can be particularly important when you are asking someone else to help you train. For example, that staple of training programs, the orientation visit to another department complete with presentation by the department head and selected staff, can be made more effective by guiding "guest trainers" to reduce lecturing and increase hands-on activities.

Having worked with the trainee to identify needs, objectives, and training methods, the identification and scheduling of specific activities should come easily. Paquette wisely recommends (1) separating orientation to local procedures from training in the more professional and intellectually challenging responsibilities such as selection decision making and (2) making sure that the basics are covered first.[5] Beyond such general injunctions, it is difficult to prescribe activities and sequencing very specifically, though there are models from which specific advice can be gathered.[6] During implementation, there should be opportunities for trainer and trainee to talk about what is working and what is not working and to adjust training objectives, methods, and schedule accordingly. There is, perhaps, no greater frustration than feeling "condemned" to complete a long, time-consuming, and largely irrelevant training process.

4. *Development of performance goals, measures, and expectations.* A key strategy for integrating the trainee into the organization is to work with the person to develop performance goals and objectives, preferably with meas-

ures of accomplishment. It is also a good opportunity for the trainer to assert the performance expectations that will form a major element in the "contract" that is being developed between the newcomer and the organization during the integration process. These are excellent activities to begin toward the end of a structured training process once the newcomer has a clear sense of organizational context, policy, procedures, and environment.

Facilitating successful performance through the development of clear goals and performance expectations is a commonplace notion in the general management literature, yet it is not consistently practiced in our libraries. According to David Null, this has importance for bibliographers with dual assignments because questions of priorities and time management are critical.[7] Betty Ann Stead and Richard Scannell remind us of the strong relationship among clear organizational objectives, clarity of individual objectives, roles, responsibilities, and job satisfaction.[8]

Although performance goals and objectives may relate to and build on the training objectives mentioned above, they are longer range; in short, they focus on "life after training." Elsewhere, this author has described a program for training library professionals in writing clear and effective goals and objectives.[9] A key concept is that the professional and the supervisor work as a team to *plan* the librarian's performance through the development of three types of goals: *organizational*, *performance effectiveness*, and *professional*. *Organizational goals* directly further the work of the organization; an example might be to assess existing collections in a specific area in preparation for writing a grant proposal. *Performance effectiveness goals* focus on the *manner* in which work is carried out; such goals might relate to communication effectiveness, time management, and interpersonal skills. *Professional goals* focus on how the librarian intends to make professional contributions. By working with the trainee in a goal-setting mode from the beginning, the trainer sends the clear message that performance planning is an important part of the person's job.

5. *Evaluation.* Evaluation of the training program derives easily from the steps outlined above. Have the identified needs been met, objectives achieved? Does the newcomer feel reasonably comfortable with roles, responsibilities, and expectations? What more should be done to complete the training? At a programmatic level, it is also important to find out from the new person what worked and what did not work in the training process; information gleaned here can be useful in refining the training program.

MAJOR COMPETENCY AREAS

With a sense of the major steps in developing a training program in place, attention can be focused on specific competency areas. What knowledge, skills, and abilities must the new librarian master to do an effective job? William Wortman groups competencies into three areas: *knowledge* (subjects, users, publishing, etc.), *activities* (community analysis and liaison, collection analysis, etc.), and *interpersonal* and *intellectual characteristics* (goal oriented, collaborative, etc.).[10] Jasper Schad looks for "highly motivated self-starters . . . first rate management skills . . . the ability to balance many diverse functions . . . [toleration of] stress and ambiguity," and awareness that an outstanding job does not necessarily mean perfection.[11]

Viewing the problem in the mode of a training needs checklist, one can identify seven competency areas in three groupings. Group I, Assumed Competencies, includes (1) command of basic functional principles and (2) subject knowledge. Most organizations assume a level of competence in these areas, basing their assumptions on information gathered in the recruitment process. Group II, Job Competencies, includes (3) knowledge of local policy and procedure, (4) understanding of work expectations, and (5) understanding of the environment. These three constitute the new information most trainees need to perform the day-to-day job and thus form the core of most orientation and training programs. Group III, Instrumental Competencies, includes (6) awareness of organizational culture and (7) management skills. These competencies usually receive the least attention in the training process, and yet for many newcomers, they may merit the most intense focus. Visible success is likely to be attributed to accomplishments in Group I and II competency areas. Outright failure, on the other hand, is more often attributable to deficiencies in Group III competencies.

Group I: Assumed Competencies

1. *Basic functional principles* are the core principles for the function of collection development. For most bibliographers, they are the background phenomena that rarely need to be articulated. We all know the reasons for building research collections; the importance of knowing our users; the factors that make for an effective selection decision; the tenets of intellectual freedom; the importance of building and preserving collections for the future as well as the present. Most newcomers have an acceptable working knowledge of these core principles. Sometimes, however, librarians make it through both library school and the interview process without betraying deficiencies in basic functional knowledge. Such knowledge can be strengthened through reading,[12] especially for the recent graduate, but it is more likely to happen through the process of close work over time with the trainer.

2. It is a common enough situation for the *subject knowledge* of the newcomer not to line up exactly with the needs of the library. More difficult to deal with is the subject competency gap that is unknown to—or unappreciated by—the newcomer. The depth and scope of subject knowledge needed is, of course, an important consideration. The need may be for high-level

"curatorial" expertise accompanied by appropriate language skills and a sophisticated knowledge of the book trade. More likely, the need will be filled by librarians who are "subject literature experts" rather than true subject experts.[13] Lynn Williams offers as a standard for basic subject expertise "an ability to recognize the important names and topics in a subject canon."[14] Even so, some newcomers may find it a stretch to reach basic competency in all areas of responsibility. To learn needs, the trainer should talk candidly with trainees, assessing their general sense of the discipline, knowledge of the key resource literature and its structure, and familiarity with key publishers, journals, series, non-standard formats. Newcomers also need to be assured of the library's support in their program of gaining further subject expertise. Reading and roaming the reference stacks are solid methods for gaining greater knowledge of the subject, as are discussions with faculty and with librarians in other libraries. Obviously, the best strategy is to focus first on subjects as they are taught and researched in the university's programs, moving on later to mastery of the broader subject area.

Group II: Job Competencies

3. *Knowledge of local policy and procedure* is what many orientation and training programs focus on. There are excellent examples of written manuals and orientation guides available for review.[15] Maureen Gleason suggests that such guides might contain organization charts, roles and responsibilities of key staff, committee structures, and recent statistics about the collections.[16] Procedural topics typically include budget preparation and monitoring, annual reporting requirements, ordering, approval plan review, gift processing, endowment fund purchases, collection assessment, and weeding. Familiarity with the library's written collection policies is, of course, especially important. Not having such documentation available makes the job much tougher, of course. In either event, the trainer needs to spend time with the newcomer in the all-important area of policy as the basis for selection decisions.

4. Having a clear *understanding of work expectations* is an important step beyond mastery of policy and procedure. Providing information about the approval review process is essential, but asserting the expectation of regular weekly review of approval receipts clarifies priorities and helps in time management. Usually there are expectations for every bibliographer that can be distributed as part of the training process. Several examples of such lists are available for review.[17] A position description with estimated percentages of effort can serve to sketch in the major areas of responsibility. From such an outline, the trainer can develop more detailed descriptions of expectations. As an example, all bibliographers in the organization may be expected to be active in the area of resource sharing within an existing consortium; for the newcomer, a specific expectation might be to develop contacts with key

bibliographers at other libraries within the consortium. Areas where expectations might need to be emphasized include faculty liaison, resource sharing, collection management routines, and gift solicitation. An understanding of expectations from the beginning can prevent problems later.

5. *Understanding the environment* within which the library builds collections and offers services is critical. Some of this environment is shared by all libraries: skyrocketing materials prices, federal information policies, the increasing availability of online resources. Yet trainees may have an inadequate grasp of some of these distant environmental factors, and the trainer needs to make sure that this basic territory is covered. One strategy is to connect the new person with selected electronic newsletters and listservs where an awareness of these environmental issues can quickly be built. Another is to encourage liaison with other librarians and key vendors, who can be a useful source of current information about the environment.

Closer to home, the environment of the campus and the political jurisdiction within which the university operates are even more important. The larger planning and budgetary context is particularly important for the new person to learn about. The first task, of course, is to master knowledge about the programs for which the newcomer will be responsible and to develop effective working relations with faculty. The university catalog and library collection profiles can be very useful, but there will be no substitute for contact with users: The trainer can help by introducing the newcomer to faculty and by monitoring progress in this area closely. Librarians who view collections work as chiefly "desk-bound" may need a push in this direction.

Group III: Instrumental Competencies

6. *Organizational culture* is not an easy concept to describe briefly. For purposes of integrating the trainee into the organization, a key question will help: What is it that the newcomer needs to know about this organization that is not easily available information but is critical to success? Some organizations answer this question by focusing on history—the principal stages in the development of the library and the key contributions of mythic leaders. If available, the library's mission statement can help, but typically it does not tell much about the culture. One way of getting closer is to complete this sentence: "This is an organization that values . . ." Answers might range from "hard work and initiative" to "promptness and clear writing." Gleason offers "mutual support" as an important climate factor in collections work, reinforcing the notion that bibliographers cannot work in isolation but must develop effective working relationships within the library.[18] Sometimes the newcomer's misreading of the culture can cause serious problems, such as when the person tries to be highly competitive and political in a collaborative culture or chronically misses deadlines in an organization where meeting them is a strong priority.

7. *Management skills* needed by staff librarians are often overlooked because it is assumed that these are chiefly the province of supervisors. Yet, as noted earlier, deficiencies in these skills can lead to trouble for the new person. In most organizations, bibliographers need to know how to plan projects, analyze problems, set goals, make cases, negotiate, contribute effectively at meetings, and manage their time. Interpersonal and communication skills are clearly essential. Moreover, creativity and leadership skills will soon be called into play.

Many people find it difficult to acknowledge need for improvement in management skills. They may be convinced that the skill is not important in their job, or they may perceive implied criticism while identifying needs in this area. Again, the trainer can provide a secure developmental context in which skill needs can be addressed. Some organizations are able to support attendance at management skills workshops or such events may be available on the campus. In any event, the trainer needs to stress the importance of management skills in achieving success and work with the trainee to develop these skills.

CONCLUSION

Wortman emphasizes the importance of an integrated collections program that is much more than the sum of isolated activities.[19] An integrated training program is perhaps the best introduction a new bibliographer can have to the integrated collections program.

The program outlined above stresses *success* as the goal for every trainee and the key role of the collections officer or other supervisor in managing the process. *Planning* is the essential concept throughout the program. The planning process begins with an assessment of the readiness of the organization, the training program, and the trainee. The collections officer and the newcomer plan the learning experience as a team by identifying needs, developing objectives, and deciding methods. Finally, the key competency areas provide a planning framework for development of knowledge, skills, and awareness over a range that is much broader than one finds in the typical training program. Careful planning assures an effective training experience; training is the medium for integrating the new bibliographer; and comprehensive integration provides the groundwork for lasting success and satisfaction.

NOTES

1. David G. Null, "Robbing Peter . . .: Balancing Collection Development and Reference Responsibilities," *College & Research Libraries* 49 (1988): 451.

2. Charles B. Osburn, "Education for Collection Development," in *Collection Development in Libraries: A Treatise*, ed. by Robert D. Stueart and George B. Miller,

Jr., Foundations in Library and Information Science, vol. 10 (Greenwich, Conn.: JAI Press, 1980), 561.

3. Null, "Robbing Peter," 451.

4. Julie Ann McDaniel, "Leading the Way: In-House Collection Development Training for New Selectors," *Library Acquisitions: Practice & Theory* 13 (1989): 293–294. This is a report of a conference presentation by Judith Paquette.

5. McDaniel, "Leading the Way," 293–294.

6. James E. Bobick, *Collection Development Organization and Staffing*, SPEC Flyer and Kit, no. 131 (Washington, D.C.: Office of Management Studies, Association of Research Libraries, 1987). See especially the Notre Dame and University of Waterloo examples.

7. Null, "Robbing Peter," 450.

8. Betty Ann Stead and Richard W. Scannell, "A Study of the Relationship of Role Conflict, the Need for Role Clarity, and Job Satisfaction for Professional Librarians," *Library Quarterly* 50 (1980), 319–320.

9. George J. Soete, "The Rhetoric of Performance Management: A Training Problem and Two Solutions," *Journal of Library Administration*. Manuscript accepted for publication in late 1992.

10. William A. Wortman, *Collection Management: Background and Principles* (Chicago: American Library Association, 1989), 212–216.

11. Jasper G. Schad, "Managing Collection Development in University Libraries That Utilize Librarians with Dual-Responsibility Assignments," *Library Acquisitions: Practice & Theory* 14 (1990): 168.

12. Wortman presents an excellent overview of collection management principles and practices in his *Collection Management: Background and Principles*. The selection decision process is well summarized in John Rutledge and Luke Swindler, "The Selection Decision: Defining Criteria and Establishing Priorities," *College & Research Libraries* 48 (1987): 123–131. All collections officers will have their favorites.

13. G. E. Gorman and B. R. Howes, *Collection Development for Libraries* (New York: Bowker-Saur, 1989), 257.

14. Lynn B. Williams, "Subject Knowledge for Subject Specialists: What the Novice Bibliographer Needs to Know," *Collection Management* 14:3/4 (1991): 37–38.

15. Bobick, *Collection Development Organization*; the documentation from Notre Dame and Penn State include indications of priorities.

16. Maureen L. Gleason, "Training Collection Development Librarians," *Collection Management* 4:4 (1982): 4.

17. Bobick, *Collection Development Organization*; also Jack Siggins, *Performance Appraisal of Collection Development Librarians*, SPEC Flyer and Kit, no. 181 (Washington, D.C.: Office of Management Services, Association of Research Libraries, 1992).

18. Gleason, "Training Collection Development Librarians," 4.

19. Wortman, *Collection Management*, 2–3.

12

The Conspectus as an On-Site Training Tool

Anthony W. Ferguson

Surely, the RLG Conspectus is one of the most exciting new collection development tools to be introduced in the last dozen years, second only, perhaps, to the collection assessment CD-ROMs prepared by bibliographic utilities containing selected holdings of a local library and some of its peer institutions. Anthony Ferguson examines the Conspectus from a trainer's perspective and explains the fundamentals of understanding user needs, existing collections, and future possibilities. To be sure, he does not overlook the value of Conspectus activities for their more obvious purpose of providing a library with an in-depth evaluation of its collections. But that purpose cannot be fulfilled unless the librarians doing the work of examining and judging materials on library shelves do so in the manner Conspectus designers intended, namely, consistently, applying uniform principles in estimating the value of materials.

As Ferguson points out, the spinoff benefits are, perhaps, as valuable for collection development as the primary benefits, provided librarians use Conspectus activities to get in touch with their users, become intimately acquainted with their materials, hone their powers of observation, and gain expert knowledge of the universe of publication in their areas of specialty. He does not stop with his review of these benefits but goes on to analyze the drawbacks involved, both in administering the training and supervising the necessary practice it requires.

Ferguson's suggestions are timely, as many libraries turn for the first time to the Conspectus to aid in their efforts to maximize the effectiveness of the money spent on materials. His suggestions offer collection development officers the potential to enhance the knowledge and effectiveness of the library's reference librarians in the process, and to avoid some major pitfalls along the way.

INTRODUCTION

Collection development is not much more than discovering what users need in the long and short term, what the collection can deliver, and then deciding what to buy or borrow to make up the difference. Unfortunately, competing demands for selectors' time in many college and university libraries have reduced their collection development activities to saying yes or no to approval plan books and assigning fund codes to faculty recommendations, titles listed in a variety of new book listing media, or review slips provided under approval plan profiles when book shipment is excluded. Discovering user needs and collection capabilities is skipped because of lack of sufficient time, and materials are purchased based on the selector's informed instincts. This works better for selectors who have been associated with an institution for an extended period and less well for new librarians. Even for the veteran, keeping up with changes in the curriculum and the research needs of the faculty is difficult, and the needs for which the selector is making purchases may no longer exist. The Conspectus can be used by collection development managers to renew the collection development process because it requires selectors to focus on user needs, what kind of collection the library has, and the type of collection that should be built, as well as the resource-sharing agreements that should be instituted to make up for collection inadequacies.

The purpose of this chapter is to illustrate how the Conspectus can be used as a self-training device to help selectors discover user needs, describe the strengths and weaknesses of their collections, and record acquisition policies. Positive by-products of the Conspectus methodology, how to deal with Conspectus weaknesses, and practical training suggestions are also presented.

THE CONSPECTUS AND DISCOVERING USER NEEDS

First, a short description of the Conspectus is in order. The Conspectus began as a resource-sharing tool but evolved into a framework for collection assessment. The WLN (formerly Pacific Northwest) version, the one discussed in this chapter, is being used by libraries increasingly for this purpose.[1] A major benefit of this version is the availability of personal computer software for local data input and sorting. The Conspectus is a survey or inventory embodying a list of more than 6,000–plus subject headings, arranged first by broad major divisions and then by narrower categories, about which the librarian is asked three questions: What kind of collection is needed to meet user needs? What kind of collection do you have on the shelf now? What kind of collection are you currently building? The librarian is asked to pick an answer from the following six possible responses:[2]

0. Nothing
1. Minimal information
2. Basic information
3. Study or instructional support information
4. Research-level information
5. Comprehensive-level information

Each of the answers is amplified with paragraph-length definitions for the collecting level.

The answer to the first question, what kind of collection is needed to meet user needs, is recorded in a Collection Goal column in the Conspectus. Although the Conspectus does not specify the survey research technique to be used to respond to the question, it does suggest the need to communicate with the user community. For academic librarians, communication with the faculty is a requisite and opens up communication between the selector and his or her most important user group. The selector should meet with individual faculty members or committees, if available, and explain the need to establish a collecting goal for the subject terms related to their field. This readily demonstrates to the faculty members that their advice is important and will become part of the public record. The selector should not stop with just the faculty, however, but also should survey students as well to understand their wants and needs better.

The value of the Conspectus is that it naturally draws the selector into needs assessment activities that focus on collection building. I have found that meetings with the faculty usually lead to joint inspections of the collection that then lead to other kinds of cooperative activities.

COLLECTION STRENGTHS AND WEAKNESSES

The answers to the second two questions, what kind of collection do you have on the shelf now and what kind of collection are you currently purchasing, are recorded in Collection Level and Current Collecting columns of the Conspectus worksheets. The definition for each possible answer or collecting level in these columns requires the selectors to analyze their collections in both quantitative and qualitative ways.

Quantitative factors include information about the size of the collection for each subject, the number of volumes added during the past year, the number of periodicals currently being received, the level of expenditure, the amount of circulation, and so on. These pieces of information help the selector understand both the Collection Level and the current collecting policies of the library. The notes field in the personal computer-based WLN version for the Conspectus makes the recording of this kind of data especially easy. Qualitative assessments rely more upon the informed judgment of the selector. The definitions for the six collection depth indicators supply the questions, which when answered teach the selector about his or her collection.[3] Among the factors the selector analyzes are the following:

- *Curricular support.* What levels of coursework can the collection support fully? Basic Information collection can support secondary school and beginning undergraduate coursework, and Instructional Support collection can support beginning, advanced undergraduate, and beginning graduate research, and a Research collection can support dissertation research.

- *Imprint dates.* Are current materials collected and are retrospective materials retained? For example, Basic Information collections are actively weeded, with out-of-date materials discarded, Study collections are reviewed for currency with "essential and significant" materials retained, and Research collections retain and preserve older materials.

- *Periodicals subscriptions.* Does the library collect only a few major journals for broad fields, are specialized periodicals collected selectively or extensively? Minimal collections lack periodicals, Basic Information collections have only a few major titles, Study collections have a selection of representative titles, and Research collections have extensive collections.

- *Monographic acquisitions.* The questions here are similar to those for periodicals. Does the library collect general survey monographs or does it collect narrower specialized monographs as well? Minimal and Basic collections include a minimum number of monographs, Study collections have a wide range of general monographs, and Research collections have a wide range of both general and specialized monographs.

- *Foreign language acquisitions.* For the subject at hand, are foreign language materials collected selectively in addition to English language materials? In all applicable languages? Are materials collected in one language only? The Conspectus classifies collections as "E" for English language if they have little or no foreign language materials, "F" for selected foreign language in addition to English material, "W" for collections where all applicable languages are collected, and "Y" for collections where all of the material is in a single foreign language.

- *Reference tools.* Are reference materials collected in the minimum number needed to define the subject? All those fundamental to the topic? All important titles? Basic collections have the minimum number needed, Study collections have all fundamental reference tools, and Research collections have very extensive reference tool collections.

- *Databases.* What kind of access to electronic databases is provided? Bibliographic only? Are numeric or textual databases provided? Basic collections must provide access to bibliographic databases while Study collections also provide access to non-bibliographic databases.

- *Authors.* Are the works of major and minor writers collected? Study collections have selections from the works of minor writers while Research collections are expected to have large collections of these works.

By the time selectors mull these questions over in their minds and seek out information to answer them, they become experts on their collections and, thereby, more valuable members of the staff. To uncover these kinds of information, selectors are trained to review the following:

- *Shelf lists.* In training sessions, selectors are taught to let their "fingers do the walking" through the shelf list looking for imprint dates, foreign language coverage, the relative number of specialized titles, the proportion of materials published in the past five years, and so on, characteristics that will help them make decisions about collecting levels for the existing collection on the shelf and the one currently being built.

- *Reports.* Library reports on expenditures generally and from vendor management reports are reviewed. Once the selector becomes familiar with the expected amount of publishing in a field, these reports can help him or her understand a library's relative standing. For example, knowing that several hundred books are produced annually in a particular field provides a context for understanding if the amount spent by a library is minimal or significant.

- *Circulation.* Circulation system reports help to evaluate recommendations on collecting goal levels. If the faculty recommends a research-level collection in a particular field as the goal but few things if any circulate, the librarian is prepared to discuss whether the collection is appropriate.

- *Library's subject catalog.* Frequently selectors assume they are evaluating the materials in the call number ranges listed in their Conspectus worksheets. Training materials, however, emphasize focusing on subject heading and using local subject catalogs to learn where materials on that subject are housed throughout the collection. Usually this will alert the selector to the materials in non–Library of Congress classified collections and in other collections, including rare and special collections.

Selectors are also encouraged to "walk the ranges," that is, to walk around in the stacks, in the reference collections, and to dig into vertical files and examine collections not included in the main catalog or library online public access catalog. This gives the selector a user's view of the collection. Too often, selectors tied to committee tables, reference desks, or approval plan review shelves lose their day-to-day contact with the collections they are assigned to build and manage. The Conspectus forces a renewed relationship between the selector and his or her collections.

Again, completing these Conspectus-related activities helps selectors understand their own collections. Moreover, using the information discussed above, selectors can classify their collections' strengths and weaknesses using the Conspectus methodology as a sort of shorthand. For example, a 3F in the Collection Level column of the Conspectus for the history of Chinese education would mean all of the following:

A collection of English and primarily Chinese language materials sufficient to support curricular needs up through beginning graduate courses. While of less than research intensity, the collection contains a wide range of monographs and a selection of periodicals focusing on this topic. The collection also includes all reference tools fundamental to the topic, with complete collections of the major writers in the field and selections from the works of minor writers as well.

POSITIVE SPINOFFS

A completed Conspectus worksheet is important because it summarizes what the library already has on its shelves, what is being purchased currently, and what users and the librarian feel the level of the collection should be. It is a detailed collection development policy statement. But this document, and the familiarity with the collection that it represents, is only one educational benefit that can be derived from a library's pursuit of a Conspectus project. Several useful by-products are obtained. First, selectors develop familiarity with the basic guides to the literature. Such knowledge not only helps the selector understand the universe of publication and facilitate the completion of the Conspectus but enhances the selector's effectiveness in performing reference duties. Second, by working with other selectors to complete the Conspectus, a library's collection development librarians develop an *esprit de corps* that can carry over to other areas of cooperation. Third, selectors are provided with a communication device to use with the faculty or other critical user groups. Fourth, selectors become involved with the collection as a physical object and not as something divorced from reality.

WEAKNESSES OF THE CONSPECTUS METHODOLOGY

The major problem with the Conspectus is that it is time consuming to conduct the necessary reviews and complete the worksheets. For new selectors, especially, it takes time to learn about the collection and the subjects for which they have responsibility. In the forty or so hours that it takes to evaluate a major Division of the Conspectus (depending upon the size of the collection and the amount of knowledge the selector already has about the collection and its subject field), a selector could probably weed a reference collection and evaluate current journal subscriptions for an area. Unable to realize the full benefits that accrue from a thorough knowledge of the collection in the short run, many selectors become frustrated with the time pressures associated with the work.

The collection manager who is in charge of training selectors can do three things to help them cope with the frustration. First, work schedules can be rearranged to allow uninterrupted blocks of time for the selector to work on the Conspectus. Second, trainees can be helped to understand that learning anything new will bring with it frustration. The trainer should not be too quick to try to erase the problem. A selector cannot quickly obtain the knowledge that comes with advanced academic training or several years of work and at the same time complete a normal forty-hour assignment. Third, the selector can be helped to use his or her considerable reference skills to identify specialized guides to the literature, handbooks, and so on, to learn their subject fields and then to do subject searches using a database such as OCLC's WorldCat or the Research Libraries Group's RLIN (Research Libraries Information Network) to understand the universe of publication. All these steps will increase selectors' speed and effectiveness when completing the Conspectus.

A second, related problem is the tendency for librarians to lose track of their reason for undertaking Conspectus activities. Instead of viewing the process as one of providing an inventory of collection strengths and weaknesses, the vision seems to become one of producing sheets of paper with meaningless numbers and words on them. If this happens, the whole process becomes drudgery and the manager has a revolt on his or her hands.

One way to combat this problem is not to allow the process to drag on too long. The Conspectus is a survey, and the value of the survey is in the information it produces. Selectors need to set realistic timeframes for each part of the project and stick to them. The magnetic-like pull of the reference desk and committee table has to be counterbalanced with the reality that if time is not dedicated to working on the Conspectus, as the process draws on, guilt about not finishing the assignment will cause the selector to become frustrated and angry.

The time-consuming nature of the Conspectus and the potential for focusing on the means instead of the ends pale as problems, however, compared to working with Conspectus subject headings. They were adopted, largely unaltered, from the Library of Congress classification schedules. Many terms are out of date, refer to archaic topics about which there are no published materials, have political or cultural biases that either over- or underemphasize the topic, or, more importantly, pass over newer topics critical to the curriculum or research being supported by the library.

The best solution to the subject heading problem is, after careful consultation with knowledgeable people who are available, to substitute one's own vocabulary for terms that detract from the usefulness of the Conspectus. The "official" vocabulary used in the WLN or the Research Libraries Group (RLG) versions is only critical when a library wants to share its Conspectus values with another institution. Thus far this has not been a real problem. The roadblocks that must be overcome before coordinated collection development can take place are so large that using non-standard vocabulary is a non-problem. The Conspectus methodology, not the Conspectus worksheets, should be seen as primary. The idea of substituting an approval plan profile or the university's course catalog for the Conspectus's list of subject headings to overcome the problem of archaic language has been suggested in the past. So far, it has been easier to change or substitute good terms for poor ones than to contemplate developing an entirely new vocabulary.

A fourth major criticism of Conspectus methodology is that the collection-depth definitions are imprecise and administered arbitrarily.[4] Without a doubt this is true to some extent. The definitions for Minimal and Basic collections sometimes blur into each other. The former is characterized as a collection of "basic titles" and the latter as a "selective collection." To avoid this problem, training exercises should emphasize the importance of selectors' learning the definitions thoroughly, considering all, not just one, of the factors stated in the definitions, and then sticking to the definitions when assigning collection-depth indicators. To get selectors to base assignments on the Conspectus definitions, a variation of the definitions has been created.[5] Selectors are encouraged to make photocopies of the checklist to carry about the library when assessing the parts of the collection for which they are responsible. It reminds them of the questions for which they are seeking answers.

PRACTICAL TRAINING SUGGESTIONS

Conspectus training is best done in a group setting because it affords each participant the chance to discuss problems and experiences others may share in the same situation. For collection development administrators the advantages are obvious: Training sessions are given once; everyone has the same deadlines; the project is more likely to have a beginning and an end and not drag on interminably. There are a variety of options available for teaching selectors the Conspectus methodology. The administrator, using a manual like the one produced by WLN Collection Assessment Services, can serve as the facilitator; a small group of selectors can function in the same way; or a consultant, brought in from the outside, can provide the training. The Association for Research Libraries (ARL) Office of Management Services can provide names of consultants able to provide Conspectus training. Whether or not the manager does the training, he or she still needs to determine the following:

- Who will be responsible for completing each Division of the Conspectus.
- When the initial training session(s) will be held.
- An action calendar, suggesting dates for the initial collection goal discussions with the faculty and other user groups, review sessions for the manager or instructor and the selectors after they have had time to complete an initial page or two of the worksheets, draft reports of completed Divisions, final drafts, and review sessions of the final data with the library director.

Once these decisions have been made, the person chosen to serve as the instructor can prepare a training agenda. The *WLN Collection Assessment Manual* provides useful lesson plans, and typically selectors take part in the following activities:

- An overview of the Conspectus, its history and uses.
- Discussion of worksheet mechanics, including the subject headings employed; the meaning of the Collection levels, Acquisitions Commitment, and Collection Goal columns; and call number ranges.
- Thorough discussion of what the collection-depth indicators mean.
- Discussion about the variety of client- and collection-centered assessment techniques that might be used to obtain the information needed to complete the Conspectus.

- Simulated exercises in which selectors, using prepared collection descriptions, assign collection-depth indicators.

- Small groups of selectors, working together, complete lines from the worksheets based upon real library materials with discussions of the results and problems.

- Discussion about the meaning and function of RLG Supplementary Guidelines and Verification Studies and how they will be used by the library.

- Discussion about the organization and deadlines to be followed during the Conspectus project.

CONCLUSION

The Conspectus is a tool for helping selectors understand their collections. It can be used with a minimum amount of instruction if training materials developed by groups like WLN Collection Assessment Services are used. It is more than a training tool, however. In the end it produces a detailed collection development policy statement that specifies what the collection is like today, what is being built for tomorrow, and what should be done in the future to meet the library user's needs.

NOTES

1. See Nancy Powell and Mary Bushing, *WLN Collection Assessment Manual*, 4th ed. (Lacey, Wash.: WLN, 1992). Copies of the *Manual* and Conspectus database software can be purchased from WLN.

2. The WLN version breaks down the first three collection levels further: "Minimal" has even and uneven categories, "Basic" has introductory and advanced categories, and "Study or Instructional Support" has basic, intermediary, and advanced categories.

3. See Appendix 1 for full definitions of the six major collection-depth indicators.

4. David Henige, "Epistemological Dead End and Ergonomic Disaster? The North American Collection Inventory Project," *Journal of Academic Librarianship* 13 (September 1987): 209–213. See also Anthony W. Ferguson, "Philosophical Arguments and Real Shortcomings," *Journal of Academic Librarianship* 17 (January 1992): 350–351.

5. See Appendix 2 for the checklist developed by the author.

Appendix 12.1
WLN Collection Assessment Manual

Collection Depth Indicators

0   OUT OF SCOPE: The Library does not collect in this subject.

1   MINIMAL LEVEL: A subject area in which few selections are made beyond very basic works. A collection at this level is frequently and systematically reviewed for currency of information. Superseded editions and titles containing outdated information are withdrawn.

2   BASIC INFORMATION LEVEL: A selective collection of materials that serves to introduce and define a subject and to indicate the varieties of information available elsewhere. It may include dictionaries, encyclopedias, access to appropriate bibliographic databases, selected editions of important works, historical surveys, bibliographies, handbooks, and a few major periodicals. The collection is frequently and systematically reviewed for currency of information.

3   STUDY OR INSTRUCTIONAL SUPPORT LEVEL: A collection that is adequate to impart and maintain knowledge about a subject in a systematic way but at a level of less than research intensity. The collection includes a wide range of basic works in appropriate formats, a significant number of classic retrospective materials, complete collections of the works of more important writers, selections from the works of secondary writers, a selection of representative journals, access to appropriate machine-readable data files, and the reference tools and fundamental bibliographical apparatus pertaining to the subject. At the study or instructional support level, a collection is adequate to support independent study and most learning needs of the clientele of public and special libraries, as well as undergraduate and some graduate instruction. The collection is systematically reviewed for currency of information and to assure that essential and significant information is retained.

4   RESEARCH LEVEL: A collection that includes the major published source materials required for dissertation and independent research, including materials containing research reporting, new findings, scientific experimental results, and other information useful to researchers. It is intended to include all important reference works and a wide selection of specialized monographs, as well as a very extensive collection of journals and major indexing and abstracting services in the field. Pertinent foreign language materials are included. Older material is usually retained for historical research and actively preserved. A collection at this level supports doctoral and other original research.

5   COMPREHENSIVE LEVEL: A collection in which a library endeavors, so far as is reasonably possible, to include all significant works of recorded knowledge (publications, manuscripts, other forms), in all applicable languages, for a necessarily defined and limited field. This level of collection intensity is one that maintains a "special collection"; the aim, if not the achievement, is exhaustiveness. Older materials are retained for historical research with active preservation efforts.

Source: Nancy Powell and Mary Bushing, *WLN Collection Assessment Manual*, 4th ed. (Lacey, Wash.: WLN, 1992), 32–33. Used by permission of WLN.

Appendix 12.2
Ferguson Conspectus Codes Checklist

0   OUT OF SCOPE
Collecting aim—Library does not collect

1   MINIMAL LEVEL
Collecting aim—Basic titles—Beyond this, few selections made

2   BASIC INFORMATION LEVEL (Everything at Minimal, Plus)
      Collecting aim—Course work support—Beginning undergraduate
      Collecting aim—Important works—Selected in the minimum number
          needed
      Databases—Bibliographic— Selected in the minimum number needed
      Imprint date—Up-to-date material—Introduces and defines a subject
      Imprint date—Up-to-date materials—Directs one to information else-
          where
      Periodicals—A few major ones in the minimum number needed
      Reference materials—Encyclopedias, dictionaries, bibliographies, hand-
          books, Minimum number

3   INSTRUCTIONAL SUPPORT LEVEL (everything at Basic Level, Plus)
      Collecting aim—Coursework support—Advanced Undergraduate
      Collecting aim—Coursework support—Graduate—Sufficient for most
      Collecting aim—Independent study support—Sufficient for most
      Collecting aim—Research intensity—Less than
      Databases—Nonbibliographic—Access to Monographs—Wide range of
          general
      Periodicals—Selection of representative titles
          Reference/Bibliographic tools—All fundamental to the subject
      Writers—Important—Complete collections of
      Writers—Secondary—Selections from

4   RESEARCH LEVEL (Everything at Instructional Level, Plus)
      Collecting aim—Dissertation support—Source material needed for support
      Collecting aim—Research intensity—Sufficient to support independent
          research
      Foreign language material—Pertinent included
      Imprint date—Older material retained for historical research
      Monographs—Wide range of general and specialized
          Periodicals—Very extensive collection
      Reference—All important sources—Very extensive
      Special collections—included where appropriate to collection
      Writers—Minor—Collected widely

5   COMPREHENSIVE LEVEL (Everything at Research Level, Plus)
      Collecting aim—Exhaustive collecting in a narrow area
      Foreign language material—All applicable languages collected
      Special collections—Manuscripts and other applicable formats—Col-
          lected exhaustively
      Special collections—Collection itself becomes a "special collection"

LANGUAGE CODES
      E—English language materials predominate, little or no foreign materials
      F—Selected foreign language material in addition to English material
      W—Material collected in all applicable languages
      Y—Material primarily in one foreign language—a vernacular collection

13

Training Existing Staff to Assume Collection Development Responsibilities

D. Whitney Coe and Joseph P. Consoli

In the chapter that follows, Whitney Coe and Joseph Consoli bring the issues surrounding the training of part-time selectors into the realm of human understanding. Coe and Consoli begin by establishing the fact that in the contemporary library environment now pervading the research library as well as the college and public library, a significant proportion of selection, if not the bulk of it, falls to staff members whose primary duties lie elsewhere. That the effectiveness in the collection development roles of part-time selectors recruited from among a library's existing staff depends squarely on the kind of training they receive is clear. But the authors go further, to address the human problems libraries often overlook.

In the first place are the problems of finding willing parties among existing staff to take on selection duties. All too often staff members may be "tapped in the dark," without warning or preparation for their new duties. The difference that good training can make is to bridge the gap between the selection tasks and librarians' primary tasks and to facilitate the perception of a synergistic whole. Otherwise, the two sets of tasks may be perceived as completely divorced from one another, and staff thus engaged are likely to feel torn apart and ill-used.

Having established the framework in which training takes place and suggested its priorities, the authors move to specifics of the training program for part-time selectors. They deal, also with the special needs of newly hired staff. Components of the training program and how they operate are discussed in detail. Alternatives for training delivery and realistic estimates of the time they require are explored and furnish a well-marked map for developing a knowledgeable cadre of selectors functioning as an integrated part of library services.

Published in 1980, the two-volume set of essays *Collection Development in Libraries: A Treatise*, edited by Robert D. Stueart and George B. Miller, Jr., quickly established itself as a major contribution in the newly-recognized field of collection development.[1] Articles by Robert Stueart and Norman Dudley describe the major shift in responsibility in book selection from faculty to librarians in the late 1950s and early 1960s, the appearance of the full-time subject specialist/bibliographer, and the growth of approval plans and blanket orders. Sheila Dowd precisely presents the need, structure, and value of the carefully written collection development policy statement. Jean Boyer Hamlin sets forth both the theoretical methodology and a practical review of sources in the selection process. Managing the library collection, preservation, collection evaluation and analysis, education for collection development, and the need for the development of theory are among the other topics discussed in this collection. However, in 1980 there was little recognition of the expanding role of the part-time library selector and no recognition of the need for a well-defined training program for such a selector.

In 1991 a second two-volume set of essays, *Collection Management: A New Treatise*, edited by Charles B. Osburn and Ross Atkinson, was published.[2] This worthy sequel reflects the changing focus and expanding responsibilities that have developed in the 1980s in the field of collection development. Four deserve mention. David Farrell notes that among the significant developments in collection development is "the emergence of the 'dual role' librarian functioning as collection specialist as well as cataloger, reference librarian, or other role."[3] He also emphasizes the value of the collection development policy statement as well as other library policies that affect collection development. Louis Pitschmann, in describing organizational and staffing patterns, recognizes the growing role of part-time library selectors and their relationships with a collection development officer. Dan Hazen, in an examination of selection, presents both the theoretical and the practical, including "macro" versus "micro" selection decisions. Jutta Reed-Scott provides an invaluable review of selection tools as a part of the selection process. This collection, in examining the new trends in the field and recognizing the role of the part-time library selector, creates a firm background for the training of existing staff for collection development responsibilities.

The contemporary crises of diminishing funds and vanishing staff lines experienced by American libraries today, coupled with the explosion of information and formats and the expansion of disciplines and subjects being formally studied, have forced libraries to look inward in an attempt to maximize personnel efforts to cover adequately more with less. Traditional lines of professional distinction, such as technical services, interlibrary loan, reference, bibliography, acquisitions, circulation, and administration, are quickly being erased, or at least modified, to profit from the potential expertise and/or interests of already in-place personnel.

For collection development, this translates into a search for subject, language, and format experience and expertise from other members of the institution's staff. Recruitment, in other words, now begins at home, and venturing outside the library's walls occurs only when there is no chance for adequate coverage from within the library. The current situation complements the historical development of collection development in academe. The last several decades have witnessed a striking shift of selection responsibility from faculty to librarians. By 1978 approximately 90 percent of all selection was being performed by librarians.[4]

Initially this led to the rise of bibliography departments, but as "libraries felt the need to increase the number of librarians working with collection development, many different organizational patterns developed."[5] These included the merging of collection development with other departments, such as acquisitions, technical services, or reference. Even those libraries that maintained an independent collection development department began to rely heavily on part-time selectors from other departments.[6] A 1987 survey by Jeanne Sohn identified only three out of seventy-three libraries surveyed that used only full-time selectors; whereas, twenty-nine libraries reported all selectors as less than half time.[7] Probably most astounding, and disconcerting, is Sohn's finding that "almost 50% [experience] dissatisfaction with the way collection development is structured in ARL [Association of Research Libraries] libraries."[8] If such a trend is to continue, and since financial and economic variables support such a conclusion, then one can assume that more librarians will begin to participate in the collection development functions of their institutions. Since the numbers will increase, yet many of those deployed will have time constraints and duties, often primary, in other departments, the need for effective and efficient training becomes paramount.

While professionals at smaller institutions have always had to wear several hats, their counterparts at larger research institutions are not always so comfortable with changes in professional responsibilities. The rigors of the information explosion demand the acquisition of sophisticated, complex skills in all sectors of librarianship. This leads to specialization, the focusing on a specific issue or concern from a particular subset of a traditional aspect of librarianship. Titles like microforms librarian, Latin American librarian, Romance languages cataloger, hypertext librarian, media specialist, systems officer, and database librarian are not uncommon in today's library hierarchy. At institutions in which librarians have faculty status, the demands of the publish-or-perish syndrome accentuate the investigation and demonstration of expertise in unique but slender slices of professional activity.

Expanding daily responsibilities into more than one traditional sphere of librarianship, then, requires the mastery of sophisticated techniques and a responsiblitity for current awareness in a much broader arena than previously demanded. This expansion is a precarious move and must be well thought out to avoid limiting the librarian's ability to contribute to library research only in the most generalized and broad-based aspects of the profession. Thus, the augmentation of any employee's job description should be consistent and complementary to the person's originally assigned position. Such a transition places an enriching, qualitative perspective on the new assignment, instead of a simple quantitative enhancement of appointed duties. Again, training is critical to the effective transition of an employee into the collection development environment. Educational programs should stress the relationship of collection development to other facets of library science. Training should be direct, not generalized, and it should encourage the effective use of previously gained knowledge in a collection development perspective. In such a program, all members have the opportunity to contribute original ideas for investigation. Simultaneously, new selectors can view their collection development assignments as extensions of their initial responsibilities, not as add-ons that, as Carol Cubberley suggests, happen frequently,[9] and that can easily be relegated to a position of secondary importance.

Selection can be a lonely business. It is rare for any institution, no matter how large or renowned, to have more than one person selecting in any given area. The nature of the business seems to nurture independence and individualism. Maureen Gleason reports that "a sense of isolation from others engaged in the same work is common."[10] It is important that this feeling of separation be addressed and rectified before an infusion of more bodies into the collection development process occurs. This "sense of isolation," when viewed from a different perspective, is often interpreted as "elitism" by colleagues laboring in more gregarious segments of the profession.[11]

While relationships with teaching faculty are encouraged, each selector will usually interact only with a unique set of professors, typically those in the teaching department(s) for which he or she holds selection responsibilities. Such relationships are critical to the health of the collections, but unfortunately they often result in a myopic, possessive approach to networking and a closed communication system that does not take advantage of the diversity of opinions other experienced librarians could contribute. Functioning as the library liaison to a given teaching department requires much time away from the library. Success in the endeavor often results in the placement of the librarian on various faculty and university committees. While all this is helpful to the library's image and reputation, it can result in alienating and isolating the selector from the quotidian exploits of her or his colleagues, which could eventually lead to job dissatisfaction and misinterpretations of performance. Again, training is essential. It is imperative that communication be opened among collection development personnel, especially in a new, multitask environment. The selection process must be portrayed as a coordinated group effort instead of a multitude of isolated processes. It should be emphasized that all selectors share the library's collection development goals and objectives, namely, to populate the library with the information resources required to meet the teaching, research, and information needs of an identified patron population given a historical, current, and future assessment of the library's general mission working within the framework of a given budget.

Cubberley believes that "in order to counter any charges of elitism, and to prevent jealousy, the collection development librarians should contribute to other activities in the library."[12] The introduction of collection development librarians into other areas of librarianship will help to neutralize any negative feelings some of their colleagues may harbor toward them. This response, however, addresses only half the problem and does nothing to allay the feelings of isolation that collection development librarians experience in the performance of their primary selection duties. This unfortunate situation, expounded upon in the literature, suggests a serious misunderstanding in the profession concerning the collection development experience and its relationship to other areas of librarianship.

Collection development, as it is known today, may be the newest department in a library's organization,[13] and as such it seems to suffer some confusion of definition and perception. After two to three decades, however, it does seem time to put these misperceptions to rest. Only education and training in the library, across the board, can remedy the situation. To deter feelings of isolation and loneliness, selectors need to understand and discuss the interrelationships of collection development and the other divisions of the library. During their particular training sessions, librarians not involved in collection development need to be made aware of the functions of collection development and its affinity to their primary responsibilities. Such exposure can dissipate counterproductive misconceptions, identify and emphasize the symbiotic nature of library duties, and create an environment where harmony replaces isolation in the pursuit of communal missions. For collection development, this state of affairs is essential if each individual's accomplishments, no matter how sophisticated, are to advance from the singular weakness of "book selection" to the collective strength of "collection development."[14]

According to Pitschmann, "A review of the literature leads one to conclude that there are apparently nearly as many organizational structures for collection development/management as there are libraries."[15] Gleason, however, better describes the current situation by stating that "the situation has changed noticeably since the 1950s when library selectors were typically area-studies bibliographers, who devoted their subject and language expertise to building collections on a full time basis." She characterizes contemporary selectors as "less likely to devote their time exclusively to selection. In fact, they often work only part-time in collection development, with a primary assignment elsewhere in the library."[16] Once a library has determined, as many seem to be doing, that decentralizing collection development responsibilities and distributing these among current on-line personnel is in the library's best interest, it should explain the decision and the events leading up to it to all current employees. In an enlightened environment, decentralization will already have been discussed in the various units, so that it will not come as a complete surprise to anyone.

Instead of then arbitrarily announcing position description changes or discussing such changes with prospective selectors, the library would find it advantageous to use an open forum to identify the specific areas in need of selectors and request volunteers, stating, of course, the prerequisites for each selector position. Such a system, or any variation on it, allows those truly not interested in collection development to refrain graciously from being drawn into an undesirable task. Employing auto-candidacy at this stage, rather than appointment from above, minimizes any assumptions of personality preference and subdues the potential for unwarranted and destructive competition. Naturally, collection development administrators should have educated themselves in the extra qualifications of employees and encourage those who may, through timidity or lack of experience, be reluctant to volunteer. The desired result of the exercise is, of course, coverage for as many disciplines as possible by current personnel who have the appropriate qualifications and/or have expressed an enthusiastic interest in selecting materials in a given area. Once fields of responsibility have been agreed upon, the task of familiarizing and integrating new selectors into the collection development process begins.

It is at this point that many libraries hand over a dollar amount to new selectors and consider the process complete. New selectors find themselves responsible for a given allocation, be it $200 or $200,000, and battered by waves of glossy fliers, pounds of commercial catalogs, dozens of patron requests, hundreds of selection slips, hours of review tools reading, and shelves of weekly approval plan books from which to select. No matter how talented the new person might be, a sense of drowning in relevant letters seems inevitable.

Some methodological form of training at this point is not just crucial but charitable. Julie Ann McDaniel suggests the implementation of a mentoring program to introduce new people to the world of selection.[17] Without a doubt such an arrangement would ease introduction into mainstream selection and significantly relieve feelings of isolation and anxiety. Yet the process contains certain inherent limitations. First, the prescribed coupling of a veteran and a novice suggests a teacher-student relationship and carries with it the restrictions imbedded in such an unidirectional canonical method of information transfer. Problems can easily arise because the model does not neatly apply to the situation. The new selector may be unaware of the methodologies of selection, but the mentor may be equally ignorant of the discipline(s) assigned to her or his mentee. Such a formalized one-to-one relationship may inhibit new collection development personnel from obtaining experienced or innovative advice from a host of other sources.

The initial learning experience in such a model is totally dependent on the knowledge gained and the ability to impart said knowledge by the mentor. Thus, the success of the program relies heavily on the premise that all mentors are well-versed, proficient teachers, a hypothesis highly unlikely to withstand the vagaries of reality. Finally, one must note that the pairing process is highly susceptible to the emotion-charged instabilities and foibles of personality—not the strongest of foundations on which to build an educational process.

Gleason adeptly remarks that "the new selector's training should encourage mutual support . . . allowing them to exchange information and ideas."[18] She goes on to suggest that "meetings of smaller groups, perhaps those in related disciplines in which the participants determine the agenda,"[19] might prove effective. Although each decision in book selection is an individual act, collection development for any given library is best defined as a group effort. It seems natural, therefore, that an understanding of the various, intricate components of the process are probably best achieved in a collective environment. Training new selectors might best be realized by employing a system of dual meetings.

At first it would prove profitable to new people to conduct a series of meetings attended by all personnel involved in selection where the universal aspects of collection development are discussed. One approach could be to have experienced bibliographers prepare brief reports introducing specific aspects common to all selectors and then open the floor to general discussion. Topics appropriate to such meetings might include profile development, approval plan selection, slip selection, faculty relationships, budget monitoring, serial-monograph acquisitions, gift collections, collection evaluation, weeding, rare books acquisition, general bibliographic publications, and trends in collection development.

Another series of smaller meetings, scheduled concurrently, could be planned around groupings of constituents according to similarities in selection disciplines. While the size of the collections, budget, and number of selectors should dictate the exact constitution of these groups, examples for a typical university library might include different meetings for selectors in the humanities, literatures, social sciences, sciences, and fine arts. Some libraries might find a special interest meeting for those heavily involved in foreign language acquisitions profitable also. These groups might address more specific functions and problems such as discipline priorities, publishing house evaluation, trends in research, duplication of effort, non-traditional sources of information, professional sources of relevant reviews, and group rankings of high-ticket items.

This system of double meetings provides a congenial, broad-based atmosphere for learning and for the exchange of ideas among collection development personnel. The process provides experienced selectors with a platform for expressing current practices. Simultaneously, they can rely upon other experienced people to enrich and enlarge upon their pronouncements for the benefit of all attending. In such a milieu, a new selector might feel more comfortable knowing that he or she is not the only person awaiting experience in the group. This should ease the educational process and efficiently diffuse common fumbles and encourage questions and comments, especially from the newer colleagues, whose fresh, original ideas could very well suggest innovative approaches to tenaciously held traditions. Most important, however, is the fact that such a training process would help to alleviate collection development isolation and to foster sympathetic feelings among the library employees, whatever their primary responsibilities.

The research cited in this chapter affirms the current decentralizing strategy of incorporating many librarians, not just full-time bibliographers, into the collection development process. However, confusion exists concerning the source of these new part-time selectors. Citing a 1986 ARL survey, Pitschmann believes the selection of selectors is diffused throughout the library. "Traditionally, part-time selectors have been reference librarians regardless of library type or size, but the 1986 ARL survey found that there was a move toward including part-time staff from non-public service units."[20] A year later, Cubberley's study showed this phenomenon was but short lived. "Although the American Library Association places Collection Development in its Resources and Technical Services Division, [Elizabeth] Futas states that most collection development is done by public services librarians. Futas is overwhelmingly supported in this survey."[21] Jeanne Sohn's survey substantiates these findings. "When the selector is not full-time, the other assignments vary greatly but focus on 'reference librarian' and 'branch librarian and/or department head.' "[22] Justification for this public services preference is often based on an ambiguous relationship between reference and collection development, yet often reference librarians are assigned selection responsibilities according to subject specialties they have achieved outside the reference arena.

Subject is not the only criterion used for materials selection. Other individuals in the library can provide significant advice, not subject specific, in deciding whether particular items should be purchased. Microforms librarians are probably the best-advised people in this unique and difficult area of publishing. Often microforms materials are exorbitantly priced, and querying an expert could elicit much pertinent information. For example, are similar sets available and being used? Are the materials available in another format? Microforms librarians can not only answer such questions but also comment on the reputation of a microforms publishing company.

Circulation librarians, also, maintain much significant information that could prove invaluable in the selection process. These individuals can generate detailed information concerning the types of materials and subjects that are consistently being used heavily and the types of users. They can identify materials that are quickly returned and those that are held for long periods of time. They can also learn which titles and subjects are no longer being requested by patrons. Of course, interlibrary loan officers can augment these data concerning requests for information outside the library system.

The learned opinions of technical services personnel could prove invaluable in interpreting cataloging information as a selection device. Their hands-on-experience in the processing of previously selected materials could be translated into a historical perspective pertinent to future selections. This division usually includes individuals accomplished in foreign languages. It is essential that these individuals be encouraged to work closely with subject selectors so that collections represent the best research from around the globe and are made available promptly.

Just as there is no library composed of only one book, so there is no function in the library that is unique to one individual. If the mission of a library is the collective dissemination of information, then performance of the obligations required to achieve that mission cannot be misanthropic by nature.

Collection development is not a profession unto itself but a subset of the profession known as librarianship. As such, all librarians, during the quotidian performance of their duties, gain information that could advance the collection development operation. It is the task of the library administration to create an environment that encourages this exchange of ideas and to perpetuate the enrichment process through the development of continuing education and training programs.

Planning is essential to the development of any successful training program, and it should be initiated by an examination of the tasks basic to collection development. In a study describing the allocation of human resources for collection development, Bonita Bryant identifies nineteen potential tasks.[23] Cubberley, in a survey of medium-sized academic libraries, lists sixteen collection development activities.[24] It is necessary for each library to evaluate and to assign priorities to these tasks for the beginning selector. The details of this list of job assignments will vary, not just from library to library but with each position within the same library. Adjustments will need to be made regularly because change, often from outside forces, is normal. However, the basic tasks of the selector should apply to most job situations.

Two written documents should be available as a basis for training. These are the bibliographer's/selector's manual and the collection development policy statement. The bibliographer's/selector's manual should help set the atmosphere for the collection development activities of the library. The

definition of the aims, tasks, and practices of the library's collection development program allows the beginning selector to interpret the priorities within
that program. It is important, especially to the selector with dual responsibilities, to clarify the administration of the program, which today so frequently
crosses traditional patterns of departmental organization. Questions such as
responsibility for training, the determination of time assignments, and the
preparation of performance evaluations must be addressed. The ARL Office
of Management Services has developed a SPEC (Systems and Procedures
Exchange Center) kit that presents the results of a recent survey of practices
related to the critical process of performance appraisals.[25]

To help in developing such a manual, a guide has been published by the
American Library Association (ALA).[26] Also available, as a practical model,
is the *Bibliographer's Manual* prepared at the General Libraries, University
of Texas at Austin.[27] This manual begins with a statement of the mission
and goals of the collection development program and thereby presents the
foundations for sound collection development procedures. The functions
and activities of the bibliographer/selector are then described in priority
order, followed by specific, but not inclusive, suggestions for implementation. The section on the administration of the collection development
program includes the responsibilities of the assistant director for collection
development and of the bibliographers, besides mechanisms for communication, recruiting, orientation, performance appraisal, and budgeting.
The appendices offer such specifics as position descriptions, an orientation
checklist, and a budget request form. It is emphasized that this document
is a "dynamic" one and, for in-house use, is published in looseleaf format.

The value of the written collection development policy statement has
received a much wider, and a much earlier, acceptance. Sheila Dowd has
described both the need and design requirements of such a document.[28]
Most frequently, it divides the collection into broad subject areas with
detailed subdivisions and assigns collecting values, such as pre-defined
levels of collecting and language requirements. This is the second important written local guideline to aid the beginning selector to meet his or her
responsibilities in collection development. It provides the foundation for
understanding the growth of the collection, past, present, and future. Like
the bibliographer's/selector's manual, as a living, changing document it
too should be available in looseleaf format.

The primary task is the selection of currently published monographic
and serial titles in a given subject area, and these two written documents
provide both the practical and the philosophical background for this activity. The new selector needs to understand this background to recognize how
his or her selection fits into that program. This understanding of the whole
should help avoid the dangers of myopic book selection, supposedly
eliminated when book selection responsibilities reverted from the faculty
to librarians. The collection development policy statement should also

clarify the levels of collecting in well-defined subject areas. The languages of materials, also any restrictions of format, need to be clearly explained. The growing trend toward interdisciplinary studies encourages consultation among selectors. The selection of titles in legal anthropology, for example, might require consultation between the selector of legal material and the selector of anthropology. These relationships should be highlighted for the new selector by references in the collection development policy statement. Finally, it must be emphasized that these statements are subject to regular review as programs and clientele undergo steady change.

Once a new selector is announced, a flood of selection tools miraculously appears on his or her desk. Jutta Reed-Scott describes the wide variety of selection tools available.[29] This material must be disposed of efficiently, and it is the selector who must make the decisions. For current selection, there are several tools that cover book publishing in the broad perspective. There are the standard book-trade publications, such as *American Book Publishing Record (ABPR)*, to aid in identifying titles published in the United States. Also available are national bibliographies, such as *British National Bibliography (BNB)*, although care is advised as to accuracy and thoroughness. The *ABPR* and the *BNB* are arranged by Dewey classification, which proves advantageous for selection in traditional, single subject specialties but does not so neatly correspond to the selection requirements of interdisciplinary subject areas. There are the many publishers' catalogs, often arranged by subject. Such catalogs contain additional information that can be helpful in making individual decisions. These can also be used to identify the book dealers who specialize in specific subjects. Flyers, brochures, and other advertisements serve a similar function in the selection of new publications. However, depending on the library's approval plans and the selector's understanding of the publishing trade, much of this paper can be discarded quickly.

Book review media provide another valuable source of information for decision making in book selection. Various types of review media are available. *New York Times Book Review, Times Literary Supplement*, and *New York Review of Books* publish a wide range of reviews that help the selector in keeping abreast of new trends and new authors. Review journals such as *Library Journal* or *Choice* offer another perspective on questionable titles. Most important are reviews from specialized subject journals. Each selector needs to recognize the major journals in his or her field and identify those journals with significant reviews. The weaknesses of this source of selection is the time lag between the publication of a title and its review and the limited number of books reviewed. In this age of short press runs and shorter stock backlogs, this method of book selection can create unpredictable gaps in the collection. Finally, the new selector needs to be reassured that a "bad" review does not automatically mean that the library should not acquire that title. A balanced collection is not developed by a selector's belief that he or she should be adding only the "good" books.

Domestic and foreign vendors, and, often but not always, approval plans, offer the new selector an additional source of information on new publications. Generally these slips are created with the book in hand so that with prompt action the librarian can expect to acquire that publication. The Library of Congress (LC) also publishes proof slips based on their cataloging output, including Cataloging-in-Publication and foreign language cataloging. Library of Congress proof slips can be selected by individual LC classification and are printed on individual cards, making them convenient to circulate among several selectors.

Because approval plans have become a major, widely accepted method of acquiring materials in the 1980s, it is important to orient the new selector to the role approval plans play in the library's collection development program. The selector needs to understand the profiles of the approval plans as they relate to his or her areas of responsibility. This includes an examination of how subjects are assigned by the vendor, when slips are to be sent instead of books, and any limitations stipulated in the profiles. Such limitations might include restrictions relating to the number of pages in the volume, the price, reprints or collections of works previously published, works based on theses, translations, textbooks, foreign language materials, editions of works, or even publishers who are not considered appropriate for the collection. Such limits would not mean the automatic exclusion of that title from the collection but would require the selector to make a specific decision on that title. With experience, the selector can be expected to suggest modifications to the profile. Reviewing approval plan books provides the new selector with an excellent introduction to the current trends in the publishing field. One difficulty selectors often face is that they do not immediately see the results of their recommendations. Approval plans present the opportunity to examine publishing output while immediately affecting the development of the collection.

Finally, all methods of book selection, including approval plans, require monitoring. The new selector must develop a workflow system that allows a reasonable time lag in the process to act as a monitoring device. Such procedures often require the efficient use of bibliographic searching of both in-house databases and those of national and international library networks. Therefore, it must be verified that the new selector has gained the necessary bibliographic searching skills.

The new selector is less likely to become involved quickly in the selection of retrospectively published titles. The selector must first develop an understanding of the strengths and weaknesses of the existing collection. He or she must also become familiar with additional selection tools such as out-of-print catalogs, the specialties of the used/rare book dealers, and the general nature of the out-of-print business. The potentials of desiderata files also need to be explored.

Fund management formulates another major segment of the training program for the new selector, who must understand the process of budget justification and allocation of funds within the library's budgeting system, especially if he or she will be a responsible participant in the development of this perennial report. A one-time budget justification might also be requested as a part of any evaluation of the collection. Monitoring of expenditures through the interpretation of the monthly fund balance is also important for the new selector. He or she must identify the major expenditure items, including the expenses incurred by serial and other standing orders, the nature of encumbrances on firm orders, and payments for the approval plans. Such reductions from the budget may leave insufficient funds available for the actual selection of new materials, creating a situation detrimental to a rational collection development program and the morale of the selector.

Effective liaison with other units within the library is an important component for successful collection development. An organized orientation program will aid the new selector in understanding his or her role in the entire process. This should advance the selector's knowledge of the important routines and everyday workflow in the order division, such as the placing of orders, the claiming of missing issues, the handling of delinquent orders, the processing of approval books, and the payment of bills. The new selector must recognize the need for the careful preparation of appropriate order forms, providing as much information as possible. Any processes built into the system, such as rush orders, priority cataloging, decisions relating to levels of cataloging, or early preservation decisions, should be explained. The role of gifts and exchanges, the value of circulation, and interlibrary loan studies and the potential of user surveys all need to be discussed with the new selector. The selector affects every part of the library's organization, so the more thoughtfully the orientation program is planned, the quicker the selector can make a contribution. This sense of positive feedback can only strengthen his or her performance.

The broader concept of collection management includes several more recently recognized tasks of collection development found in many libraries. The new selector needs to be aware of these responsibilities, although the level of involvement may vary. The processes of deselection include programs of weeding the collection and the cancellation of serial and other standing orders. It may include procedures for the transfer of lesser-used materials to a remote storage facility or a branch library site. Increasingly, in many libraries collection management reflects the growing concerns of preservation, as materials deteriorate in the library stacks. Therefore, the new selector must become familiar with the preservation policies of the library to comprehend the most effective means of preserving the collection.

Many responsibilities of the selector, such as the selection of out-of-print titles, budget justification, deselection, and preservation decisions, depend upon the library's practices of collection evaluation and are a response to the question, "Is the collection meeting the needs of the user?" If the library has an established program of periodic reviews of the collection, the details must be explained to the new selector. Outside forces also may be involved, such as the development of a network conspectus or a national shelf reading project.

A final important responsibility of the new selector is the establishment of effective relations with the academic department(s), including the teaching faculty and the students, both graduate and undergraduate. Initially, introductions to appropriate faculty members should be arranged and invitations to orientation meetings for the faculty and the department's students should be sought. Descriptions of course offerings should be reviewed. These contacts are essential to the understanding of the research interests of the academic community and allow the new selector to then prove how he or she can help these primary users more effectively employ the library's resources. An extra slip from the approval books can be used to notify a department of newly arrived titles. Faculty and students can be instructed to request needed titles through the appropriate selector. Assistance can be requested with budget preparation and collection evaluation. Finally, specialized bibliographies and library use instruction designed for specific courses may be developed. The rewards of strong relationships between the library and the academic departments are considerable, but the new selector must recognize that building these contacts can be a slow process, so persistence must be encouraged.

Information relating to other libraries, such as library network commitments or cooperative acquisition plans, needs to be identified. The new selector may benefit from being linked with a selector having similar responsibilities at a neighboring institution.

To some degree each of these tasks must be included in the new selector's training program. Order and emphasis will change with each position. Additional elements will need to be included and others eliminated. Each library will establish its own priorities to meet each job situation. The cornerstone to successful training is the preparation of a program that provides all selectors with the critical information needed to perform their collection duties, cultivates an atmosphere of shared responsibilities, and places the collection development process in a sympathetic relationship with all other aspects of the library environment.

NOTES

1. *Collection Development in Libraries: A Treatise*, ed. by Robert D. Stueart and George B. Miller, Jr., Foundations in Library and Information Science, vol. 10 (Greenwich, Conn.: JAI Press, 1980).

2. *Collection Management: A New Treatise*, ed. by Charles B. Osburn and Ross Atkinson, Foundations in Library and Information Science, vol. 26 (Greenwich, Conn.: JAI Press, 1991).

3. David Farrell, "Policy and Planning," in *Collection Management: A New Treatise*, 51.

4. Norman H. Dudley, "Organizational Models for Collection Development," in *Collection Development in Libraries*, 20–24.

5. Jeanne Sohn, "Collection Development Organizational Patterns in ARL Libraries," *Library Resources & Technical Services* 31 (1987): 123.

6. Ibid., 124.

7. Ibid., 127.

8. Ibid., 130.

9. Carol W. Cubberley, "Organization for Collection Development in Medium-sized Academic Libraries," *Library Acquisitions: Practice & Theory* 11 (1987): 298.

10. Maureen L. Gleason, "Training Collection Development Librarians," *Collection Management* 4 (1982): 3.

11. Cubberley, "Organization for Collection Development," 299.

12. Ibid., 320.

13. Louis A. Pitschmann, "Organization and Staffing," in *Collection Management: A New Treatise*, 131.

14. Ross Atkinson, "The Conditions of Collection Development," in *Collection Management: A New Treatise*, 31–32.

15. Pitschmann, "Organization and Staffing," 129.

16. Gleason, "Training Collection Development Librarians," 3.

17. Julie Ann McDaniel, "Leading the Way: In-House Collection Development Training for New Selectors," *Library Acquisitions: Practice & Theory* 13 (1989): 293–95.

18. Gleason, "Training Collection Development Librarians," 4.

19. Ibid.

20. Pitschmann, "Organization and Staffing," 133.

21. Cubberley, "Organization for Collection Development," 310.

22. Sohn, "Collection Development Organizational Patterns," 127.

23. Bonita Bryant, "Allocation of Human Resources for Collection Development," *Library Resources & Technical Services* 30 (1986): 149–62.

24. Cubberley, "Organization for Collection Development," 297–323.

25. Jack Siggins, *Performance Appraisal of Collection Development Librarians*, SPEC Flyer and Kit, no. 181 (Washington, D.C.: Office of Management Services, Association of Research Libraries, 1992).

26. American Library Association. Resources and Technical Services Division. Collection Management and Development Committee, *Guide for Writing a Bibliographer's Manual*, Collection Management and Development Guides, no. 1 (Chicago: American Library Association, 1987).

27. University of Texas at Austin, General Libraries, *Bibliographer's Manual*, Contributions to Librarianship, no. 7 (Austin: General Libraries, 1982).

28. Sheila T. Dowd, "The Formulation of a Collection Development Policy Statement," in *Collection Development in Libraries*, 67–87.

29. Jutta Reed-Scott, "Typology of Selection Tools," in *Collection Management: A New Treatise*, 301–11.

14

Continuing Education for Collection Management and Development: Professional and Survival Imperatives

Gay N. Dannelly

Commonly accepted characteristics of a profession include a specific body of knowledge conveyed through a professional school program, a professional association, dominance of individual achievement, and collective occupational orientation. To these can be added the need for continuing education. Professional practice, regardless of field, is not static. The best-prepared, most well educated library school graduate of ten, or even five, years ago is seriously hindered if he or she has not continued to learn. Practitioners need to keep up with developments in their social, political, and economic environments along with developments in their field.

Gay N. Dannelly suggests that continuing education is not only a professional concern, it is a matter of professional survival. She begins by exploring the changing environment that influences and affects collection management and then describes the responsibilities of collection management librarians. Effective execution of these responsibilities presents a challenge and an obligation: continuing development of knowledge and skills. Lifelong learning cannot be merely a buzz word used in community education catalogs.

Dannelly concludes her chapter with a list of opportunities for continuing education for collection development librarians. She suggests options that include, but are not limited to, courses, conferences, and institutes. Dannelly calls the less formal alternatives entrepreneurial opportunities and advises librarians to make the most of them. In these days of reduced travel budgets, entrepreneurial opportunities—particularly those available free electronically—may be our best option.

The rapid transformation of the methods and means of access to information and knowledge is changing the practice of librarianship fundamentally. Not only is this transformation changing the profession, it is affecting the nature of our collections dramatically and the responsibilities of the librarians who are charged with the stewardship of these resources. Continuing education is no longer "just" a professional concern, it is a matter of professional survival.

As society reconsiders and seemingly increases the value of information, not only for education and work but also for recreation, libraries are faced with decreasing financial, personnel, and operating resources and with concomitant increases in costs. In addition, rapidly expanding numbers and kinds of information sources, coupled with escalating equipment requirements to provide access, are multiplying the demands on already hard-pressed library budgets.

While attention is being lavished on new technologies and resources, the traditional formats continue to increase significantly in both cost and numbers produced. Although monograph publishing has been restrained somewhat by economic conditions, serials, media formats, and their costs have all increased, seemingly exponentially. In addition, "the uncertainty about durability of records in modern forms . . . means that the printed text (on durable paper) has a continuing role in preserving the records of our civilization."[1] The managers of library collections cannot ignore the past any more than they can ignore the developing records of contemporary society and the issues of capturing and fixing the historical record in electronic formats that are changing constantly.

These pressures make the nature of collection management and development a significant consideration for all libraries. The changing world of information requires that those responsible for collection management seek appropriate educational opportunities to enable them to deal more effectively with the expanding variety of information resources and the changing world of technology.

The literature on education for collection responsibilities is limited in its coverage, despite recent discussions on several electronic listservs. There is an even smaller literature on continuing education for collection management and development. During a recent review of *Library Literature*, from December 1984 to June 1992, only thirty-two articles addressed the specific issues of continuing education for collection management and development; this averages barely four articles a year in an area of significant growth within the discipline and of particular importance to those charged with managing financial resources. The issues have hardly been addressed. To identify the character of continuing education needs and opportunities properly, it is important to consider the present environment in which collection management and development occur, to understand the development of the subdiscipline and the institutional pressures that influence its nature, and to understand the professional context in which such education takes place.

INFORMATION AND KNOWLEDGE: GENERAL
CHARACTERISTICS OF THE CHANGING ENVIRONMENT

Charles Osburn has described the emphasis on context as a recognition of "the importance of the interrelationship between collection management and its environment, especially the influence of the latter upon the former."[2] He identifies several factors that influence this environment: "scholarly activity at the national level; the publishing industry; technological innovation and adoption; higher education policy; federal and foundation funding policy; the general economy; the academic and research library world; and the local community to be served."[3] In the non-academic community, the growing reliance on publicly available information resources, the local and regional economy, and the increasing appetite of the public and private sectors for electronic and traditional resources are also factors in the current milieu. A further influence on collection activity is the increasing reliance on cooperative arrangements to augment local resources. Cooperation has long been a hallmark of librarianship, but its effectiveness has been limited not only by local priorities and institutional competition but by the lack of adequate technology to provide identification of and access to needed information in a timely fashion. Richard Dougherty notes that "the importance of convenience and timeliness can hardly be overstated in a society so accustomed to rapid communication and online systems."[4]

Among the environmental concerns that influence the practice and process of collection management are several over which librarians have little or no control. The societal implications of "information as a social good versus information as an economic commodity" and the "information rich versus information poor" have been eloquently addressed by Ellen Detlefsen.[5] These differences—the value and the cost of information and the availability or unavailability of access to new information resources—are both social and professional issues of particular concern to librarians. Many libraries, committed to the provision of information to those who want it, find the current climate of privatization of government information, restrictive licensing by publishers, and unequal access to many forms of information (due to inadequate funding and an inadequate technological infrastructure) particularly difficult.

The maintenance and growth of established print collections, the additional applications of changing technology to traditional resources, along with the development of new kinds of information resources and consequent implications for broadened access and service, are a major challenge. As Michael Gorman notes, "New technologies do not always abolish previous technologies."[6] They certainly provide new demands on both services and budgets.

The changing technological capabilities of information resources are also changing the methodologies and foci of faculty and students. "Innovations in the ways scholars work and inventions of new technologies and new text forms challenge academic librarians to accept new responsibilities and to design new requirements for themselves."[7] With the typical library user's increasing reliance on information, these changes are of great concern to all libraries.

While it has always been important for the library to understand how it fits the priorities and needs of its constituents, it becomes increasingly imperative that the library and its staff "understand the mission and goals of their own institution . . . know how their library fits in the institutional design for supporting scholarship [and other library uses] . . . know how to manage the library as an effective, integral part of the local structure."[8] In the present evolving environment, the library and its collection management librarians must consider how the library's mission to provide information will be carried out. Detlefsen points out that the change is viewed in many places as "collections versus connections . . . how do libraries transform themselves from social institutions which collect forms of information into social institutions which connect users and information but without the physical collections of the past."[9]

Dougherty predicts that "at the heart of this transformation will be a fundamental change in what is expected of libraries. Researchers will attach more importance to locating and obtaining information and less importance to where the information was obtained."[10] Those charged with the responsibility for collection management and subsequent access must be aware, however, that if no public resource owns desired information, then access may be denied, very limited, unavailable, or simply disappear over time. It is this latter concern that is prompting the developments in shared electronic journal archives.

Libraries are generally considered responsible for "selecting, organizing, describing, preserving and disseminating texts or information, as well as with designing effective systems of access to texts and information."[11] The challenge is to carry out these responsibilities in a time when nearly all the practices that have governed the profession are in a state of flux. While change is fundamental to growth and development, the financial chaos and incredibly rapid change in information resources create a dilemma for libraries. These conditions suggest an important new role for libraries while simultaneously undermining their ability to carry out their present primary obligations. The potential strategic role of the library will increase if it is able to take advantage of these present developments. As Pauline Wilson has stated, "Information is not the best game . . . knowledge is."[12]

COLLECTION MANAGEMENT AND DEVELOPMENT: HISTORY AND CHARACTERISTICS

The subdiscipline of collection development and collection management has expanded and become established as a specialty in the profession over the last twenty-five years. Charles Osburn explains:

Now we are at the point of crossing the threshold to a new era in research and thought devoted to collection management . . . wherein the fundamental considerations are global accessibility, rather than local ownership, and the generic book, rather than the paper codex; wherein scholarly communication, rather than librarianship is our business, and distinctions between information and knowledge have a new importance. We will need to test old models, measures, and principles at a fortunate time when it seems likely that information systems made possible by technology will be of much greater value to collection management than they have been heretofore.[13]

Osburn's comments project a theoretical context for the evolution of collection management and development. Equally important are practitioners' current priorities to define present and short-term needs as they cope with decreasing resources, increasing responsibilities, and users' demands and to provide "the systematic, efficient and economic stewardship of the library's resources."[14]

The professional specialization of collection development is a relatively recent development in the evolution of librarianship. Although librarians traditionally held responsibility for selection of materials in public libraries, most academic libraries relied on faculty to select materials. Although many great university collections were formed during this era, most were narrowly focused and often the needs of students or of long-term, broad-based development were not addressed.

During the last forty years, however, bibliographers—subject specialists responsible for working with faculty and students and monitoring and selecting the most appropriate literature in support of specific subjects, programs, or constituents—have become prevalent in large libraries. During the past two decades, the assignment of collection responsibilities to specific librarians has been accepted widely at most academic institutions. This shift is reflected in changed staffing patterns as budgets decrease and bibliographer/selector assignments are combined with reference responsibilities. This has been particularly true in the research library setting. In addition, the collection development officer position has evolved, responsible not only for collection management but also for directing preservation activities and, more recently, public or technical services units.[15]

Paul Mosher has defined collection management librarians as "sociologists of library behavior, studying and establishing patterns of need for and use of library materials."[16] To carry out this role, they must analyze, evaluate, and contrast the expressed needs of users with the actual circulation and use of information resources. Automated systems may help with this analysis, but the knowledge required to ask the appropriate questions and interpret the resulting data will still demand an informed and experienced librarian. To participate in the evaluation of user needs, librarians must be very aware of the universe of information, the segments of that universe appropriate for most library user needs, the structure of those information resources, and methods of accessing other, less frequently needed, resources.

Several objectives must be accomplished to establish an effective collection management and development program. These include the following:

- Becoming knowledgeable about the information needs of the users of the library collections for which the selector is responsible
- Becoming knowledgeable about related collections in the library and elsewhere
- Developing consulting relationships with other selectors in these areas
- Assessing the collection, evaluating its contents for usefulness
- Identifying those materials that should be considered for addition to the collection, particularly new formats
- Establishing a collection management plan and development policy
- Consulting with users and colleagues as appropriate
- Evaluating the collection development policy against available resources
- Identifying priorities and, if necessary, developing a projection of unmet needs and costs of meeting those needs
- Establishing a collection management program
- Evaluating holdings for preservation, replacement, withdrawal, and housing in remote locations
- Evaluating the appropriateness and feasibility of interlibrary cooperative collection management agreements
- Reviewing and evaluating the acquisitions programs in place to determine if they are effective and appropriate
- Reviewing and evaluating the effectiveness of the collection development policy, including evaluating interlibrary loan requests and unfilled purchase requests
- Considering development possibilities through grant, gift and donation support[17]

THE NEED FOR CONTINUING EDUCATION

The changes in the library environment reflect changes in social, economic, and technological expectations, and they influence institutional, professional, and individual values, priorities, and expectations. To meet these expectations, or even to cope with them, librarians must be able to establish personal goals and objectives, not only to create a satisfying and useful career but to survive the rapid changes in the environment in which they work.

The American Library Association (ALA) midwinter 1992 meetings included an open hearing on the ALA Code of Professional Ethics. More than two hundred people attended the hearing, whose primary theme, running through the remarks of several speakers, was the need to recognize an ethical commitment to continuing education. This theme was not an issue solely for academic libraries, but was addressed by individual speakers from a variety of libraries and by representatives of associations within ALA. Given that librarianship is a profession, governed in principle by a code of ethics, the explicit value of continuing education is not just an issue of individual value; it must also be a significant concern for the institutions in which librarians work. The need for libraries to provide continuing education opportunities for their employees, at all levels, is particularly critical if libraries are not to be overtaken and left behind by the rapidly evolving information revolution. The ethics of providing skilled, up-to-date services and resources and of professional survival are directly linked in the minds and actions of many librarians.

Recently the Association of College and Research Libraries (ACRL) Professional Education Committee addressed the definition of the professional academic librarian. The association's definition applies not only to the librarian in an academic setting but to every librarian:

As professionals, academic librarians are characterized by the attributes identified in accepted and tested definitions of a professional. Besides mastery of specific areas of expertise and mastery of complex tasks, academic librarians are expected to use the principles, concepts, analytical techniques, and metholodologies of librarianship to identify and address problems facing the library and its user community and to plan for the future.[18]

The committee also addressed the issue of continuing education, stating that "education for the profession of academic librarian is a career-long process that begins in the master's degree programs in library and information studies . . . [but] librarians must then meet the challenge of maintaining and developing their knowledge and skills throughout their careers."[19]

In a recent communication on the electronic *Library Collection Development List*, Ruth Wallach noted that there was "no uniform way to manage a collection" and that many collection managers switch subject responsibilities over time.[20] Consideration of these points makes clear our need for a specific model by which to evaluate the needs and the opportunities for professional education.

A useful construct is to conceive of two parallel paths of education. The first is the education that is received in "traditional" library and information curriculums—that is, the presentation of theoretical bases and models and the underlying principles that govern a wide range of areas and methodologies for the analysis, evaluation, and development of problem-solving mechanisms. The second is the presentation of applications of theories—the translation of principles into practice and the employment of specific methodologies to specific situations resulting in improved processes and services.

Formal education, the M.L.S. and the Ph.D., should emphasize the first approach, using the second path to illustrate and clarify specific situations. Continuing education is more likely to concentrate on the second path, at least at the primary levels, although formal programs that return the librarian to the classroom or are specifically aimed at the extension of current knowledge certainly provide opportunities to expand theoretical approaches.

Detlefsen suggests that

our best strategy is (1) to work for a coordinated planning process, and (2) educate ourselves about advances in information technology. If we can be ready to partici- pate in the planning process and lead the way in using new technologies effectively and for the common good . . . [then] individuals, institutions, and governments are thus necessary for the efficient, effective and planned use of the information that flows around us.[21]

The changing universe of information and information services makes it crucial that librarians take full advantage of continuing education oppor- tunities. Although writing about academic libraries, in the following state- ment the ACRL Professional Education Committee was addressing the situation faced by all librarians:

The rapid development of library technologies and substantial expansion of the tools and services offered through . . . libraries are factors which make continuing education imperative. In selecting career-long educational opportunities, the pro- fessional judgment and dedication of an individual . . . librarian are also essential elements . . . librarians must then meet the challenge of maintaining and developing their knowledge and skills throughout their careers.[22]

THE PROFESSIONAL CONTEXT OF CONTINUING EDUCATION

There are a variety of means of expanding professional competencies, although many possibilities are usually not considered when defining continuing education. To expand and enhance collection management capabilities, librarians must seek both systematic and opportunistic means of continuing professional education.

Systematic Opportunities

The most consistent and important influence on collection management and development education has been the continuing role of a series of Collection Management and Development Institutes, sponsored by ALA's Association for Library Collections and Technical Services (ALCTS), for- merly the Resources and Technical Services Division. Based on a planning pre-conference held in 1977 in Detroit, the first of the institutes was offered at Stanford University in 1981. It was a successful attempt to begin a consistent educational program for the new specialty of collection management. It was followed the next year by an institute at George Washington University. Since then, institutes have been held irregularly and more than 1,100 attendees have taken advantage of the opportunities offered. Using a general outline of basic topics, each institute has varied in the specifics and the speakers. Many people have attended more than one due to the shifting treatments and the expansion of the curriculum. At the time of this writing, an advanced institute is being planned that will test the need for a more focused, higher-level curriculum directed at the experienced collection manager and collection development officer.

With the recent division of ALCTS's Resources Section into two separate sections—the Acquisition Section and the Collection Management and Development Section—opportunities for more continuing education programs should be enhanced. The establishment of ALA's Reference and Adult Services Division (RASD) Collection Evaluation and Development Section in 1988 has provided another venue for collection concerns aimed at those librarians whose primary responsibility is public service, but who also have collection management responsibilities.

In addition to these, other ALA divisions have programs at conferences that address collection management issues on either a regular or irregular basis. The Special Libraries Association, American Association of Law Libraries, and regional, state, and discipline-specific associations also often include programs of interest to collection management. This is becoming more frequent as collection management broadens its scope to include the delivery and preservation, along with the selection and acquisition, of information. The addition of cooperative and collaborative resource agreements also expands the horizons of concern as collection managers consider the implications, complementaries, and conflicts of access and ownership.

There are many conferences, institutes, and programs in collection management from a variety of sources offered regularly. Among the best known is the Charleston Conference, held each November at the College of Charleston, which combines acquisitions and collection development topics, particularly those issues related to vendor relations and materials costs. Another program with a continuing history is the University of Oklahoma Conference on acquisitions and collection development, held each February. Recently this conference has begun to change its focus to specific topics of primary interest to collection managers. Other regional institutes and conferences, like the Feather River Institute (held the last few years in May), offer possibilities for those interested in collection development topics. Fortunately for those unable to attend, most of the papers presented at these conferences are summarized or printed in full in the professional library literature.

The Research Libraries Group has a tradition of giving strong support to collection development for its members and has recently begun to give programs concentrating on the North American Collections Inventory Project (NCIP) for librarians from non-member institutions. OCLC, Inc., and its regional organizations, particularly AMIGOS, also occasionally provide programs on collection issues. The Association of Research Libraries (ARL) has a regular program of management institutes specifically directed at collection assessment and NCIP applications. The ARL Office of Scientific and Scholarly Publishing supports joint programs on information issues with the Society for Scholarly Publishing, American Council of Learned Societies, and recently with the American Mathematical Society.

To address issues of cooperative collection management and development and to define its role in these areas, the Center for Research Libraries offers tours, provides seminars at member and potential member institutions, and participates in programs to make its holdings and services better known to potential users. This is particularly useful for new bibliographers who may need orientation to the broad array of sources available for their patrons.

Besides the continuing education opportunities provided by professional organizations and associations, commercial organizations also develop programs of interest. The Faxon Institute, usually held in May each year, has proven to be an effective professional conference for addressing the identification of user needs and the implications of electronic information, and bringing together librarians, information providers, and information users.

Entrepreneurial Opportunities

Continuing education should be pursued not only in traditional ways; librarians should also be entrepreneurial in seeking such opportunities. Many regular activities are continuing education situations even if generally not perceived in that framework. Although there are undoubtedly many of these, the following are among the most readily available and most useful:

1. *Informational focus groups*. It is becoming common practice for library consultants to establish focus groups before surveying a wider selection of librarians about various issues. This is particularly true in acquisitions and collection development. Although these are primarily meant to be a means of gathering information for the consultants, such situations also can serve as educational opportunities.

2. *Advisory groups*. Several vendors and publishers have established advisory boards for everything from title selection for reprinting or digit-

izing to business practices. Electronic information vendors, in particular, are having "seminars" on product identification, development, and application in libraries. The meetings of these groups are excellent sources of information about collection priorities and practices.

3. *Library "Friends" groups.* Participation in a library's constituent and Friends groups also enhances the knowledge that a librarian brings to collection management. These can range from local book clubs to college department faculty meetings to Friends committee support. Each of these can improve the understanding of users' needs and preferences and can, perhaps, provide a chance to improve our users' understanding of the library.

4. *Library committees.* Committee service within the library and the home institution is also a superb educational opportunity. As staff resources decrease in many libraries, the role of committees has become stronger and more central to the running of the library. Committees offer a way to learn many things that are not within a particular position's direct responsibilities. Besides the need to represent collection management concerns, committee service is an excellent method of learning more about the library and the institution and their respective priorities, needs, and personalities.

5. *Professional associations.* Service on professional association committees is not only a means of education but a professional obligation. There are many associations and organizations that are important to collection management concerns. Not only library and information but also discipline and specific interest organizations provide means of enhancing professional competencies. These exist at the local, state, regional, national, and international level; each provides a particular and important layer of educational opportunity. Most librarians seem to view committee service as contributing to the profession, but service also contributes to and enhances an individual's professional development.

6. *Collegial interactions.* Visits to other libraries, vendors, publishers, and related organizations, no matter what kind of library one works in, are also great opportunities to broaden professional perceptions. Visits also can lead to cooperative collection management programs, improved publisher and vendor relations, and increased knowledge of available resources. Visits that provide direct interaction with staff also allow potential development of a broader professional network. These networks are not just of personal benefit but can help by providing an informal consultant pool for future reference.

7. *Electronic communications.* With the recent proliferation of electronic mail, another opportunity for continuing education has become a regular part of daily activities for many librarians. Listservs, rapid electronic communication, and networking with both known and unknown colleagues are presenting the profession with a remarkable tool for continuing education. Even for "lurkers," a network term for those who read but do not contribute

to listservs, the educational opportunities are enormous. Easy access to a remarkable variety of subject and interest areas provides a wealth of "consultants" that would not have been possible five years ago. The ability to provide greater numbers of digitized resources is of great benefit to our users, but it is also a challenge to the management of collections that are becoming increasingly dependent on rapidly changing technology. What could be more appropriate than using that technology to continue to educate ourselves in and about the changing world of information?

NOTES

1. Michael Gorman, "The Academic Library in the Year 2001: Dream or Nightmare or Something in Between?" *Journal of Academic Librarianship* 17:1 (1991), 4.

2. Charles B. Osburn, "Collection Development and Management," in *Academic Libraries: Research Perspectives*, ed. by Mary Jo Lynch with Arthur Young (Chicago: American Library Association, 1990), 25.

3. Ibid.

4. Richard M. Dougherty, "NEEDED: User-responsive Research Libraries," *Library Journal* 116 (January 1991): 62.

5. Ellen Detlefsen, "User Costs: Information as a Social Good vs. Information as a Commodity," *Government Publications Review* 11 (1984): 386.

6. Gorman, "The Academic Library," 6.

7. ACRL Professional Education Committee, "Education for Professional Academic Librarianship," *College & Research Libraries News* 53:9 (October 1992): 590.

8. Ibid.

9. Detlefsen, "User Costs," 386.

10. Dougherty, "NEEDED," 59.

11. ACRL Professional Education Committee, "Education," 591.

12. Pauline Wilson, "Mission and Information: What Business Are We In?" *Journal of Academic Librarianship* 14:2 (1988): 86.

13. Osburn, "Collection Development," 30.

14. Paul H. Mosher, "Collection Development in Collection Management: Toward Stewardship of Library Resources," *Collection Management* 4:4 (Winter 1982): 45.

15. Osburn, "Collection Development," 1.

16. Mosher, "Collection Development," 45.

17. See Mosher, "Collection Development," 46–47; and Bonita Bryant, "Allocation of Human Resources for Collection Development," *Library Resources & Technical Services* 30:2 (April/June 1986): 154, for further discussion.

18. ACRL Professional Education Committee, "Education," 591.

19. Ibid.

20. Ruth Wallach, "Education for Collection Development," *Library Collection Development List* [electronic listserv], moderated by Lynn Sipe (October 27, 1992). Available from: COLLDV-L@VM.USC.EDU.INTERNET or COLLDV-L@USCVM.BITNET.

21. Detlefsen, "User Costs," 390.
22. ACRL Professional Education Committee, "Education," 591.

SUGGESTED READINGS

Association of College and Research Libraries Professional Education Committee. "Education for Professional Academic Librarianship." *College & Research Libraries News* 53:9 (October 1992): 590–591.

Bone, Larry. "Noblesse Oblige: Collection Development as a Public Service Responsibility." In *Reference Services & Technical Services: Interactions in Library Practice*, ed. by Gordon Stevenson and Sally Stevenson, 65–73. New York: Haworth Press, 1984.

Bryant, Bonita. "Allocation of Human Resources for Collection Development." *Library Resources and Technical Services* 30:2 (April/June 1986): 149–162.

Detlefsen, Ellen. "User Costs: Information as a Social Good vs. Information as a Commodity," *Government Publications Review* 11 (1984): 385–394.

Dougherty, Richard M. "NEEDED: User-responsive Research Libraries." *Library Journal* 116 (January 1991): 59–62.

Gorman, Michael. "The Academic Library in the Year 2001: Dream or Nightmare or Something in Between?" *Journal of Academic Librarianship* 17:1 (1991): 4–9.

Gould, Constance. *Information Needs in the Humanities: An Assessment*. Stanford, Calif.: Research Libraries Group, 1988.

Mosher, Paul H. "Collection Development to Collection Management: Toward Stewardship of Library Resources." *Collection Management* 4:4 (Winter 1982): 41–48.

Osburn, Charles B. "Collection Development and Management." In *Academic Libraries: Research Perspectives*, ed. by Mary Jo Lynch with Arthur Young, 1–37. Chicago: American Library Association, 1990.

Wallach, Ruth. "Education for Collection Development," 27 October, 1992. *Library Collection Development List* [electronic listserv]. Moderated by Lynn Sipe (October 27, 1992). Available from: COLLDV-L@VM.USC.EDU.INTERNET.

Wilson, Pauline. "Mission and Information: What Business Are We In?" *Journal of Academic Librarianship* 14:2 (1988): 82–86.

Part V

IMPLICATIONS FOR THE FUTURE

15

Collection Development
in the Year 2025

F. W. Lancaster

What does the future hold for collection development librarians? This is, perhaps, the biggest question of all for those who have chosen a career in this specialty. F. W. Lancaster addresses this topic in a paper that surveys the views of several authors. He begins by identifying changes in collecting and accessing information sources that have occurred in libraries in the last few years and goes on to speculate on what collection development may mean at some future date.

Among the significant trends Lancaster notes are the following: Catalogs have become gateways to resources beyond the walls of individual libraries and the speed of developments is increasing with no signs of a future slowdown. Libraries have always been dependent on development in the publishing industry and in scholarly research and communication—but now they face the radical possibility that scholarly publication could become the direct responsibility of universities and other research institutions. Although the role of the library has the potential to continue to be as important as in the past, care must be taken that alternatives to it are not glorified as able to perform information services libraries are limited or bound by the tradition to provide.

He stresses that the library must continue to take a lead in the exploitation of information sources in electronic form, at the same time acknowledging the problems of doing so. Electronic resources present problems—problems of integrating them with more traditional forms, problems of costs of acquisition versus access, and the most critical problem of determining what "collection development" really means in an electronic environment. The role of collection development in dealing with distributed electronic sources may be little different from the print-on-paper world. However, the processes involving remote resources are where the future is less clear. Several options are explored—node, mediation point, or selecting, downloading, and protecting sources, gatekeeper—and the ultimate importance of resource sharing, archiving, and preservation is thoughtfully assessed.

In 1976 the author presented a paper in Helsinki that predicted that technological developments would cause scholarly communication to become
increasingly "paperless."[1] This was expanded upon in books published in
1978 and 1982.[2] In the scenarios presented, the library was seen as becoming
increasingly "disembodied," meaning that access to electronic information
resources would to a large extent replace ownership of physical artifacts.

These ideas were not widely accepted by librarians in the 1970s. Today,
however, access rather than ownership has become virtually the motto of
the profession. For example, a recent Research Libraries Group (RLG)
report refers to the "transition from the physical library to the logical
library."[3] The authors of the report, Richard Dougherty and Carol Hughes,
point out that "the concept of the virtual library, i.e., a library that provides
access to electronic and print materials from many sources, both local and
remote, has achieved a widespread popularity."[4] In the same report, Jim
Michalko stresses that the research library "must move with minimal
disruption from a library model directed primarily at ownership of materials to one in which access and delivery play a more central role."[5]

This message has been presented, in one form or another, by others
prominent in the library field. For example, David Penniman argues that
libraries must be active, not passive, emphasizing the delivery of information rather than its storage.[6] Maurice Line agrees that libraries should be
evaluated based on the services they provide rather than the collections
they own,[7] and Kenneth Dowlin refers to the need to transform the library
from a "fortress" to an information "pipeline."[8]

This chapter will look at the changes that have occurred in libraries in
the last few years, in terms of the collecting and accessing of information
sources, and will speculate on what "collection development" may mean
at some future date—perhaps the year 2025. The views of other authors will
be surveyed and the emphasis will be on the academic library.

It is obvious that electronic technologies have already had considerable
impact. Virtually all libraries, at least in the most-developed countries, are
members of networks that greatly ease locating sources of information and
gaining access to them. Card catalogs have largely been replaced by online
catalogs, and these are being expanded through the inclusion of materials
not previously included. The whole idea of what a catalog should be is
changing; it is no longer seen as a tool bounded by the collections of a single
library but one that reveals the availability of resources in a network of
libraries or even one that is essentially a gateway to a universe of information resources in printed, electronic, or other forms. Use of terminals or
workstations to access databases of various kinds is now routine for many
libraries, and most libraries now add electronic resources to their collections in CD-ROM or other forms.

These developments have occurred with surprising speed, suggesting that the changes of the next decade will be more dramatic and rapid than those of the past decade, a point made clearly by James Govan:

It is startling to realize that in 1983, as I recently read, no library owned a CD-ROM. . . . When one thinks of the widespread use of them today, one wonders about the future proliferation of other forms of digitized information: intelligent workstations, optical scanners and optical discs, expert systems, artificial intelligence, hypertext, broadbands and satellites, and local area networks (LANs) and other kinds of networks, as well as devices yet unknown.[9]

That this electronic revolution in libraries has occurred, of course, is due to developments over which the library profession has had little direct control, most obviously the growth of electronic publishing and of networks that facilitate scholarly communication—BITNET, Internet and, in the future, the National Research and Education Network.[10]

Of course, some libraries have been much faster than others in turning the technology to their advantage and thus offering innovative services to their users. One that has been at the forefront is the Butler Library at Columbia University. Its Electronic Text Service (ETS), established in 1987–88, integrates electronic primary research materials into the library's collections and services. ETS includes several thousand texts and hypermedia research tools in many languages.[11]

ELECTRONIC PUBLISHING AND SCHOLARLY COMMUNICATION

What happens to the library in the future will to a very large extent depend on developments in related sectors, most obviously the publishing industry. One must assume that the proportion of the world's publications issued in some electronic form will increase and, thus, the proportion issued as print on paper will decline. Less clear is the form that the electronic publishing will take. How much will consist of resources that can be accessed only through networks and how much will actually be distributed, for purchase or lease, as CD-ROM, videotape, videodisk, electronic book (e.g., the SONY Data Discman), or formats yet to be devised?

Of course, what happens to the format depends on what occurs in the creative process itself. Electronic publishing is still in a largely "simulation" stage of development in that most authors tend to think in terms of the static printed page and the static illustration.[12] Hypertext and hypermedia capabilities free the author from static representation, allowing publications that are dynamic and interactive. In the future, authors, whether research scientists or poets, will increasingly exploit the full capabilities of the electronic media (sound, movement, animation, simulation, color, and so on), thus changing the nature of many publications and determining the format in which they are best issued. The truly dynamic and interactive publication brings with it other important implications, not least of which is the fact that it cannot be printed out on paper.

The subject of electronic publishing cannot be divorced from the broader issues of scholarly research and communication. Scholarly endeavors are being profoundly affected by technology. As Edward Shreeves points out, "The emergence of machine-readable texts, of computer-based networks, and of all the attendant technological apparatus, has provided the means to alter radically scholarly communication and scholarly method."[13] Shreeves was speaking specifically of the humanities, but the observations are also true of the other disciplines, perhaps even more so.

The influence of technology on scholarly research extends much further than the obvious effects of word-processing capabilities. Scholars now use a variety of networks to access sources needed in their research, to exchange information with colleagues, and to collaborate with them in research and publishing activities. Some more subtle changes are also taking place. The scholarly journal in printed paper form has not yet been replaced by electronic journals, although experiments with new electronic forms continue and electronics obviously offers the potential for more effective dissemination of information—for example, journals tailored to individual interests. What has happened is that network resources have caused a significant increase in informal communication—informal "journals" now exist within electronic mail and computer conferencing facilities. Such resources diminish the role of the conventional printed journal as a vehicle for the dissemination of research results; increasingly it exists solely to satisfy social (publish-or-perish) and archival requirements.[14] One obvious sign of the increasing importance of the informal electronic sources is the fact that we now see them cited in the conventional printed journals.[15]

The existence of text in electronic form even alters the nature of scholarship. For example, Shreeves has mentioned how the ability to manipulate text by computer has changed the types of research that can be undertaken and the types of research questions that can be asked. This point has also been made strongly by Marianne Gaunt:

The potential research activities using the electronic version of a text are limited only by the interest and ingenuity of the individual researcher. As social science data in machine-readable form is valuable to the researcher for analysis of trends, for hypotheses and conclusions, so too is the literary text in machine-readable form for similar ends, and for particular work perhaps even more valuable.[16]

The changes in scholarship that have occurred so far may be merely cosmetic compared with changes that could take place in the future. Most radical is the possibility that scholarly publication could become the direct responsibility of the universities and other research institutions. This possibility has been clearly described by William Britten:

Virtually every college and university requires publication as evidence of scholarly achievement and the advancement of knowledge. Sustaining the publishing process is not only in the self-interest of academic institutions, but is also their obligation. In the current publish-or-perish model, the academic community has hired the commercial sector to provide editorial review, indexing and abstracting, printing, and distribution of faculty publications. However, the continuing trend toward cancellation of journal subscriptions indicates that the costs of the practice of paying scholars to produce knowledge and then paying a second time to acquire it from publishers needs reevaluation.[17]

ROLE OF THE LIBRARY

The library profession does seem fairly unanimous in the belief that libraries and librarians will continue to have important functions to perform vis-à-vis electronic resources. Indeed, several writers have warned that unless the library takes a lead in this, its role will be usurped by other bodies—other departments on a campus or other organizations entirely. For example, Margaret Johnson has said:

Libraries, in their central role as providers and organizers of information, cannot afford to ignore computer files or to approach them in a piecemeal fashion. To do either places the library at risk of becoming less valuable to and less supportive of the academic community. Libraries will no longer be regarded as the focal point for information as more of it slips outside their purview. Researchers will no longer think of the library as the first resort because they will be unable to depend on its catalogs, collections, and directional tools to provide access to the universe of information resources. The library's significance to the administration will diminish as well.[18]

A similar message has been delivered by Ralph Alberico:

If we don't become involved at all levels, there is a very real possibility that resources will shift to other segments of the economy that can deliver the electronic services that academic and post-industrial organizations will need to survive. It is already happening in some places.[19]

D. W. Lewis has also pointed out that users will demand more from the library than they have in the past:

Students may expect the library to be as powerful and easy to use as electronic teaching tools. Unfortunately, libraries are rarely easy to use. If analysis with new computer tools becomes easier and more productive than library research, students can be expected to use the new tools rather than the library. If libraries do not improve their services so that they remain an essential teaching tool, they risk becoming irrelevant to the teaching process. If this is allowed to happen, it is easy to predict a decline in library funding.[20]

Finally, one should recognize the fact that the compilers of one influential report seem to feel that it is almost inevitable that the library will decline. John Martyn and others suggest that individual academic departments will provide their own electronic resources and the library will decay into little more than a study hall.[21]

COLLECTION DEVELOPMENT AND MANAGEMENT

Given that the library *must* continue to take a lead in the exploitation of information sources in electronic form, what exactly does this imply for collection development? Obviously, electronic resources, particularly those that can be accessed only when the need for them arises, present a set of problems that have not been encountered by librarians in the past. As Alberico points out: " 'Collecting' electronic information is more problematic than collecting printed texts. And, as we all know, collecting printed texts is not without its own problems."[22] Erwin Welsch warns that the entire approach and philosophy of collection development must change: "Simply duplicating the collection practices we evolved for print materials in the network environment does not seem responsive to current needs or capabilities."[23] Nevertheless, collection development, whatever form it takes, still requires policies, as Craig Summerhill has noted: "The advent of networked resources does not eliminate the need for a formal policy governing the acquisition of electronic resources."[24]

An obvious challenge is the problem of how to integrate electronic resources with more traditional forms. The need for complete integration seems taken for granted by librarians and library users alike, at least in the scholarly community, as Dougherty and Hughes report, "Provosts and librarians . . . prefer a future in which there is universal access by faculty and students to multiple information sources in all possible media via a single multifunctional workstation."[25]

Mary Ghikas points out that the future library must be a combination of "actual" and "virtual" materials:

The twenty-first century collection will, I believe, be an accumulation of information-bearing objects—printed, aural, graphic, digital—housed within the physical library, *and also* indices, abstracts and catalogs through which, using electronic channels, the library user has access to *pre-identified* resources held by other libraries and information providers. The twenty-first century "collection" thus combines the actual and "virtual" collection. The "virtual collection" is an *electronically browsable* collection. In contrast, tomorrow's library, like today's, will go beyond the limits of its own collection—*both* actual *and* virtual—in response to specific information requests. In this case, neither location nor delivery time and channel will be preidentified.[26]

The integration issue is also dealt with by Welsch:

Technology and technological resources need to be integrated as closely as possible with traditional resources within a unified approach to information founded on principles derived from studies of information seeking and use. Users want to be able to identify information through one access point and not through a series of separate catalogs or information utilities with varying search strategies and command structures that complicate as much as they help. Until a search device, a dynamically updated online guide, or satisfactory resource guides are created, we will have to continue to depend on that hypermedia, intelligent (but not artificial), semi-robotic system that is known as a "librarian."[27]

An obvious problem in collection development is that of the costs involved in acquisition or access. John Haar has pointed out that reference sources in optical disk form are very popular with library users, yet they tend to be more expensive than their print counterparts.[28] The addition of several optical disk systems might well mean that monograph purchases would have to be further reduced, perhaps drastically, in many libraries. Moreover, one must recognize the fact that different formats actually interact with each other. For example, an index to periodicals in CD-ROM form may increase demand for periodicals in printed form.

It is true, of course, that electronic resources, particularly network-accessible resources, are economical in space. However, the saving in space is unlikely to compensate for cost increases elsewhere. Moreover, while the costs of computer/telecommunications technologies have obviously declined dramatically, and are likely to continue to do so, such cost reductions do not apply to all the technologies of concern to libraries. The equipment needed to implement hypermedia systems is very expensive, and it will be for a long time.

Another consideration is that in the electronic world, libraries have much less to show for their expenditures. Some resources are leased rather than owned, and others do not exist within the library at all. The bodies that fund libraries must recognize and accept this fact.

It is undeniable that access to electronic resources reduces the funds available to acquire other formats. As Shreeves indicates, "Taking the cost of electronic information from current resources is not a pleasant prospect, but it may be the only strategy available for many."[29]

It is Govan, however, who has been most forceful in warning of the economic dangers facing the library in a research setting:

If any transformation of our present intricate system of acquiring materials should come about, it would change drastically both the practices and the structure of academic libraries. The larger point is that the present system is not working economically for those libraries. The combined costs of assimilating electronic technology, recent printed materials, and preservation, have eaten deeply into their infrastructures. For all the professed recognition of information as a commodity, legislators and university administrators have offered little relief, and much of the new funding seems to have gone to computing services elsewhere on campus. Any prognostication about libraries' future would be irresponsible if it did not lay heavy emphasis on their perilous fiscal state today and the economic problems that lie ahead. All that we have discussed carries a large price tag, and the parent institutions must face the question squarely as to the very considerable costs of supporting a contemporary academic library in a world awash with information.[30]

He goes on to suggest that libraries will become vastly more expensive or they will become useless.

Costs are not the only issues facing the collection development librarian. Gaunt identifies other significant problems:

1. Finding out what is available,
2. Evaluating the sources available, and
3. Acquiring and servicing the sources required.[31]

As she explains, electronic resources are not adequately controlled bibliographically, they are not easy to identify, and they are not well reviewed. The problem has also been recognized by Shreeves:

A major obstacle for the selector of electronic texts is the difficulty of defining the available universe. The usual selection tools (reviews in scholarly journals, national bibliographies, publishers' catalogs, etc.) do not cover such resources effectively, nor is there a developed system of publication and distribution. Finding out about electronic texts requires attention to a number of specialized sources of information.[32]

The critical problem, of course, is access and what collection development really means in an electronic environment. Jutta Reed-Scott, for example, sees the role of the collection developer as altering dramatically: "Because electronic texts are fluid and interactive and are changed frequently, it will be difficult to capture information. Building collections will move from a static process of acquiring library resources to a more fluid position of providing access to information."[33]

Sheila Creth claims that the collection development librarian will continue to do many things he or she is now doing, at least in the foreseeable future, but also will take on new responsibilities:

The context for the future library suggests that rather than relinquishing functions that are currently an integral part of university library activities (e.g., selecting and organizing materials, assisting and educating users in locating information) these will continue, although in different ways, along with new activities that will emerge.[34]

In dealing with electronic sources that are distributed, of course, the collection development role is little different from the situation in the print-on-paper world, although some sources acquired may not really be "owned" by the library. It is in dealing with the remote sources, those that can be accessed only through telecommunications, that the collection development function becomes ambiguous. Ross Atkinson, for example, raises the important question, "What role does the research library play, if most research consists primarily in the searching and downloading of information from a distant database by a scholar at a personal workstation?"[35]

He hopes that libraries will restructure their operations around three basic functions: mediation, primary record definition, and secondary record definition. *Mediation* involves helping users to identify needed information and to download this to local storage facilities. In a sense, this can be considered as a kind of deferred collection development operation—locating information sources as they are needed rather than trying to predict the needs in advance. Nevertheless, some prediction will be required, according to Atkinson. The *primary record definition* role Atkinson identifies would consist of identifying resources that are likely to be of greatest interest locally and downloading these to a local database. His *secondary record definition* function is the most unconventional; it is an uploading rather than a downloading activity. In essence, the library becomes the publisher and disseminator of scholarly information:

When a scholar at an institution has written something which is deemed by a select group of peers to be worth communicating broadly to other scholars, that communication should take place by the library's uploading that publication into the library database, thus disseminating it to other libraries, and thereby to other scholars, throughout the nation and the world. The ultimate purpose of the academic library is to provide bibliographic support for education and to serve as a basis for communication among scholars—in short, to disseminate significant information. . . . The library—in conjunction with the computer center and the academic press—must assume direct responsibility for disseminating information among scholars. Providing scholars with the channels through which to communicate, working with scholars to establish the technical and bibliographical standards and procedures for online publication in this fashion— these are responsibilities which should therefore also be assumed by the library in the online era.[36]

The mediation role, in one form or another, is one that seems fairly widely accepted. Welsch describes it in these terms:

This is where librarians should find their niche: identifying resources regardless of format and encouraging suppliers of network information to make their products readily and easily available. Focusing their future role not on being a warehouse of electronic or printed information, but on becoming an information utility that locates data in diverse sources seems more appropriate.[37]

The view that libraries should build local databases from network resources elsewhere is not one that appears widely held. More commonly, the library is seen as more of a switching center, possibly also having such value-added responsibilities as user education. For example, Britten has said: "Libraries should not think primarily in terms of collecting information stored on networks, but should instead pursue strategies for teaching users how to locate and retrieve this information."[38] This agrees with several prominent librarians who see the library of the future as primarily a node in a vast information network. F. G. Kilgour, for example, believes that a major function of such a library node will be to build local indexes to aid users in accessing remote sources.[39] Atkinson, on the other hand, claims that the view of the library as a switching center is a shortsighted one:

What we have perhaps failed to recognize, however, is that the library must also continue to maintain its responsibility for record definition—for collecting . . . and thereby stabilizing that information for future reference. The most serious error the library could make at this time would be to assume that its role in a predominantly online environment will be mainly that of a switching point. That role as switching point belongs not to the library side, but rather to the computer center side of information service. The library's function has always been—and will remain regardless of changes in technology—to select, stabilize, protect, and provide access to significant or representative graphic texts.[40]

Atkinson is supported in this by Summerhill:

Clearly, groups of local users will have an ongoing need for the proximate location of heavily used data. Thus, achieving a balance between local "collections" of heavily used electronic resources and the provision of network access to less frequently used resources should be the goal of the library acquisition process in a networked environment.[41]

A few other writers agree with Atkinson's view that the library, in association with other segments of the research community, should become publisher and disseminator of information. Welsch has said: "Yet, the concept of individuals and organizations, including libraries, as self-publishers of new information, who would then make it available through networks, is so tantalizing that I am reluctant, despite obstacles, to surrender it."[42]

Alberico is more specific:

The "electronic book" of the future is as likely to be a composite as it is to be a single coherent entity. Scholars will compile their own electronic books by gathering separate pieces of information from different parts of the network. Libraries may become publishers simply by using the network to build customized multimedia documents for clients or by providing the technology, training, and facilities to allow clients to build their own composite documents.[43]

To become an effective creator and disseminator of new information composites, the library must be more active than it is now. In the words of Welsch: "Unfortunately, the image that emerges for me when I think of scholarly societies, universities, and libraries and their roles in the creation of information systems of all kinds is, with rare exception, one of passivity."[44]

One specific problem to be faced in the future is how to deal with electronic journals, assuming that these journals are accessible through networks. Michael Stoller identifies three options:

In simple terms, those options are: first, to print the journal either directly from the online file or with the intermediate step of a download and manipulation by word processing software; second, to download the online file to an electronic medium, usually a diskette, manipulate the file with word processing software, and provide access through personal computers; third, to maintain the file on a mainframe computer and provide access through a local area network.[45]

He goes on to discuss the pros and cons of each of these options. Unfortunately, he seems to assume that electronic journals will be little more than print on paper displayed electronically. If, as seems likely, completely new forms emerge—for example, with analog models or other forms of animation—certain options, such as printing out on paper, remove themselves from consideration.

The University of Pennsylvania libraries concluded, perhaps not surprisingly, that there is no one best method of providing access to machine-readable data files.[46] All forms of access—remote time sharing, CD-ROM, and locally mounted files—are needed. Factors influencing the choice for a particular set of data include timeliness, expected volume of use, the probable number of simultaneous users, and whether remote access (from offices, laboratories, classrooms, and so on) is needed.

ARCHIVING AND PRESERVATION

Preservation of materials is an important facet of collection management. What are the library's responsibilities for preservation in an electronic environment? Summerhill seems to believe that libraries collectively should strive to preserve almost everything communicated: "Computer conference logs, electronic serials, even archived exchanges of electronic mail transmissions may all be appropriate for a library to acquire and preserve, given sufficient interest on the part of the user community."[47]

He goes on to defend the position that even "ephemeral" communications need preservation:

Those who doubt the suitability of personal exchanges of electronic mail might consider what value such materials would be to a historian of the twenty-first or twenty-second century faced with the task of restructuring the correspondence of an individual (or organization) who ceased writing letters on paper late in the twentieth century.[48]

A very similar claim has been made by Stoller.[49] Not everyone holds this view. For example, Shreeves, quoting a speaker at a Symposium on Scholarly Communication held at the University of Iowa in 1991, introduces the argument that not all communication among scholars is scholarly communication and that much of what is transmitted by electronic mail or computer conferencing is nothing more than "high level, high-tech cocktail party conversation"; only peer-reviewed communication can be considered scholarly and thus worth preserving.[50]

RESOURCE SHARING

Technology has already had a profound beneficial effect on resource-sharing activities. What form will this take in the future? Few doubt its importance. For example, Dougherty and Hughes report: "It was also observed that libraries and library services were no longer individual university problems and that a collective approach is now absolutely essential."[51]

Summerhill has given some specifics:

Striking the delicate balance between local ownership and network access will be aided by, if not achieved by, a formal acquisition process that accounts for network access. Librarians must shift the focus of their acquisition policies from the collection of materials by and for an individual library to policies that weigh the merit of acquiring the same resource by consortia of local libraries, regional library cooperatives, and/or state library networks. The funding agencies that back libraries must come to accept this type of cooperative venture. At the same time, vendors of commercial data products must understand the imperative facing libraries to enter cooperative collection development agreements. Accordingly, they must develop fee structures that accommodate such ventures.[52]

To what extent will what we now think of as an interlibrary loan (though most of it is not) continue in the future? The topic is dealt with by Stoller:

Electronic sources, at least those remotely accessible, do not need to be acquired, nor do they need selection. Instead, the selection activity is of a different kind: librarians select what to access to satisfy a known demand rather than what to purchase in anticipation of future demands.[53]

To a very large extent, he still agrees with this. However, in the last ten years, and particularly in the last two or three, the profession has given much more thought to what collection development and collection management really mean when electronic communication is the focus of attention. As we have seen in this chapter, views range from the librarian as primarily mediator between users and network resources to the librarian as creator and publisher of new information resources.

One does not really know what the world will look like in 2025. It is possible that the whole system of scholarly communication will be very much different from the situation today. Shreeves considers the collection development librarian as primarily a gatekeeper—one who identifies that portion of the universe of information resources that is likely to be of greatest value to a particular user or group of users.[54] Whatever happens to scholarly communication, and whatever happens to the library as an institution, clearly gatekeepers of this type will still be needed in the future. Indeed, they will be even more important than they are today.

NOTES

1. F. W. Lancaster, "The Dissemination of Scientific and Technical Information," *Proceedings of the 1976 Conference of NordData* (Helsinki: NordData, 1976).

2. F. W. Lancaster, *Toward Paperless Information Systems* (New York: Academic Press, 1978), and *Libraries and Librarians in an Age of Electronics* (Arlington, Va.: Information Resources Press, 1982).

3. Richard M. Dougherty and Carol Hughes, *Preferred Futures for Libraries* (Mountain View, Calif.: Research Libraries Group, 1991).

4. Ibid., 4.

5. Ibid., 2.

6. David W. Penniman, "Shaping the Future for Libraries through Leadership and Research," in *Libraries and the Future: Essays on the Library in the Twenty-first Century*, ed. by F. W. Lancaster (New York: Haworth Press, in press, 1993).

7. Maurice B. Line, "Libraries and Information Services in 25 Years' Time: A British Perspective," in *Libraries and the Future*.

8. Kenneth E. Dowlin, "The Neographic Library," in *Libraries and the Future*.

9. James F. Govan, "Ascent or Decline? Some Thoughts on the Future of Academic Libraries," in *The Future of the Academic Library: Proceedings of the Conference Held at the University of Wisconsin in September 1989*, pp. 24–44. Graduate School of Library and Information Science Occasional Papers nos. 188 & 189, ed. by Eugene P. Trani (Urbana: University of Illinois, Graduate School of Library and Information Science, 1991), 24.

10. See Brett Sutton and Charles H. Davis, eds., *Networks, Open Access, and Virtual Libraries: Implications for the Research Library* (Urbana: University of Illinois, Graduate School of Library and Information Science, 1992), for a full discussion of the network picture.

11. Anita Lowry, "Electronic Texts in English and American Literature," *Library Trends* 40 (Spring 1992): 704–723, and her "Machine-Readable Texts in the Academic Library: The Electronic Text Service at Columbia University," in *Computer Files and the Research Library*, ed. by Constance C. Gould (Mountain View, Calif.: Research Libraries Group, 1990), 15–23.

12. F. W. Lancaster, "Electronic Publishing," *Library Trends* 37 (Winter 1989): 316–325.

13. Edward Shreeves, "Between the Visionaries and the Luddites: Collection Development and Electronic Resources in the Humanities," *Library Trends* 40 (Spring 1992): 579.

14. A. Herschman, "The Primary Journal: Past, Present, and Future," *Journal of Chemical Documentation* 10 (February 1970): 37–42.

15. See, for example, the Spring 1992 issue of *Library Trends*.

16. Marianne I. Gaunt, "Machine-readable Literary Texts: Collection Development Issues," *Collection Management* 13:1/2 (1990): 89.

17. William Britten, remarks in "Symposium on the Role of Network-based Electronic Resources in Scholarly Communication and Research," ed. by Charles W. Bailey, Jr., and Dana Rooks, *The Public-Access Computer Systems Review* [serial online] 2:2 (1991): 50. To retrieve this article, send an e-mail message to LISTSERV@UHUPVM1 (Bitnet) or LISTSERV@UHUPVM1.UH.EDU (Internet) that contains the command GET BAILEY PRV3N2 F-MAIL.

18. Margaret Johnson, "Adding Computer Files to the Research Library: Issues in Collection Management and Development," in *Computer Files and the Research Library*, ed. by Constance C. Gould (Mountain View, Calif.: Research Libraries Group, 1990), 12.

19. Ralph Alberico, remarks in "Symposium," 6.

20. D. W. Lewis, "Inventing the Electronic University," *College & Research Libraries* 49 (July 1988): 293.

21. John Martyn, Peter Vickers, and Mary Feeney, eds., *Information UK 2000* (London: Bowker-Saur, 1990).

22. Alberico, remarks in "Symposium," 36.

23. Erwin K. Welsch, remarks in "Symposium," 44.

24. Craig A. Summerhill, remarks in "Symposium," 41.

25. Dougherty and Hughes, *Preferred Futures for Libraries*, 3.

26. Mary W. Ghikas, "Collection Management for the 21st Century," *Collection Management* 11:1/2 (1989): 123.

27. Welsch, remarks in "Symposium," 26.

28. John M. Haar, "The Reference Collection Development Decision: Will New Information Technologies Influence Libraries' Collecting Patterns? *Reference Librarian* 22 (1988): 113–124.

29. Shreeves, "Between the Visionaries and the Luddites," 581.

30. Govan, "Ascent or Decline?" 37.

31. Gaunt, "Machine-readable Literary Texts," 92.

32. Shreeves, "Between the Visionaries and the Luddites," 587–588.

33. Jutta Reed-Scott, "Information Technologies and Collection Development," *Collection Building* 9:3/4 (1989): 49.

34. Sheila D. Creth, "Personnel Realities in the University Library of the Future," in *The Future of the Academic Library*, 48.

35. Ross Atkinson, "Text Mutability and Collection Administration," *Library Acquisitions: Practice & Theory* 14:4 (1990): 356.

36. Ibid., 357.

37. Welsch, remarks in "Symposium," 44.

38. Britten, remarks in "Symposium," 39.

39. F. G. Kilgour, "The Metamorphosis of Libraries during the Foreseeable Future," in *Libraries and the Future*.

40. Atkinson, "Text Mutability and Collection Administration," 356.

41. Summerhill, remarks in "Symposium," 41.

42. Welsch, remarks in "Symposium," 55.

43. Alberico, remarks in "Symposium," 49.

44. Welsch, remarks in "Symposium," 53.

45. Michael E. Stoller, "Electronic Journals in the Humanities: A Survey and Critique," *Library Trends* 40 (Spring 1992): 659.

46. University of Pennsylvania Libraries, "Providing Local Access to Machine-Readable Data Files: Choices and Tradeoffs," in *Computer Files and the Research Library*, 59.

47. Summerhill, remarks in "Symposium," 41.

48. Ibid., 42.

49. Stoller, "Electronic Journals in the Humanities," 647–666.

50. Shreeves, "Between the Visionaries and the Luddites," 579–595.

51. Dougherty and Hughes, *Preferred Futures for Libraries*, 9.

52. Summerhill, remarks in "Symposium," 41.

53. Lancaster, *Libraries and Librarians in an Age of Electronics*, 167.

54. Shreeves, "Between the Visionaries and the Luddites," 579–595.

Selected Bibliography

Alemna, A. Anaba. "Acquisitions and Collection Development Education in Ghana." *Library Acquisitions: Practice & Theory* 14:1 (1990): 53–59.

American Library Association. Resources and Technical Services Division. Collection Management and Development Committee. *Guide for Writing a Bibliographer's Manual.* Collection Management and Development Guides, no. 1. Chicago: American Library Association, 1987.

Atkinson, Ross. "The Citation as Intertext: Toward a Theory of the Selection Process." *Library Resources & Technical Services* 28:2 (April/June 1984): 109–119.

———. "Text Mutability and Collection Administration." *Library Acquisitions: Practice and Theory* 14:4 (1990): 355-358.

Biancofiore, Piera, and Lucilla Vespucci. "Acquisitions and Collection Development in Italy." *Library Acquisitions: Practice & Theory* 13:3 (1989): 303–313.

Bobick, James E. *Collection Development Organization and Staffing.* SPEC Flyer and Kit, no. 131. Washington, D.C.: Office of Management Studies, Association of Research Libraries, 1987.

Bone, Larry. "Noblesse Oblige: Collection Development as a Public Service Responsibility." In *Reference Services & Technical Services: Interactions in Library Practice*, edited by Gordon Stevenson and Sally Stevenson, 65–73. New York: Haworth Press, 1984.

Bryant, Bonita. "The Allocation of Human Resources for Collection Development." *Library Resources & Technical Services* 30 (1986): 149–162.

———. "The Organization Structure of Collection Development." *Library Resources & Technical Services* 31 (1987): 111–122.

Bucknall, Carolyn. "Organization of Collection Development and Management in Academic Libraries." *Collection Building* 9 (1988): 11–17.

Cogswell, James A. "The Organization of Collection Management Functions in Academic Research Libraries." *Journal of Academic Librarianship* 13 (1987): 268–276.

Creth, Sheila D. "The Organization of Collection Development: A Shift in the Organization Paradigm." *Journal of Library Administration* 14 (1991): 65–85.

Cubberley, Carol W. "Organization for Collection Development in Medium-sized Academic Libraries." *Library Acquisitions: Practice & Theory* 11 (1987): 297–323.

Edelman, Hendrik. "Selection Methodology in Academic Libraries." *Library Resources & Technical Services* 23 (Winter 1979): 33–38.

Evans, John. "Education for Acquisitions and Collection Development in Papua New Guinea, with Reference to Courses at the University of the South Pacific." *Library Acquisitions: Practice & Theory* 14:1 (1990): 43–52.

Ford, Karin F. "Interaction of Public and Technical Services: Collection Development as Common Ground." In *Library Management and Technical Services: The Changing Role of Technical Services in Library Organizations*, edited by Jennifer Cargill, 45–53. New York: New Haven Press, 1988.

Futas, Elizabeth, and David L. Vidor. "What Constitutes a Good Collection?" *Library Journal* 112 (April 15, 1987): 45–47.

Gaunt, Marianne I. "Machine-Readable Literary Texts: Collection Development Issues." *Collection Management* 13:1/2 (1990): 87–96.

Ghikas, Mary W. "Collection Management for the 21st Century." *Collection Management* 11:1/2 (1989): 119–135.

Gleason, Maureen L. "Training Collection Development Librarians." *Collection Management* 4:4 (1982): 1–8.

Gorman, G. E., and B. R. Howes. *Collection Development for Libraries.* New York: Bowker-Saur, 1989.

Haskell, John D., Jr. "Subject Bibliographers in Academic Libraries: An Historical and Descriptive Review." *Advances in Library Administration and Organization: a Research Annual* 3 (1984): 73–84.

Hazen, Dan C. "Is Money the Issue? Research Resources and Our Collections Crisis." *Journal of Academic Librarianship* 18:1 (March 1992): 13–15.

Henn, Barbara J. "Acquisitions Management: The Infringing Roles of Acquisitions Librarians and Subject Specialists—An Historical Perspective." *Advances in Library Administration and Organization* 8 (1989): 113–129.

Higginbotham, Barbara Buckner, and Sally Bowdoin. *Access Versus Assets: A Comprehensive Guide to Resource Sharing for Academic Librarians.* Frontiers of Access to Library Materials, no.1. Chicago: American Library Association, 1993.

Johns, Cecily, ed. *Selection of Library Materials for Area Studies, Part I. Asia, Iberia, the Caribbean, and Latin America, Eastern Europe and the Soviet Union, and the South Pacific.* Chicago: American Library Association, 1990.

Johnson, Margaret. "Adding Computer Files to the Research Library: Issues in Collection Management and Development." In *Computer Files and the Research Library*, edited by Constance C. Gould, 3–13. Mountain View, Calif.: Research Libraries Group, 1990.

Kanazawa, Midori. "Organization Theory and Collection Management in Libraries." *Collection Management* 14 (1991): 43–57.

Kennedy, Gail A. "The Relationship between Acquisitions and Collection Development." *Library Acquisitions: Practice & Theory* 7:3 (1983): 225–232.

Krzys, Richard. "Collection Development Courses." In *Internationalizing Library and Information Science Education: A Handbook of Policies and Procedures in*

Administration and Curriculum, edited by John F. Harvey and Frances Laverne Carroll, 201–214. Westport, Conn.: Greenwood Press, 1987.

Lowry, Anita. "Electronic Texts in English and American Literature," *Library Trends* 40 (Spring 1992): 704–723.

―――. "Machine-Readable Texts in the Academic Library: The Electronic Text Service at Columbia University." In *Computer Files and the Research Library*, edited by Constance C. Gould, 15–23. Mountain View, Calif.: Research Libraries Group, 1990.

Magrill, Rose Mary, and John Corbin. *Acquisitions Management and Collection Development in Libraries*. 2nd ed. Chicago: American Library Association, 1989.

McClung, Patricia A., ed. *Selection of Library Materials in the Humanities, Social Sciences, and Sciences*. Chicago: American Library Association, 1985.

McDaniel, Julie Ann. "Leading the Way: In-House Collection Development Training for New Selectors." *Library Acquisitions: Practice & Theory* 13 (1989): 293–95.

Metz, Paul, and Bela Foltin. "A Social History of Madness: Or, Who's Buying This Round? Anticipating and Avoiding Gaps in Collection Development." *College & Research Libraries* 51 (January 1990): 33–39.

Mosher, Paul H. "Collection Development to Collection Management: Toward Stewardship of Library Resources." *Collection Management* 4:4 (Winter 1982): 41–48.

Null, David G. "Robbing Peter . . .: Balancing Collection Development and Reference Responsibilities." *College & Research Libraries* 49:5 (September 1988): 448–452.

Osburn, Charles B. "Collection Development and Management." In *Academic Libraries: Research Perspectives*, edited by Mary Jo Lynch with Arthur Young, 1–37. Chicago: American Library Association, 1990.

―――. "Toward a Reconceptualization of Collection Development." *Advances in Library Administration and Organization* 2 (1983): 175–198.

Osburn, Charles B., and Ross Atkinson, eds. *Collection Management: A New Treatise*. Foundations in Library and Information Science, vol. 26. Greenwich, Conn.: JAI Press, 1991.

Rahman, Afifa. "Acquisitions and Collection Development Education in Bangladesh." *Library Acquisitions: Practice & Theory* 12:1 (1988): 43–51.

Reed-Scott, Jutta. "Information Technologies and Collection Development." *Collection Building* 9:3/4 (1989): 47–51.

Rutledge, John, and Luke Swindler. "The Selection Decision: Defining Criteria and Establishing Priorities." *College & Research Libraries* 48 (1987): 123–131.

Schad, Jasper G. "Managing Collection Development in University Libraries That Utilize Librarians with Dual-Responsibility Assignments." *Library Acquisitions: Practice & Theory* 14 (1990): 165–171.

Schad, Jasper G., Michael A. Keller, Donna M. Goehner, Herbert S. White, Katina Strauch, Dan C., Hazen, and James F. Williams, II. "The Future of Collection Development in an Era of Fiscal Stringency." *Journal of Academic Librarianship* 18:1 (March 1992): 4–16.

Shapiro, Beth J., and John Whaley, eds. *Selection of Library Materials in Applied and Interdisciplinary Fields*. Chicago: American Library Association, 1987.

Shreeves, Edward. "Between the Visionaries and the Luddites: Collection Development and Electronic Resources in the Humanities." *Library Trends* 40 (Spring 1992): 579–595.

Siggins, Jack. *Performance Appraisal of Collection Development Librarians*. SPEC Flyer and Kit, no. 181. Washington, D.C.: Office of Management Services, Association of Research Libraries, 1992.

Sohn, Jean. "Collection Development Organizational Patterns in ARL Libraries." *Library Resources & Technical Services* 31 (1987): 123–134.

Sommer, Susan T. "Teaching Collection Development in Context." *Fontes Artis Musicae* 35 (July/September 1988): 195–197.

Stueart, Robert D., and George B. Miller, Jr., eds. *Collection Development in Libraries: A Treatise*. Foundations in Library and Information Science, vol. 26. Greenwich, Conn.: JAI Press, 1980.

Tóth, Gyula, and Beáta Bobok. "Educating and Training for Library Collection Development in Hungary." *Library Acquisitions: Practice & Theory* 12: 3/4 (1988): 313–323.

Williams, Lynn B. "Subject Knowledge for Subject Specialists: What the Novice Bibliographer Needs to Know." *Collection Management* 14:3/4 (1991): 31–47.

Wortman, William A. *Collection Management: Background and Principles*. Chicago: American Library Association, 1989.

Yaple, Henry M. "Gunfight at the O.K. Corral: Holding Your Own with Collection Development." *Library Acquisitions: Practice & Theory* 15:1 (1991): 33–37.

Index

About the Contributors

TERRY L. ALLISON, Collections Librarian, California State University, San Marcos, recently presented a paper at the 1992 Sager Symposium, Swarthmore College, on "AIDS Obituaries: Editing Gay Lives." His grants include a UCSD Librarians' Association grant resulting in a paper that appears in the Proceedings of the Western European Studies Section of the ALA Conference, Florence, 1988, on shared preservation program possibilities between U.S. and European libraries. Allison is also chair of the ALA Social Responsibilities Round Table Gay and Lesbian Task Force Program Planning Committee.

D. WHITNEY COE, Anglo-American Bibliographer, Princeton University, is responsible for selection of current English language monographs in most non-science subject areas. His recent publications include a contribution to *Cataloging: The Professional Development Cycle*, edited by Sheila S. Intner and Janet Swan Hill (Greenwood, 1991), and "Recruitment, A Positive Process" in *Recruiting, Educating and Training Cataloging Librarians: Solving the Problems*, edited by Intner and Hill (Greenwood, 1989). He has served as member and chair of several Association of Collections and Technical Services committees, including its International Relations Committee, Esther J. Piercy Award Jury, and Education Committee.

JOSEPH P. CONSOLI is a Humanities Bibliographer at Rutgers University, responsible for collection development in classics, Italian, French, comparative literature, gay studies, and medieval studies. Consoli is the author of *Giovanni Boccaccio: An Annotated Bibliography* (1992) and is a book review contributor to *Conservation Administration News*. His forthcoming works include a new translation, with notes and bibliography, of *Il Novellino* (in press, 1993), as well as a bibliographic article on Umberto Eco for *Style*. He is a member of ALA's Social Responsibilities Gay and Lesbian Book Award Committee and has recently been awarded a Faculty Research Council Grant from Rutgers University.

GAY N. DANNELLY is Collection Development Officer at the Ohio State University Libraries. She has served on and chaired numerous committees in ALA, including chairing the ALCTS Acquisitions of Library Materials Section and the Resources Section. Dannelly has also been active in continuing education for collection development, co-chairing planning committees for the ALCTS Collection Management and Development 1989 Institute and the Advanced Collection Management and Development 1993 Institute. Her publications include "The E's of Vendor Selection" in *Understanding the Business of Acquisitions* (1990) and "Justifying Collection Budget Costs" in *Declining Acquisitions Budgets* (in press, 1993).

ANTHONY W. FERGUSON, Resources and Specials Collections Group Director, Columbia University Libraries, is responsible for coordinating the collection development activities of Columbia's twenty-three libraries. Formerly an Asian studies librarian, he has taught numerous collection assessment workshops in the United States and Canada. Ferguson recently served as chair of the Chief Collection Development Officers of the Large Research Libraries Discussion Group (ALCTS). Publications include "(The Conspectus) Philosophical Arguments and Real Shortcomings" (*Journal of Academic Librarianship*, 1992) and "The Conspectus and Cooperative Collections Development: What It Can and Cannot Do" (*Acquisitions Librarian*, 1991).

ELIZABETH FUTAS is Director and Professor of the Graduate School of Library and Information Studies of the University of Rhode Island. Her recent publications include "The Faculty Vanishes: Who Will Educate New Librarians?" (*Library Journal* 116, September 1, 1991), "Faculty Replacements in Library Schools" (*Education for Information*, March 1993), and *Library Acquisition Policies and Procedures*, 3rd ed. (in press). Professor Futas was awarded a Council on Library Resources grant in 1990 and served on ALA Council 1991–94. She became a member of Phi Kappa Phi in 1990.

SHEILA S. INTNER is Professor at the Graduate School of Library and Information Science, Simmons College, Boston. During the 1992–93 academic year, she was awarded a Fulbright grant to Israel, where she taught Collection Development at the University of Haifa and Hebrew University in Jerusalem. Her recent publications include "Access to Patron Use Software" (in press) for the *Encyclopedia of Library and Information Science* and *Encyclopedia of Microcomputers*, *Subject Access to Films and Videos* (1992),

Standard Cataloging for School and Public Libraries (1990), and *Cataloging: The Professional Development Cycle* (Greenwood Press, 1991). Intner recently completed a study of collection development decision making funded by the Council on Libraries Resources. She also serves as editor of a monographic series published by ALA titled *Frontiers of Access to Library Materials*.

PEGGY JOHNSON, Assistant Director, St. Paul Campus Libraries, University of Minnesota, was awarded a Samuel Lazerow research fellowship by the Association of College and Research Libraries and the Institute for Scientific Information in 1987. She has consulted on library development in Uganda, Rwanda, and Morocco. Her recent publications include *Automation and Organizational Change in Libraries* (1991), "Technological Change in Libraries" (*Encyclopedia of Library and Information Science* 48, 1991), *Guide to Technical Services Resources* (1994), and journal articles. Johnson writes a bimonthly column on collection management for *Technicalities*.

BILL KATZ is Professor at the School of Information Science and Policy, State University of New York, Albany. Katz is editor of the Magazine column in *Library Journal* as well as of the journals *The Reference Librarian* and *The Acquisitions Librarian*. Among his recent works are *Introduction to Reference Work*, 6th ed. (1992), and *Magazines for Libraries*, 7th ed. (1992).

MICHAEL A. KELLER is Associate University Librarian and Director of Collection Development in the Yale University Libraries. "Re-treaded" from musicology to music librarianship in 1970 and from music librarianship to collection development and library administration in 1986, he was Music Librarian and Senior Lecturer at Cornell and Head of the Music Library at the University of California, Berkeley. He compiled the fourth edition of Vincent H. Duckles's *Music Reference and Research Materials: An Annotated Bibiliography* (1988) and has authored several articles.

F. W. LANCASTER is Professor Emeritus in the Graduate School of Library and Information Science, University of Illinois, Urbana-Champaign, where he was appointed University Scholar for the period 1989–92. He serves as editor of *Library Trends* and is the author of eight books. Lancaster has been awarded three Fulbright fellowships for research and teaching abroad and has received the Award of Merit and the Outstanding Information Science Teacher Award from the American Society for Information Science. Lancaster has been involved in a wide range of consulting activities, including service for UNESCO and other agencies of the United Nations. His recent book on indexing and abstracting was awarded the Best Information Science Book award by the American Society for Information Science.

PAUL METZ is Principal Bibliographer at the Virginia Polytechnic Institute and State University Libraries. He is the author of *The Landscape of Literatures: Use of Subject Collections in a University Library* (1983). His recent articles include "Thirteen Steps to Avoiding Bad Luck in a Serials Cancellation Project" (*Journal of Academic Librarianship* 18, May 1992) and, with Paul Gherman, "Serials Pricing and the Electronic Journal" (*College & Research Libraries* 52, July 1991).

THOMAS E. NISONGER is an Assistant Professor in Indiana University's School of Library and Information Science, where he teaches collection development, library automation, and introduction to cataloging. For more than a decade previously he was an academic collection development and acquisitions librarian. His recent publications include *Collection Evaluation in Academic Libraries: A Literature Guide and Annotated Bibliography* (1992). Nisonger serves on the editorial board of *Library Acquisitions: Practice & Theory* and on the ALA's Education for Collection Development Committee.

MARION T. REID has served as Director of Library Services, shaping the development of the library's staff, collection, and facility at California State University, San Marcos, since its founding as the twentieth campus in the State University System in 1988. She serves as a member of the Beta Phi Mu National Board, the California Library Association Assembly, and the California Library Association Executive Committee. Her recent publications include chapters in *Understanding the Business of Acquisitions* (1990) and *Technical Services in Libraries: Systems and Applications* (1992).

MICHAEL T. RYAN is Director of Special Collections in the University of Pennsylvania Libraries, where he moved after holding similar positions at the University of Chicago and Stanford University. He has been active in the Association of College and Research Libraries Rare Books and Manuscripts Section and the Association of Library Collections and Technical Services for over a decade and has published widely on the topic of special collection librarianship in the larger library and university context. He also has particular interests in the relationships between academic disciplines and library collections. In 1992, he participated in the University of California, Los Angeles, Graduate School of Library and Information Sciences Senior Fellows Program.

GEORGE J. SOETE is an Associate University Librarian at the University of California, San Diego, where the collections and staff training programs are among his responsibilities. He is a frequent organizational consultant and trainer for the Office of Management Services, Association of Research Libraries. His recent articles have focused on planning strategically for resource sharing (*Advances in Library Resource Sharing* 2, 1991) and training professional library staff in goal-based performance planning (*Journal of Library Administration*, special issue announced for 1992).

EUGENE L. WIEMERS, JR., is Assistant University Librarian for Collection Management at Northwestern University Library. He has been a bibliographer in economics at Virginia Tech and in Latin American and Hispanic studies at the University of Minnesota. Wiemers has held administrative positions in collection development and public services at Minnesota and at Michigan State University. He is the author of works in collection development, preservation, Latin American bibliography, and Latin American history.

ISBN 0-313-28561-6

90000>

EAN

9 780313 285615

HARDCOVER BAR CODE